Alec John Dawson

God's Foundling

Alec John Dawson

God's Foundling

ISBN/EAN: 9783337059385

Printed in Europe, USA, Canada, Australia, Japan

Cover: Foto ©ninafisch / pixelio.de

More available books at **www.hansebooks.com**

BY
A. J. DAWSON
AUTHOR OF MERE SENTIMENT, MIDDLE GREYNESS,
IN THE BIGHT OF BENIN, ETC.

NEW YORK
D. APPLETON AND COMPANY
1897

CONTENTS.

CHAPTER	PAGE
I.—THE MASTER	1
II.—THE MAN	6
III.—"TO MEET MR. BARNARD'S FRIEND"	18
IV.—MR. MORLEY FENTON'S PROTÉGÉ	26
V.—THE PHILOSOPHY OF MOLESEY REGATTA	34
VI.—MORNING SUNSHINE AND FRUIT	48
VII.—A MATTER FOR MR. FENTON TO DECIDE	52
VIII.—MR. MORLEY FENTON'S DECISION	62
IX.—CROSS-CURRENTS AND CARISSIMA	68
X.—FROM NORWOOD TO TROUVILLE	76
XI.—SOME REMINISCENCES, AND A BIG MAN CALLED CARROLL	88
XII.—AFTERNOON TEA AND SCANDAL	99
XIII.—TWO MEETINGS AND A LITTLE SLEEP	109
XIV.—IN THE MATTER OF A STRAIGHT LINE	120
XV.—"UP AT A VILLA, DOWN IN THE CITY"	126
XVI.—MATTERS OF EXPEDIENCY	134
XVII.—PROVIDENCE AND MR. MORLEY FENTON	145
XVIII.—THE WEARINESS OF HAROLD FOSTER	153
XIX.—HOUSE	168
XX.—COLD SUPPER, AND A BREATHING SPACE	177
XXI.—ON A WAYSIDE SLOPE	186
XXII.—A QUESTION OF DIAGNOSIS	199
XXIII.—INTERVENTION	204
XXIV.—REACTION	213
XXV.—PHASES	225
XXVI.—AFTER MANY DAYS	236

CHAPTER	PAGE
XXVII.—Between two worlds.	247
XXVIII.—Morley Fenton's foundling	255
XXIX.—Harold Foster loses his way.	270
XXX.—Harold Foster finds his way.	273

CONSEQUENCES:

Part I.—The passage of time.	294
" II.—The triumph of time.	309

GOD'S FOUNDLING.

CHAPTER I.

THE MASTER.

"You saw go up and down Valladolid,
A man of mark to know next time you saw."
ROBERT BROWNING.

THE 4.30 train from Waterloo was a little late. When it did draw up beside the down platform at Sunbury the stationmaster had been standing waiting for it for quite five minutes. Consequently, when he opened the door of a first-class smoking carriage, and touched his hat to Mr. Morley Fenton, his expression suggested apologetic regret.

"Good-evening, Mr. Fenton. Little late this evening, sir. It's those race-trains again."

"Good-evening, Johnson. Yes, we are a little late, I think."

And Mr. Morley Fenton, slim, erect, precise, passed down the narrow platform on his way home.

This little scene was one of the standing, the outstanding, features of the stationmaster's daily life, and one into which the only variation that ever crept was caused by the punctuality, or otherwise, of the 4.30 train from Waterloo. He did not make a point of opening carriage doors for other passengers, not even for Sir Graham Willoughby or Lord Lesby, who were both fairly regular in their comings and their goings. And he would have found it hard to have given any valid reason for his unvarying daily tribute of respect to Mr. Morley Fenton. He simply paid it as a matter of course, and would no more have thought of omitting the small attention than would the man at the station-gate of asking to see Mr. Fenton's ticket, when that gentleman passed out with his usual slight inclination of the head.

On this particular evening Mr. Morley Fenton's face wore a somewhat more serious and abstracted expression than was usual. Midway between the station and his riverside home Mr. Fenton paused, raising his head with the air of a man recalling some half-forgotten circumstance. Then, turning sharp round, he walked back some twenty paces in the direction of the station. A strip of banana peel lay on the curb. Having flicked it into the roadway with the point of his neatly-rolled umbrella, Mr. Fenton turned once more and resumed his walk towards Weir Lodge.

The evening was one beautifully typical of the soft radiance of summer in the Thames Valley. Air and sky and gently rustling leaves were unusually full of lusty summer's glory. Mr. Morley Fenton was a man upon whom, as a rule, one's eyes fell as upon a piece of one's surroundings. He looked as much an expected section of his environment as the figure in a portrait seems of its canvas. On this radiant evening Mr. Fenton's appearance might have suggested to a close observer some fleeting thought of coming autumn, or, more probably, of a previous summer's ending.

When he reached the garden-gate of the quaintly pretty, rambling white house called Weir Lodge, Mr. Fenton paused a moment to throw away the end of a Trichinopoly cheroot, which he had lighted, as his custom was, when leaving his office in Lombard Street. Then he walked, more briskly than before, along the trim gravel drive to the porch of the white house. The swinging glass doors in the lobby stood open, and as the master of the house entered a maidservant came forward to take his umbrella. Mr. Fenton handed the girl a compact little grass-mat bag which he had been carrying.

"Here is some fish which you might take to the kitchen, Mary. And, Mary, tell your mistress, will you, that I am expecting Mr. George Barnard to dinner."

"Yes, sir," said the maid, as she retired kitchenwards with the salmon, repeating to herself for the hundredth time at least that she had quite the nicest master in England.

"He's a real gentleman, he is," was the opinion held and expressed by most people of Mary's class who were brought into contact with Mr. Morley Fenton.

Having divested himself of a neutral-hued, extremely light top-coat, and deposited the same in an oak cabinet, Mr. Fenton walked quietly across the hall—for a house of its modest dimensions Weir Lodge possessed a remarkably fine hall—holding in one hand his silk hat, and in the other an evening paper, which latter had apparently not yet been opened. Arrived in his study, a small, pretty room overlooking the lawn and the bend of the river towards which this lawn sloped, Mr. Fenton laid his hat carefully in a case left open for its reception. Then he placed his evening paper on the centre of the writing-table, and, turning again, closed the door by which he had entered the room.

As the master of the house regained the centre of his study, and paused there, gazing out through one of its low windows, he sighed languidly, and murmured a word which seemed to be merely the articulation of the sigh. The lines of his fine face seemed in a way to droop inward, his lower lip to recede from its sweeping covering of silver-pointed brown moustache, and his eyes to be half-closed. His sigh had framed itself into the word "Sanctuary!" An odd word this, from such a man, at such a time.

Then Mr. Fenton coughed, and, passing two well-kept hands slowly over his face, as though to restore its usual impassivity, sat down restfully in a low wicker chair.

"After all," he murmured. And then the relaxation which his two hands seemed to have pressed out of his face crept over it again. He drew a slim Russia-leather letter-case from an inner pocket, and took out of it a letter on the top of which was printed, "St. Ann's Vicarage, Norwood." He read the letter carefully, and then, allowing it to fall on to his knees, he raised both hands, resting the finger-tips of each on those of the other, as a lawyer who listens, or a child who prays.

"Flesh and blood, and mother's milk: they are stronger than teaching and environment," he murmured slowly. "Or—but then, the teaching and environment must be strengthened. That is all. Yes, yes. They must be made the strongest. Yes, and penitence is at best a poor thing. The only atonement is living, breathing, creative atonement—that is, re-making, evil-effacing. Yes, yes."

Almost an hour passed, while Mr. Fenton sat perfectly still in the wicker chair, his hands resting one against the other, his eyes on the golden glamour of the strip of western sky, which seemed to run right down to the dappled surface of the river wherein its glory was reflected. And as he sat there the man's face regained all its habitual smooth serenity, and with it there seemed a light of added strength and fixity of purpose.

Then a tap on the door of the study elicited a quiet "Come in!" from the master of the house, and Mr. Fenton replaced the letter he had been reading in the case from which he had drawn it. The case he slipped into his coat-pocket as he rose and stood facing the door.

"Mr. George Barnard, sir, to see you."

The speaker was Mary, and as she drew back from the door its opening seemed to be filled, dominated, by the presence of a big fair man with a flowing russet beard, and wide blue eyes which in their expression were like those that in a horse are called "kind." He carried a dark-blue cloth crush hat in one hand, and a short briar pipe in the other.

"Ah, Fenton, old chap, how are you? I made sure I should find you in the garden."

The man's voice, like his presence, was big and sweet and clean in its suggestion. Delivered in such a voice, even the words with which he addressed Mr. Morley Fenton did not seem strikingly ill-suited to the subject of them.

"Come in, George—come in. I'm glad to see you, and—it was good of you to come."

CHAPTER II.

THE MAN.

> " Ask, ere the youngster be rated and chidden,
> What did he carry, and how was he ridden?
> Maybe they used him too much at the start;
> Maybe Fate's weight-cloths are breaking his heart."
> *Life's Handicap.*

GEORGE BARNARD was a briefless young barrister, aged forty-five. He lived, and assisted sundry other persons to achieve the same laudable end, on a private income of some hundred and forty odd pounds per annum, and the casual earnings of an uncertain, but cleverly-wielded pen. He had his headquarters in a roomy, shadowy, untidy set of chambers in Furnival's Inn. The shabby saddle-bag chairs in these rooms had for the most part served different occupants at different times as beds.

Some twenty years before this summer evening on which Mr. Morley Fenton welcomed George Barnard in the study at Weir Lodge, he had occupied a portion of the same set of shabby chambers in which his friend, the big-bodied, big-hearted barrister, had lived ever since. The two men had purchased their wigs and gowns together, and at one and the same time had been called to the Bar, and earned the right to accept the briefs which never came to either.

Then there had been happenings, and Mr. Morley Fenton had subsequently entered his father's counting-house, and become one of the well-known banking and financial house of Morley Fenton, Son and Co. So George Barnard, his friend's senior by a year or so, had remained the sole tenant, nominally at all events, of the Furnival's Inn chambers. And this was by no means the only tie between the owner of Weir Lodge and his lion-headed guest, who, by the way, looked a good deal younger than his host.

George Barnard was the only man in England who, having known Mr. Fenton in his early barrister days, had met him subsequently as a member of the Lombard Street firm, and a householder. He was one of the very few who were aware that the owner of Weir Lodge ever had been called to the Bar. He was the sole connecting link between young Morley Fenton who was "sent down" from Oxford and matured Mr. Morley Fenton upon whose opinion in matters commercial many leading lights in London financial circles were always prepared to risk money. And there were other bonds of union between the two widely-differing men.

Mr. Morley Fenton mixed his friend a glass of sherry and bitters; and then, after a carefully-worded apology, left the room for the purpose of making some change in his dress before dinner. Later on, he led George Barnard into the long drawing-room where his wife, his two daughters, and Norah, his niece, were discussing the forthcoming Molesey Regatta.

Mrs. Fenton, tall and stately, with a miniature head, and the bird-like, winsome face of a *petite* woman, rose to greet her husband's friend, whom she had known during all her married life.

"I am so glad to see you again, Mr. Barnard," she said, in the trilling small voice which, whilst in admirable accord with her flower-like face, seemed always out of keeping with her queenly figure. "It is positively a whole year since you last honoured us."

"It is—it is, Mrs. Fenton, a whole year since I indulged myself. But, as you know, I have been a good deal out of England, and really—er——"

His hostess took advantage of George Barnard's pause to bring forward Norah, whom the barrister had never met.

"This is dear Norah, Mr. Barnard. Our daughter now, you know, since——"

And this time it was the guest's turn to fill a pause. He did so with a certain manly grace, made half tender by reason of his noticing, as he bowed over the girl's hand, that she was dressed in black. He remembered then that, some six or eight months before, his friend's elder brother had died in rather poor circumstances, leaving a pretty and wholly insignificant wife, and a seventeen-year-old daughter. Norah he now rightly assumed to be the daughter, and he noticed, with Bohemian quickness of perception in such matters, that the girl's pale face was a very charming one. His recollection of his one meeting with Norah's mother made him sum the situation up in his mind by a thought which, if put into words, would have been:

"Charming girl, with an encumbrance — her mother."

He did not know the facts of the case, or he would have been aware that Norah had no encumbrances, and, to all intents and purposes, no mother. Her dead father's widow, whom Barnard would have called, "a thread-paper creature," had eagerly accepted Mrs. Morley Fenton's offer to adopt Norah, and herself had left England to travel as companion to a wealthy spinster relative.

George Barnard shook hands warmly with Maud and Lucy Fenton, two graceful girls, very much their mother's daughters, with whom the barrister was a prime favourite. A few minutes later the small party adjourned to the dining-room.

Just as everything else about Weir Lodge was the best which English orthodoxy provides and suggests, so the dinner that evening was thoroughly and conventionally good and patriotically British, from its healthy infancy of thick ox-tail to its sturdy final stages of jellies, Cheddar, and wall-fruit. The hock was poor, the claret was good, the port was perfection, and the coffee was infamous. Mr. Fenton was serious and a little abstracted, whilst never ceasing to be an attentive host. Mrs. Fenton was charming, and full of the most sympathetic of small talk. Norah was subdued, but in occasional flashes struck the barrister as being very interesting. Maud and Lucy unaffectedly demanded to be amused; and George Barnard complied with these demands to perfection, whilst mentally flagellating himself at intervals for being lacking in any of the topics of conventional small talk.

"If only one could talk to 'em about the affairs of our kinds of lives!" Barnard had been known to say to a journalistic chum, whilst speaking of ladies and of the rare occasions upon which he felt called upon to show himself in the society whose members call the circle of their acquaintance collectively by that name. As a matter of fact, he always did talk of the affairs of Bohemia, though he was never conscious of so doing. And in this way George Barnard rarely failed to amuse, even where he could not interest. And the most rigidly orthodox hostesses had found it absolutely impossible, when their gaze had met his great, sailor-child-like blue eyes, to be displeased with one whose devotion to their sex was always apparent, even to smart folk.

"You'll excuse my selfishness in not letting George join you, dear? We have a matter of business to discuss," said Mr. Fenton to his wife, as the ladies were leaving the table.

"Well, I don't know. We shall expect to see you for a little while, anyhow, Mr. Barnard."

"Yes, do come," added Mrs. Fenton's younger daughter. "And I will have that awful drinking-song ready for you to sing."

Mr Fenton did not resume his seat, but, having handed his old friend a cigar, proposed an adjournment to his study. This was acted upon, and when George Barnard had made himself comfortable before one of the open French windows, Mr. Fenton made some very good coffee, using for the purpose a special apparatus which stood on a side table.

"Ah, Morley, your hand's lost none of its cunning, I see," said the big man, tasting his Mocha, as his friend sat down in a low chair before him.

"It's fairly good coffee, is it not? Fairly good, I think."

A little twinkle of responsive appreciation of Barnard's compliment had lighted up the City man's eyes, and shown all sorts of new possibilities in his face. It was only a faint gleam, and a fleeting, but in passing it revealed more of Morley Fenton, the man, than had been shown since his arrival at Weir Lodge that evening. So a stray quotation wakes to ecstasy a renegade scholar, or a sunset glow an apostate artist. And the cause in this case was a careless comment on a man's ability as a maker of coffee.

"And now you've something special to tell me, haven't you?" asked Barnard, stroking his brown beard as he spoke, with the luxurious air of a man possessing to the full that rare faculty of seizing and appreciating comfort. "Gad! it's quite like old times, your wanting a yarn with me. I was very glad to get your wire."

"Yes"—the younger man looked distinctly the senior now. "Yes, I particularly wanted to see you, George. How long is it since you had a talk with Harold Foster?"

The barrister looked up sharply through the cloud of blue smoke which hung round his head in the still night air.

"Eh—Harold? He was with me on Saturday; he always lunches with me on Saturdays, you know. Then we generally go to a matinée, and I dine him somewhere, and yarn till it's time to see him off to Norwood. As a matter of fact, I'm ashamed to say it was my breakfast last Saturday, not lunch. I was in my tub when the boy came. But why?"

"Did you—did he seem changed in any way, George?"

"Why, no! Changed? No; I didn't notice any difference in him. He talked a good deal about the sex, bless 'em! but that's only natural. If I remember rightly, I'd had at least half a dozen serious affairs before I was his age. True, I wasn't brought up in a parsonage, but—by Gad! yes—I might have had a dozen if I had. Dangerous places—very. But why do you ask, old man?"

Mr. Morley Fenton drew his letter-case from his pocket, and handed Barnard the letter which he had read on first entering his study that evening.

"Read that, George."

"I wish you'd read it to me, old man; you're close to the light."

"Well, it is from the Reverend Winthrop at Norwood, and he says: 'I feel it my duty to tell you that your protégé has of late been causing me a good deal of anxiety. Of course, I have no means of judging of his conduct during the day, when he is presumably occupied in his studies at the hospital. Latterly, however, he has fallen into a habit of reaching home considerably later in the evening than was the case when he first took up his abode with me. His tone and attitude towards myself and the family seem changed. He frequently absents himself from the ordinary church services, and is at no pains to excuse this. His correspondence, too, has increased of late, and he shows some contempt for the simple pleasures and relaxations in which I have always encouraged the members of my household. As you know, my dear Mr. Fenton, your protégé has attained the years, if not the discretion, of manhood, and it is therefore impossible for me to enforce any rules for the guidance of his daily life. Only, as a matter of conscience, I feel bound to inform you of the impression which my careful study of young Mr. Foster gives me, and that unfortunately is, that some change, by no means toward his worldly or spiritual welfare, is at work in him.'"

Mr. Morley Fenton replaced the letter in his case, and sighed as he said:

"That is the reason, George, of my asking you, who know everything—er—all that Mr. Winthrop does not know—whether you have noticed any change in Harold Foster."

"My dear Fenton, I think, as I thought and told you when Harold first went to Norwood, that, with all respect to Mr. Winthrop, a parsonage is no place for a medical student, least of all for—for a lad like Hal."

"He is under very careful, watchful eyes there, and in the atmosphere of thoroughly good family life."

"So well watched that I expect it's getting on his nerves, old man. Such an infernally good atmosphere that I expect it makes him choky. I thought he seemed a little stale and flat on Saturday, now I come to think of it."

"Old friend, you know my hopes for Harold Foster, and—you know the fears that live with me. You know all I want to shield him from."

"My dear Fenton, believe me, you can't put old heads on young shoulders. This home-shelter business is the worst kind of foolishness. Fancy how we should have felt at his age if we'd been the subjects of a parson's careful study—and he's a medical student! You know how medicals talk. My dear fellow, the world you want him to be a man in is not a Norwood vicarage—not much!—and who knows that better than you? Let him learn the world he has to live in."

"And come unassisted into contact with—with all things that bring ruin. George, I have the two lives always before me—his and mine. God knows there's been enough similarity. You know how his college days came to an end."

"And yet you put him now, at three-and-twenty, practically in the position of a school-boy. My dear old man, let the lad live as the young fellows around him live, more or less in Bohemia. Let him live with me, if you like. Good heavens! if there's no open devilment in a young man's life, there's sure to be something a deuced lot worse. It isn't healthy for a youngster to have no appreciation of wickedness: it makes him cultivate nastiness. Let him live a worker's life among workers, and find out that green apples make a man's stomach ache; and if he drinks a glass of wine too many, and has a head in the morning, do you mean to say it's not cleaner than listening to talk of such things and wishing for them, or getting them in secret, and lying to a parson's wife about the morning's head? It is such rot, this cant about pure lives! Why, hang it, Fenton, you know it is—no man better!"

The barrister's ardour made the other man cold and calm.

"There are some matters, George, upon which individual opinions must necessarily differ. What seems cant to one man may be a thoroughly wholesome and genuine belief to another. And a third man, again, may neither believe nor disbelieve, and yet be wise enough to uphold certain standards because in the end they are the best policy."

"H'm! Well, of course, I long ago gave up trying to understand you, Fenton. I just accept you as a marvel, a very fine one, and my old friend. But I don't ask a youngster to be a marvel. I just ask him to be white, and to grow up a clean, strong man. Gad, Fenton! Think what young blood is. Let him live a complete life. There's not enough oxygen for a youngster in the odour of sanctity and week-night services. Why, why—think of our young days, you know!"

"I am thinking of them, George. In connection with Harold Foster, I never cease thinking of them."

If the stationmaster at Sunbury could have seen Mr. Morley Fenton's face now, as the light from the green-shaded lamp fell upon the veins which throbbed on each side of the high forehead with its fringe of grey-shot hair, want of recognition might have led to the omission of his usual deferential greeting. In dealing with some one feature of their lives the inwardness of most men comes to the surface—at least, more so than at other times. In its vibratile force and fulness, Mr. Morley Fenton's voice as he continued speaking was a revelation of a man not known to Mr. Morley Fenton's circle of acquaintance.

"When you talk of my letting Harold Foster live in Bohemia, George, you forget much that I remember. If I speak now as a narrow-living man of conventions and orthodoxy—let me speak as such. I, at all events, see some things clearly, and I remember. I do not think of Harold Foster simply as Harold

Foster, a young man in the doorway of his life. I think of him in the light of the past, which is stronger, if not brighter, than the light of the present, or of Bohemia. A young man is first a child, and draws in —God knows what a child draws from its mother's milk, and—and its father's loins. We do not all start fair, George, and those who have been responsible for the overweighting may at least try to lessen its effects."

The barrister stretched out one hand; but, as though to check any words which might accompany the gesture, Mr. Morley Fenton leaned forward in his chair, and continued speaking more rapidly than before.

"Your wide tolerance, George, is a far more intolerant thing than what you regard as my narrow conventionality. Prague is not a walled city. Byzantium spreads its colour for all beholders. Bohemia is open to all comers; but all men are not Bohemians, George. Let your thoughts run back to where something holds mine fixed, so far as Harold Foster is concerned. Bohemia was never to me the land it was and is to you. To you it is a living-room—a working, playing, feasting, starving place, but, first of all, a working place. Was it ever that to me? It is clean, breezy moorland—workshop camaraderie—to you, your life's oxygen. It was abandon, dancing exhilaration, or drowsy narcoticism, life's wine, the world's luridity, to me, and straying along its paths brought me—— But there! this is mere reminiscence to you. Forgive my—my unnecessary warmth; but you follow the line of my judgment. No, Harold Foster must not be helped into Bohemia."

Mr. Morley Fenton leaned far back in his chair, and the light from the green-shaded lamp, playing about his head, made fantastic livid hollows, as irresponsible lamplight will, where smooth reposeful lines were wont to be. Both men were silent for a full minute, and then George Barnard said:

"Yes, I suppose you're right, old man. Anyhow, I understand; but you want to make a change of some sort. You must introduce some interest in his life— something in the way of a condiment, to take with the week-night services, eh?"

Mr. Morley Fenton smiled slightly. It was the faintest, most tentative glimmering of a smile. Then both men were silent till George Barnard leaned forward to throw away his cigar end.

"Yes, there must be a change," said Barnard's host slowly. "An added interest, to give the quiet life's white light shade and colour. George, the boy must visit some comfortable homes, and mix with people who find happiness in a kind of life you rather despise. And for a beginning—for a beginning, why shouldn't he visit here?"

"Why indeed? I have often wondered. Why shouldn't a young man in whose life you take an interest visit your house? And then it will give you the opportunities you have found it so difficult to make of seeing him in a perfectly natural way."

"Yes. That is undoubtedly the thing to be done. It might have been done before, but I—— However, it can be done now. Look here, George! Bring him down to dinner next Saturday, and stay till Monday. That will break the ice. Will you?"

"Delighted, old man! Of course I will. I'll write him to-morrow. And now I think I must be getting down to the station. Will you walk down with me?"

"Yes, certainly. And—er—my wife——"

"Will you make my excuses afterwards, and bid the ladies good-night for me?"

"Well, perhaps it would be simpler—yes. Thanks, George! Then we'll go through the garden. Your hat is here, you know."

So the two walked out together into the scented summer night.

CHAPTER III.

"TO MEET MR. BARNARD'S FRIEND."

> "Evil or good may be better or worse
> In the human heart, but the mixture of each
> Is a marvel and a curse."
> *Gold Hair.*

As Mr. Morley Fenton lowered his first cup of breakfast coffee from his lips on the morning following his talk with George Barnard, he said quietly, addressing his wife:

"Oh, by the way, my dear, George Barnard is coming down again on Saturday, to stay till Monday, so perhaps I may be forgiven for monopolizing him last night."

"And I shall make him sing that drinking-song, though there really isn't a note in the piano deep enough."

Maud Fenton looked up from a letter, the contents of which she was imbibing with toast and watercress.

"But, father," interposed the elder sister, "Saturday is Molesey Regatta day. You must ask Mr. Barnard to lunch. We're having lunch at half-past twelve, and then he can go down with us in the gondola. He would look perfectly lovely in the bow, if he would only wear brown velveteen."

"You absurd child!" trilled the mistress of the house, raising her chin from the foamy neck of a morning gown. "As though Mr. Barnard dressed to suit your boats. Besides, I don't suppose he would care for such frivole as a regatta. You children——"

"Now, little mother"—the incongruity of her favourite appellation never struck Maud Fenton—"if you want to play at being middle-aged, you really mustn't wear that skittish wrapper with the chiffon."

"Well, I don't know," said Mr. Morley Fenton, who had been making steady, though not very vigorous, progress with his kidneys and toast.

"Why, father?" Maud still dwelt mentally on her mother's chiffon.

"Eh? Well, I was going to say that I think the regatta would suit George very well. The fact is, I have told him to bring down a friend of his, a young fellow named Foster—Harold Foster—a medical student, in whom I am rather interested. I think you heard me speak of him, my dear, some time ago, when he left college. He had a rather severe illness, and Mr. Barnard very kindly took him to the Riviera. I—I should like you all to be kind to him, you know, and —er—he will stay till Monday, too."

Mrs. Fenton raised her pretty eyebrows slightly. This was quite a new departure for her husband. He was not given to bringing friends to Weir Lodge.

"Of course, dear," she said, "we will do the best we can. Will Mr. Barnard and his friend come to lunch?"

"Oh yes, please, father, else we shall be out!"

"Yes, yes, certainly; I will ask George to come down with me. You needn't worry about room in the gondola; I shall have some letters to write, and shall leave our friends to you."

"But there's heaps of room, father. Mossop has put the new seat in now, you know."

"Yes, there is plenty of room," added Mrs. Fenton. "I was just going to ask you girls who we could invite to meet Mr. Barnard's friend. There really ought to be another man, you know."

"H'm! How about the Colonel?" suggested Mr. Morley Fenton, as he rose to leave the room.

"Father, de-ear," protested Lucy—"a single eyeglass in a gondola is too dreadful!"

"Oh, as you like; but, in spite of the glass, the Colonel's a very fine fellow."

"Don't you think, girls, that that delightfully wicked Mr. Tarne would be interesting? It's true he is dreadfully clever, but I thought him very good company at Sir Graham's on Tuesday. He has taken that funny little pagoda place, you know, for the rest of the season."

"Yes, little mother, he's splendid; he told me how people wrote novels and things. Do ask him."

"Tarne, Tarne?" queried the head of the house. "Do I know him?"

"No, dear, I don't think you do. He is a literary man, and quite a young lion, I believe."

"Oh, of course—Tarne. It must be Leo Tarne, the man who wrote that—er—— My dear, is he——"

"Oh perfectly, Morley—a charming man, really; and Lady Graham said some very nice things about him."

"Ah! Well, of course you know, and if you like him, by all means invite him, my dear. I think you will all like young Foster. I must really run away. Is there anything I can bring you from town? No? Good-bye, then; good-bye, girls. You're looking pale this morning, Norah; you must spend plenty of time on the river this weather, you know. Good-bye, dear."

And a minute afterwards the feminine portion of the household saw Mr. Morley Fenton walk past the window of the breakfast-room, and down the winding drive to the garden-gate. A moment later a thin curl of blue smoke floated in through the open window, as though to announce that his business day had begun for the head of the house, his Trichinopoly, that permanent herald of Mr. Fenton's home-comings and out-goings, being lighted.

"Isn't he a dear?" inquired Maud of Norah. Her audience nodded unqualified assent. "And," continued Maud, with fine feminine irrelevancy, "the gondola will really be pretty full if we are going to have tea in it."

"Well, you know," said Norah tentatively, "it wouldn't be so very bad for me to miss it, because I hardly know any of the people, and—— Don't you think so? Then there would be three gentlemen and three ladies, you know."

"My dear, I shouldn't think——"

"Oh yes—a delightful idea!"

Maud was given to interruptions.

"Yes, you wicked, deceitful Norah—dear! We'll leave her at home, little mother, won't we? and lock her in her bedroom."

"Nonsense, children! I am sure there will be lots of room if we leave Gyp at home and sit up properly, Maud, instead of sprawling over four cushions."

"Three, little mother—three, and then only when it was almost dark."

"Ah well, we shall see. I dare say it will be very nice. And I hope Mr. Foster is not scientific, or anything, because I am sure that Mr. Tarne will make fun of him if he is. Mr. Tarne is dreadful. He said dear Lady Graham suggested a retired Joan of Arc addressing an advanced Mothers' Meeting. I don't in the least know what he meant; but she is—a little pronounced in that drab costume—the tailor-made one —isn't she?"

And then the autocrat of Weir Lodge—Mrs. Fenton's latest discovery in cooks—demanded, through Mary, the housemaid, her mistress's immediate attendance in the hall.

Late in the afternoon of this same day, as Mr. Leo Tarne—novelist, and, some said, poet—was lying in a hammock on the verandah of the pretty bungalow of which he had recently become the tenant, he received from the hands of Carlos, his invaluable Spanish servant, a note addressed to him in the writing of Mrs. Morley Fenton.

"Pardon me a moment, Tritton," he said to a pale, somewhat puffy-looking young man, who sat beside the hammock in a crimson-lined wicker chair.

The young man nodded languidly. His own speech was to Tritton one of the few things in life which justified economy as a habit. There were people who regarded this feeling of Tritton's as the most commendable trait in his character. Tritton was a minor poet, who led a life of child-like guilelessness, and wrote luridly decadent verses at a low rate of remuneration. Originally of a peaceful, even happy, disposition, a shadow had been cast over Tritton's life by the persistent refusal of his friends to regard him as other than a thoroughly respectable young man.

"Now, here," said Leo Tarne, as he allowed Mrs. Fenton's note to fall on the boards of the verandah beneath him, "is a vivid example of the inexorable brutality of our—what-d'ye-may-call-it—what is the expression, Tritton?"

"Commercial classes?" suggested the younger man bitterly. He had not glanced at the envelope in which his friend's letter came. And Tritton had found tradesmen's bills a serious item in a poet's life.

"No, no; it's a lady."

"What? The expression?"

"No, 'social system'—that's it, 'social system.'"

"TO MEET MR. BARNARD'S FRIEND." 23

As I was saying, your unselfish and agreeable man's Nemesis is certain and pitiless. Here is a woman who is not even ugly. So far as I know, she is more wholly lacking in interest than—than the novels of writers who have not yet imitated me. Yet because in my fatal good-nature I paid her preposterous compliments at that garden-party the other day, and slandered our hostess—the only woman there of whom she was at all jealous—because of that, here comes my man to-day, like a what's-his-name, you know, from Scotland Yard, and forces a pale-blue writ on me to secure my appearance in a boatful of girls and collie dogs at Molesey Regatta. Tritton, believe me, if it were not for the horrible inconvenience and exertion it would involve, I would give up unselfishness and being agreeable—I would really—and study myself."

"You needn't go."

There was recklessness in the younger man's tone. For an entire week now he had hovered about the Thames Valley without securing a single invitation. The summer wore on apace, and Tritton found river lodgings expensive.

"Exactly. There speaks the man-about-town. Ah, Tritton, how I envy you your finished worldliness! To you life contains practically no conscience-born bugbears, no gruesome episodes born of duty by boredom."

Tritton's face lighted up.

"*You* needn't be so oilily self-satisfied," he said.

"No, I assure you I bitterly regret my verdancy. However—yes, I shall go to their massive lunch—shortly after daybreak, I think it is. It smacks of ploughed fields and bacon, does it not? And I shall afterwards make myself useful among the girls and collies and shin-breaking seats of the hearse they call a gondola. Shades of the Grand Canal! I suppose the young men's institutes and 'conducted tours' are responsible for that. I shall burn my fingers at an evil-smelling spirit-lamp, drink cold tea and eat cake—cake, Tritton!—and hand things about, and very possibly fall into the river. And all this, mark you, Tritton mio, in penance for ten minutes' good-natured unselfishness the other afternoon, and because of my fatal want of callousness. Oh, I am made to suffer! You, I know, would treat the pale-blue writ of Nemesis with silent and scornful indifference. But I—— And there is a rather charming girl in that Fenton family. I can't make out whether she is a parentless heiress or a poor relation. Heigho! would that I could slough —that's an extraordinarily ugly word, is it not?—some of my boyish chivalry, and pay a little more attention to my own comfort. How do you manage it, Tritton —eh? Are you really going already? So good of you to look me up, my dear Tritton! You'll forward me a copy of your 'Sins that are Scarlet,' won't you? Send Carlos along if you see him. Good-bye, my dear fellow."

Leo Tarne turned in his hammock as the minor poet disappeared and Carlos stepped on to the verandah.

"I should have thought, Carlos, that under the circumstances you might have perceived that I was not at home. I am afraid this same thing occurred once before, when we were in town. I don't wish to be severe, but I beg you will use more discrimination in future. A—— By the way, bring me something to drink, please, Carlos—something yellow with ice in it, and straws."

Leo Tarne moved again in his hammock and yawned slightly as his rebuked servant withdrew. The servant felt penitent and very much to blame for something. He was not quite clear as to the exact nature of his wrong-doing. But he felt that he had done wrong, and that thereby his master had suffered. This was very typical of Leo Tarne's attitude toward the world, and of the world's attitude toward Leo Tarne.

CHAPTER IV.

MR. MORLEY FENTON'S PROTÉGÉ.

> " I see the coming light,
> I see the scattered gleams,
> Aloft, beneath, on left and right,
> The stars own ether beams ;
> These are but seeds of days,
> Not yet a steadfast morn,
> An intermittent blaze,
> An embryo god unborn."
>   EMERSON.

" I REGARD this as a clear gain to us of two shillings, Harold."

" Regard what? "

" Why, this going to Lombard Street on a penny bus. Gain of one and tenpence, anyhow. We'll tack it on to next Saturday's dissipation, Hal—that's what we'll do, and have a most prodigious splash. Anyone else, you know, would have taken a hansom, which wouldn't have been half so airy. There's no doubt it's a clear profit of one and ten. You'll see now, Mr. Fenton will take a cab to Waterloo. True, he's more or less of a bloated capitalist, but still——"

" Yes, I suppose Mr. Fenton is rich. I've often thought, you know, that he must probably stand a good deal of my expenses himself. My father didn't leave very much, did he? It's a funny thing, you know, the way in which I have always accepted it as a matter of course that you and he should provide me with everything. Yet I don't know in the least how I stand."

"H'm! yes., Well, you see, Mr. Morley Fenton was your father's closest friend, so I expect he feels he has a right in the matter. As a fact, I don't think your father did have anything much; and goodness knows, I've never been able, even if it were necessary, to do anything for you in that way. But you can rest assured that in everything a real father could do for a son you have the best of fathers, and one who will never change, in Mr. Fenton."

"Yes, in everything a father can do for a son—in everything."

"By Gad, it's true! I don't believe there's anything he wouldn't do for you."

"And I'm sure there's nothing you wouldn't do."

"H'm! little enough—little enough I can. By the way, Hal, you have never been to Weir Lodge, have you?"

"No, I don't think so."

"Because I know Mr. Fenton wants to see more of you than he has done. This is only a beginning. He means to get you the entrée of several comfortable sort of houses, you know, as well as his own."

"He is good. By Jove! if you and he knew some of the things I——"

"We must get down here, Harold, and turn up Lombard Street. Steady! Your coat's caught in the rail. What was it you were saying?"

"Saying? I forget now. Nothing of any importance. By Jove! we're ten minutes late over that one-and-tenpenny find of ours."

"H'm! yes, so we are. And, of course, there's Mr. Fenton waiting on the doormat. His one vice, I think, is punctuality. How are you, old man? We came down by bus for the sake of the moral effect, and as a consequence I'm afraid we're a little late."

"Glad to see you, George. Harold, how are you?

A little unfair to morality, George, to expect it to make up in Cheapside for a late start. However, I think we have plenty of time for our train. Can we all three get into a hansom? I am afraid we must abstain from the moral luxury of the omnibus this time, to avoid the demoralization of missing a train." And the two older men giving each a knee towards the support of Harold Foster, the three started in a hansom for Waterloo.

Harold Foster, a handsome, very fair young Saxon, the weakness of whose mouth by no means overshadowed the strength of his high, wide forehead, had reached Furnival's Inn from Norwood that day in time to find George Barnard at a critical stage of his morning shaving operations. The barrister, who jovially boasted that all his life he had abstained from, at all events, one evil habit—early rising—had then proceeded to dress and breakfast in haste. He had cut himself twice whilst shaving. He had with extraordinary ingenuity contrived to mislay every small article pertaining to his toilet, and finally, by a crowning inspiration of brilliancy, had tilted a poached egg into the small bag which contained his boating clothes and other matters of detail connected with his week-end visit to Sunbury.

Then, in that fine frenzy which accompanies the desire to make up for lost time, or any other striving after the unattainable, Barnard had crammed such necessities as he could call to mind, and hand, into Harold Foster's bag, and by the time the pair reached the street on their way Citywards, had been brimming over with the blithest of good spirits. And, with the moral triumph of the omnibus thrown in, the barrister had been more nearly punctual in the meeting with Mr. Morley Fenton than his habit was in engagements with others among his friends.

Harold Foster was transparently less at ease in the presence of Mr. Morley Fenton than when alone with George Barnard, though his admiring respect for the former gentleman was an even deeper-rooted sentiment than was his affection for the big-hearted Bohemian; or, perhaps, because of this. In the train between Waterloo and Sunbury, George Barnard occupied a corner, and gazed steadily out through the carriage window, his feet crossed on the seat opposite him and his briar pipe slanting slightly upwards from the white teeth which gripped it. Occasionally he interpolated a brief remark, which was always breezy and seldom germane to anything under heaven, outside the speaker's clean fancy.

In the middle seat, on the same side of the carriage, his long fingers clasped over one raised knee, his uncovered head pressed against the dark blue of the cushions behind him—there was a Scandinavian glint in the fine lines of Harold Foster's hair—sat the man of a younger generation. His eyes were fixed on the seat facing him; his red lips, sensitive as an Æolian harp's strings, reflected every fleeting thought which crossed his mind, and seemed to tinge with hesitancy's greyness the vivid pertinence of much that he said. In the light of the high, white forehead, round the edges of which his hair clung in this summer noonday, like damp gold floss, his answers to Mr. Morley Fenton's questions were as full of meaning and understanding as a man might desire, and were enriched sometimes by nervously thrown out dramatic colour.

In the corner seat, on Harold Foster's right, was Mr. Morley Fenton. The two flaps of his dust-coat faced one another in geometrical alignment on his thin knees. The ash on the end of his half-smoked Trichinopoly was an inch and a half in length. No single hair among the many grey and the few brown under his glistening hat's brim had changed its position since Mr. Fenton had stood waiting on the doormat in Lombard Street. But where this hat's brim's little shadow fell across either side of Mr. Morley Fenton's forehead, thin, knotted, pale veins were throbbing and writhing, like baby snakes in the sun-warmed hollow of a fallen tree. Such things mean often nothing, and Mr. Morley Fenton never turned his head to look at Harold Foster. Yet his eyes, in sidelong seeingness, seemed never to leave the young man, who gazed at the seat facing him, and Mr. Fenton was conscious not only of every movement, but of every change of expression in Harold Foster's face and of every separate shade and tone in his dress.

The compartment had only one other occupant, and he wore a conspicuous amount of massive jewellery, and was immersed in the columns of a stock and share journal. But to anyone interested in human habits and idiosyncrasies, as keys to human complexities, these three men, their attitudes and bearing, would have afforded a study of rare interest. The stationmaster at Sunbury, for instance, had he been more analytically and less intuitively a student of humanity, would have keenly appreciated the opportunity.

"How do you get on now, at Mr. Winthrop's, Harold?" asked Mr. Morley Fenton, carefully tilting the ash of his cheroot through the open carriage window; gazing at the cheroot, yet seeing only Harold Foster, as one gazes at the top of one's paper, whilst seeing only a face opposite one.

"Oh, fairly well, I think, thanks. I can't take quite the absorbing interest in affairs of the vicarage which I fancy Mr. Winthrop expects me to take. They interest me so much less than—than other people's affairs."

"Ah! yes, I expect the home life there is a little confined. Very quiet, very quiet, I expect."

"No, it really is not quiet. On the contrary, there's always a host of little movements; but they are very little, as compared to the movements of places outside. They seem like the affairs of the students at Bart's, by the side of the affairs of the hospital."

Illness and other causes had carried Harold Foster's medical-student days into years somewhat more advanced than those of most of his contemporaries at the hospital.

"Yes. I was really thinking of the possible monotony of the Norwood life, when I asked George to persuade you to join us at Sunbury to-day. The life there is quiet enough, you know, but it will be a change, and if you have one or two different places to visit now and again, it may make the vicarage life more interesting. They are all really warmly interested in you there, you know, and the Winthrops are very excellent people."

"Very—very. Please don't think I blame them for any want of interest I may have in their home-life; but—you asked me."

"Yes, yes, exactly. I quite understand. But there is no excitement in their life, and you naturally look for incident and movement. But, believe me, Harold, I am speaking from a life's conviction when I say that the most beautiful thing in this world is simplicity, the most admirable state—and the strongest—is a reposeful one, and the happiest, never far from the domestic circle, with its innumerable inner wheels. Outside is a great deal of froth and bubble, some colour, and a lot of pain. Inside is responsibility, absolutely the only foundation of that happiness or content which lives. Outside is irresponsibility, a double-edged thing, which, if it gleams and laughs for an hour, wounds meanwhile for a life-time—wounds for a life-time, Harold, and wounds its lovers more deeply than its mere casual friends."

The big Bohemian in the farther corner of the carriage moved uneasily in his seat, drummed his fingers on the window-ledge, and remarked that the trail of the jerry-builder had fallen like a plague upon the Thames Valley.

Mr. Morley Fenton assented mechanically, and asked Harold Foster if he had made many friends at Bartholomew's.

"I don't think I have made any," said the young man, with some hesitation. "They seem to me rather like school—well, anyhow, I don't think I have made any friends. Do you know, I don't think I am very good at making friends."

"Ah! well, it is not a thing to do carelessly; but it is worth doing occasionally—well. This is our station."

The Sunbury stationmaster, not quite understanding Mr. Morley Fenton's appearance at 12.25 instead of at 1.48, was hurrying towards the carriage door, as the owner of Weir Lodge, with his friends, stepped on to the platform.

Ten minutes afterwards, the three, followed by one of the Weir Lodge gardeners who had met them at the station and was carrying the guests' joint belongings, were met on the verandah of the white house by Mrs. Fenton, the three girls, and Mr. Leo Tarne.

George Barnard nodded very stiffly over his presentation to Leo Tarne, and muttered something in an impossibly bass key about—" Pleasure before, I think."

Leo Tarne responded in a musical baritone to the effect that to him tried pleasures were quite the most delightful things in the world, because, unlike new ones, they were so full of illusions.

Harold Foster shook hands with the writer. He found instant interest in Leo Tarne's voice, his appearance, and the courtesy-cloaked insolence which his words suggested. On the very surface of things, Leo Tarne seemed the embodied antithesis of all that Harold Foster had, more of late than ever, found it difficult to interest himself in.

"Well, I hope you gentlemen will not find it very painful to lunch at half-past twelve. You see it takes some time to get down to Molesey in the gondola," said Mrs. Fenton.

"And really, what has time to do with meals, save to be focussed by them?" Leo Tarne appealed frankly to the summer air and sky. "Lunch creates the luncheon hour, don't you think; whereas the luncheon hour never creates lunch, does it?"

"And I know poor Mr. Barnard always breakfasts dreadfully early," suggested Maud, from over her mother's shoulder. "You can't possibly have tea before four, you know, on the river."

The barrister's smile was beautiful to see.

"Yes," he said, as the party filed into the house. "By Jove, Harold! you must tell Maud about that poached egg."

But Harold was speaking to Leo Tarne, and Leo Tarne was whispering to Norah, and Norah was examining Harold Foster with feminine subtlety of vision.

CHAPTER V.

THE PHILOSOPHY OF MOLESEY REGATTA.

> "Soft and softlier hold me, friends!
> Thanks if your genial care
> Unbind and give me to the air.
> Keep your lips and finger-tips
> For flute or spinet's dancing chips;
> I await a tenderer touch,
> I ask more or not so much:
> Give me to the atmosphere."
> *Maiden Speech of the Æolian Harp.*

GEORGE BARNARD did not gratify Lucy Fenton's æsthetic desires in the matter of boat furniture to the extent of appearing in brown velveteen; but he sat in the bows of the gondola, and, in a snowy duck-suit with flowing crimson sash, his blue cloth hat riding far back on his tawny head, and his great arms raised to serve, should occasion demand it, as fenders, the barrister was a strikingly picturesque figure in that sombre-looking craft. His knees, too, so Maud said, when covered by a cushion, formed a useful and reliable back-rest. Harold Foster and Mrs. Morley Fenton occupied the principal stern seat; Lucy Fenton and Norah sat facing them; and Leo Tarne, his blue-black hair and olive skin set off to perfection by a dark-green boating jacket, lounged on a couple of cushions between the two seats.

The gondola was fast jammed now in an interlocked flotilla of river craft of every shape and size, near the island opposite Garrick Villa. One of George Barnard's strong hands rested defensively on the gunwale of Lord Arthur Rendlesom's electric launch, the other on the stern of a rough punt, in which two tastefully attired and masked girls, with one good-looking cavalier, were singing songs from a popular comic opera, and accompanying themselves on different instruments. Later on, the boy who navigated their punt passed round an old banjo, in which a goodly collection of silver coins was taken. A little farther on, a low-caste conjurer made money by the antics of a dispirited guinea-pig, two white rats, and a blackguard monkey. On a well-kept lawn opposite the island a military band was playing a beautiful, if hackneyed, selection from a master's operatic work.

The air was full of that warm insidiousness which seems peculiar to the lower Thames, and which enables one to temporarily forget the pitiless bitterness of one half the northern year, and the flaunting insincerity of the other half. One could not see them, but one knew that midsummer roses and climbing yellow glories hung in heavy festoons about cottages near at hand. The whole world seemed drunk from the ripeness of things—ablaze with the passion of summer.

Where one could see the river's surface, it had absorbed the sky's beauty, and, rich in its wealth of blue, laughed back at the fathomless heavens. British fear of colour seems forgotten wholly on the river, and in all the densely-massed craft at this regatta were fair women and sunny-eyed maidens, decked in gauzy bravery, the very beauty of which would have frightened its wearers if seen elsewhere than in that bright carnival place of orthodox heterodoxy—the Thames in summer.

"I think Molesey is perfectly delicious," murmured Leo Tarne, addressing Norah. "It is so unlike Henley."

"But I think Henley delightful," replied the girl,

colouring slightly, from what cause it would have been hard to say.

"Do you really?" This was the class of question or remark into which Leo Tarne always seemed to put serious thought. Even the tone of his question, his differing from Norah, was made to sound in some way like a delicate compliment to the girl. Or, at least, Harold Foster thought so, as he sat listening in the stern of the gondola.

"But surely Henley is so big, so like the Derby, or a Drury Lane pantomime," continued Tarne. "It always strikes me in that way. Henley seems to take itself seriously"—he waved one graceful hand in the direction of the conjurer's boat, and the mass of varied colour beyond it—"whereas Molesey is so charmingly irresponsible."

Harold Foster leaned forward suddenly. Floating through his mind, as from quite a distant past, came Mr. Morley Fenton's words of that morning: "Irresponsibility, a double-edged thing, which if it gleams and laughs for an hour, wounds, meanwhile, for a lifetime."

"And is that really an advantage?" he asked, surprised and half ashamed at his own seriousness.

"Oh, surely!" replied Tarne, without turning his head from Norah.

"Even apart from regattas?"

Harold had hardly intended to give utterance to this. Perhaps something in the medical student's tone, or in his attitude when they first met, had roused interest in Leo Tarne. At all events, he moved slightly on his cushions now, and his dark eyes lighted up with half-amused surprise, as, looking into the younger man's eager face, he said:

"Certainly, Mr. Foster. Nothing is enjoyable without irresponsibility; just as, I take it, life holds no other responsibility worth recognising than the finding out and enjoying of the enjoyable. That seems to me fundamental and—surely—elementary."

"But would you take nothing seriously?"

"Nothing but the avoidance of the serious."

"And duty?"

"Is enjoyment; and knowing that, is life; and life is delightful, unless one is misguided enough to fall into bad habits, and find seriousness, as the men who wear red jerseys 'find' religion."

"But, Mr. Tarne"—again Norah coloured when she heard her own voice—"if no one took anything seriously, nothing would ever be done."

"Then people would have time to live, instead of doing things. It is because so many people insist on doing things, Miss Fenton, that so few people, comparatively, have any happiness nowadays."

"Well, but I'm sure that cannot be right, Mr. Tarne. For instance, we should not have this. There would be no judges and umpires and secretaries and things."

"Then we should have none of these stupid races to interrupt the regatta."

"But they are the regatta."

"Hardly. Surely the colour, and the music, and the river, and the sunshine—you and I and the summer, together, are the regatta."

"That is true," said Mrs. Morley Fenton; "because you know, nobody takes any notice of the races. But your doctrine is false, Mr. Tarne, delightfully untrue. You know it is. He is not in the least serious, Norah dear."

"Heaven and the summer forfend, my dear Mrs. Fenton! That would be the basest kind of apostasy, and at Molesey—sacrilege. Mr. Foster is serious at this moment; but that is unavoidable, a catastrophe.

Mr. Foster is listening to the man in burnt cork, who is making jokes. The burnt cork men who make jokes! There you have the real criminal class; the men who throw a shadow of gloom over the life of a comparatively innocent community. Such men should be placed under restraint, or in the House of Commons."

"Mrs. Fenton!" George Barnard's big voice came booming breezily along from the gondola's bows. "If you don't let me have some tea or some lemonade or some other gentle stimulant, I shall throw up my position as chief fender, and come down there on a filibustering expedition."

"Mr. Barnard, you are not to move. If you do, you will knock my hat off, and our friendship will be ended. Little mother, for the sake of peace, and my hat, send some lemonade along, please."

"I will, Maud dear, I will. Lucy, protect your sister and her hat. Mr. Barnard, I think you take a very unfair advantage of your indispensable position."

Waking suddenly from the fit of abstraction into which he had been thrown by the suggestive influence of Leo Tarne's personality, and his carelessly expounded mock philosophy, Harold Foster came to the conclusion that he was neglecting people in general, and his hostess in particular. So he began to bestir himself in finding lemonade for the barrister, in spasmodically interesting conversational efforts, and in preparations for tea. Hence it was that in the course of the next half-hour Mrs. Morley Fenton arrived at the conclusion that Mr. Barnard's friend was really a most excellent young man, when once his shyness had been penetrated by her tactful diplomacy. Lucy Fenton formed the same opinion, giving to her own tact the credit of having broken through the young man's reserve. Norah had, from a much earlier pe-

THE PHILOSOPHY OF MOLESEY REGATTA. 39

riod, shared the first half of Mrs. Fenton's conclusion.

Leo Tarne, being considerably vainer and more centred on himself than anyone else in the party, came very much nearer to discerning the true cause of Harold Foster's sudden opening out, and felt a thrill of pleasure and gratification in connection therewith. He felt that in some only half-understood way he was exerting the first great personal influence which had entered into the life of this young man with the viking-like head and the femininely beautiful mouth. And Leo Tarne was right in his conclusion. He generally was right in his unspoken opinions, just as he was wrong in almost all those thoughts to which he gave utterance. It was Leo Tarne's habit to put most of his thoughts into words, though perhaps the man himself seldom believed anything that he said.

Now, his decision in this matter was an interesting and pleasing discovery to Leo Tarne, for it was an axiom of his that " all interesting people lead illustrated lives," and here to his hand was the possibility of appearing in a creative rôle. But yet he was interested in Norah and her pale budding womanhood; in the dark wonder of her eyes, set in the goldleaf frame of her nineteen-year-old dainty freshness. And then, he told himself, Harold Foster with his tense eagerness for revelation—Harold Foster would come to him. Norah could only allow him to come to her.

So Leo Tarne, thinking of his illustrated life, talked for the most part to Norah, though to some extent for Harold Foster. And Harold conversed nervously, yet far better than was his wont, with Mrs. Morley Fenton and with Lucy; only occasionally throwing, as from sheer necessity, a sentence, a suggestion, or a question, into the current between Leo Tarne and Norah; a current in which brilliant, soulless banter carried earnest, girlish wonder along its glistening surface into whirlpools of mazed perplexity, where vivid lights baffled resistance. And in return for these outthrown interpolations grateful looks were shot at him from Norah's soft eyes; looks which never reached Harold because he saw only Leo Tarne's inscrutable smiles, and heard only Leo Tarne's unanswerable cynicism, which seemed to mock reason, and to laugh behind a veil at itself.

At last the late summer's evening, having passed through night's purple-draped ante-chamber, merged into blue darkness. Some few of the illuminations the Weir Lodge party waited to see, Mrs. Fenton having purposely ordered dinner that evening to be at half-past nine. Then came the slow passage up stream, past the places where a hundred lights multiplied themselves in the river's glamour to a thousand ropes of rippling, ever-changing colour; past the camping-ground, where singing and playing were made musical by distance and the night's soft harmony; on past the range of scattered, twinkling lights into the hushed, billowy blackness of the backwater below Sunbury, where the lisping stream kissed the hidden feet of the trees, and the trees rocked and sighed out their murmurings of love to the night which clung around them.

Immeasurably the superior of Tritton, the minor poet who practised silence from economical motives, Leo Tarne was generally made intuitively aware of those moments in which silence is golden in an artistic sense. He did not allow the light of this sweet darkness to make naked the source from which his whimsicalities were drawn. Among his sins the making of discords had no place.

When dinner was over that evening, the men of the party elected to take their coffee with tobacco on the verandah which skirted the front and one side of Weir Lodge. The ladies gathered about the open windows of the drawing-room, where Norah, a born musician and by education a most accomplished pianist, played dreamy music by the light of one crimson taper. The day had been one full of interest and of new impressions to pale, dark-eyed Norah.

On the verandah it seemed natural that Mr. Morley Fenton and George Barnard should enjoy their cheroots in the two great hammock-chairs which stood near the porch, and as natural that the two younger men should loungingly betake themselves and their cigarettes to the farther end of the verandah, where the moon, lately risen, poured broad streams of glistening tenderness over bloom-fragrant trellis work and climbing rose-trees.

"It is very beautiful, very clean-smelling; and—this Thames is a wonderful place."

Harold Foster was just then too saturated by all the night's beauty to be very lucid in speaking of it.

"It is, is it not?" assented the writer, who was perfectly cool and at peace with himself. "And is it all new to you, Mr. Foster?"

"Perfectly new. Oh yes, it is quite new to me. I don't know why. I have often been on the Thames before, but yet it is all quite new to me to-day."

Leo Tarne smiled slightly as he took his cigarette from his lips. Apparently, then, he had not only been revealing Harold Foster to Harold Foster. He had unintentionally revealed much else beside. The process was extremely interesting, he thought. And his thinking that he had done these things was not mere vanity but truth, though the fact that he, Leo Tarne, and no other, had done them was possibly merely an accident of circumstance. But, as Leo Tarne would have said, the very existence of the young man was no more than that. He was very much older, apart from years, than Harold Foster, and knew very much more, though the limits of his understanding's possibilities may have been far narrower.

"And you are glad you came down here to-day, Mr. Foster, are you not?"

"Very glad."

"You have seen and felt more than you would if you had spent the day at the hospital."

"Oh, the hospital! I see nothing there but realities, and feel nothing but facts."

"And reality does not interest you?"

"Because those realities seem to me so small. They make me feel that there must be far more reality and beauty in what are called fancies and trifles, outside."

"There are no realities, Mr. Foster, and there is certainly no beauty, save in what the average man either does not see at all, or brushes aside as trifles, or rigidly abstains from as improper, because fascinating. The average man takes seriously nothing that he cannot understand, and understands nothing which is beautiful. That is why ugliness is so respectable, and the lives of respectable folk so ugly. On the other hand, the classes we consider not respectable have no understanding at all, and are simply ugly by instinct."

"But according to that there is no beauty left in the world at all."

"Oh, the world! I think it has just as much beauty as it ever had; but the really beautiful, like the essentially ugly, exists in the mind of the man who feels and sees it. That is the basis of society's morality, Mr. Foster. An individual with ugliness in his mind looks upon a certain thing, and sees in it, of course, only ugliness; you look at the same thing, your mind being free from ugliness, and see in it only beauty. Consequently, you desire to enjoy it. But the other man,

THE PHILOSOPHY OF MOLESEY REGATTA. 43

representing, unfortunately, the majority, having looked at the thing through the curtain of his soul's ugliness, has labelled it immoral, or absurd, or bad form, as the case may be. Therefore, the thing is not to you a new delight, but a temptation to be resisted. If you resist it, you sicken with desire for it—that makes it a really immoral and unnatural thing to you; if you yield to it, you do so in the face of the label, and forthwith the thing we call conscience tells you plainly that you are immoral, or absurd, or guilty of bad form. So a system of morality is built."

"Do only those ostracized by society enjoy life's beauties, then?"

"No; but only those who themselves ostracize society from their inner lives have any conception of life's chiefest beauties."

"But how can a man do this?"

"Ah! that is a question for a man's individual senses to answer. I should say he would achieve it by never speaking as he thought, and never acting in opposition to a thought. You see, the average man says what he thinks, and acts as society tells him to. Consequently, his inner self lives hungry and dies starved, and beauty does not enter into his life. But there is colour—a wealth of colour—and life, and tremulous, vivid beauty, in a world some men discover, and their discovery of it entails what I mean by a man's ostracizing society from his inner life. And if society should ostracize him from itself, so much the worse for society, for the very casual outward contact into which conventional men and women may be brought with him affords humanity a fresh impetus, and gives to the cramped world of tired-out orthodoxy little flash glimpses into unknown worlds of colour, sound, and beauty; little suggested whiffs of freer air, which fill men's veins like wine, and tinge with faint rose-light the bloodless drab of their existence. Oh, believe me, there is beauty, warmth, and poetry—not depicted in dead imagery, but in the living, in the red, throbbing life, of sound, and touch, and sight—for him who, having beauty, can beauty see!"

The man who said these things raised one cool hand to his lips, and puffed delicately at his cigarette, pouring out then into the sheen of the moonlight a cloud of yellow, aroma-cloyed smoke. The man who listened dropped his cigarette from between damp, nerveless fingers, which he raised and passed quickly across his forehead. He felt all the other man had said, and felt it the more intensely because it seemed to him not an expression of Leo Tarne's opinions, but the shaping, the voicing, of all his own most deeply-felt thoughts, and vaguest hot longings. But the expression, the shaping, the voicing, were those of one who had achieved all that he, Harold Foster, had dreamed and thought. This dark, handsome man at his side, with his low, mellow voice, and his deep-set, impenetrable eyes, had revealed to Harold Foster many of the hidden, cloudy possibilities of his nature, and this by mere suggestion. That is because he has lived these possibilities, thought Harold. And he felt full of gratitude to the young man lounging beside him, and of desire to know more of him and of his life.

"Mr. Tarne," he began, "you have shown me much to-day and suggested more, but will you——"

"Harold! Mr. Tarne! If you can tear yourselves away from your moon-worship, the ladies want us to go and hear some music."

Mr. Morley Fenton was speaking from the porch at the other end of the verandah.

"The moon's attractions grow misty and fade, Mr. Fenton, in the light of those you offer," said Leo Tarne. And then, as they strolled down the verandah, he added in a whisper to Harold Foster: "We have enjoyed some beauty out here, where the moon drapes all things, let us go and find more now, of another kind, in the drawing-room. It is there, I am sure, and in addition to what came out to us through the window. And, thank Heaven! the vulgarity of constancy never appealed to me. Fidelity is the unoriginal man's excuse for his inability to discover."

"Then I am glad you have no fidelity," returned the younger man.

"That is, you are not sorry we met."

"That is, I am very thankful we met, and—that you have no need of the excuse you mentioned."

"You must come and see me at the little place above the weir; I shall be back in town in a month or six weeks."

And then they entered the drawing-room behind Mr. Morley Fenton, and Leo Tarne, with a little smile as of understanding, left Harold by Mrs. Fenton's side, and himself took a place close to where Norah sat at the piano.

Later on, when George Barnard was finishing a final smoke in his host's study, Mr. Fenton said to him:

"By the way, George, what do you think of young Tarne? Clever fellow, isn't he?"

"Ye-es, I should think so—very. Of course, every man lives and works according to his lights, and Leo Tarne's may be truer and better than mine. Personally I don't like 'em. I can't tell you why, but they don't seem to me the thing. Leo Tarne and his work represent what I call 'elimination,' which perhaps conveys nothing to you. But, as I say, every man lives and works according to his lights. He wrote 'Where Wings are Singed,' you know."

"Yes, yes, I know; but my wife assures me he is really a most excellent young fellow. I know he comes of very good people—in the accepted sense, I mean."

"Quite so. Please don't let me prejudice you against him. That would be very absurd, coming from me. But I confess I don't like him. To me he is like the cigarettes he smokes—medicated Egyptian, I suppose."

"H'm! I think Harold enjoyed his day. Do you think he did, George?"

"Very much, I should imagine; and, at all events, there's no doubt Mr. Leo Tarne pleased him."

"Upon my word, George, I believe you are jealous of the writer."

"Say of the man," replied the barrister with an abrupt laugh. "I don't admire his writings."

While these two talked in the study, Leo Tarne was strolling idly along in the moonlight, cigarette in hand, towards his bungalow.

"I must cultivate Harold Foster," he murmured to himself. "He is like some rare old wine, new-discovered—like a beautiful stringed thing with a thousand new chords and strange melodies, lying waiting for my fingers to play on. He is as responsive as the trees to the wind, and as sensitive as a thought unborn, a poem half conceived. And then there's that girl, with her Botticelli head and her dainty face. Such eyes, too! Heigho! it's a charming world, if one could only remain long enough in it without being bored."

At the bedroom window immediately above Mr. Morley Fenton's study, Harold Foster was standing. He was looking out into the beautiful night, to where the river curled like a silver snake past the knoll, above which was visible the quaint Oriental turret of Leo Tarne's bungalow.

"He will show me that life he has found, where

THE PHILOSOPHY OF MOLESEY REGATTA. 47

the colour is and the beauty. I almost grudge that girl the time he devotes to her, because—and she's a charming girl, too. She is a charming girl."

"It's been a beautiful day," said Norah in parting from Maud Fenton that night; "it's been a delicious day. But do you know, Maud, I think that Mr. Tarne would have left a sort of nasty taste in my mouth if—if it hadn't been for Mr. Foster."

CHAPTER VI.

MORNING SUNSHINE AND FRUIT.

> "I saw where the sun's hand pointed,
> I knew what the bird's note said ;
> By the dawn and the dewfall anointed,
> You were queen by the gold on your head."
> *An Interlude.*

By her last speech to Maud Fenton on the night of the Molesey Regatta, Norah frankly implied that Harold Foster had produced a favourable impression upon her. It was not a daring implication, and almost any girl might have ventured as much; yet, on the morning following this same night, wild horses, whose persuasive powers, as every mere phrase-vendor is aware, are practically irresistible, could not have drawn from Norah the admission that Harold Foster had impressed her in any way whatsoever. She faced the world on that Sunday morning, bearing conspicuously about her shapely person announcements as to her absolute ignorance of even the existence of this same Harold Foster.

Between the evening of Molesey Regatta and the bright, sweet-smelling morning of Sunday, a whole peaceful night had passed. And if in a single night a baby mushroom may reach maturity, or a man travel from England to France, surely in the same period there may be such happenings in the closely-allied mind and heart of an English girl in her twentieth year as will produce almost any development from the previous day's condition.

MORNING SUNSHINE AND FRUIT. 49

But such transitions lend themselves not to man's coarse analysis—less still, perhaps, to that of woman. Words record them, and, being themselves clumsy things, may be made to set off the delicacy of these fairy growths. But words do not describe or explain them.

Having parted from Maud Fenton on Saturday night, Norah had seated herself at the window of her own room, and gazed out over the quiet river to the sleeping country beyond. For a long while she had sat there, thinking of things and people that had come into her life during the day. And when every other thing and everybody beside had faded away from her mind into the soft, black night, Harold Foster had remained. Long afterwards, when one side of her face was pillowed on her rounded right arm, like brown cream on snow, when her great eyes slowly closed and she drifted into light sleep, the last milestone of consciousness which her mind passed had indicated that Harold Foster would be reached next morning.

When morning came, Norah, the warm flush of sleep still in her cheeks, spied George Barnard's friend walking in the garden. It was Norah's invariable custom to gather flowers in the garden before breakfast. Now she might have done so in the company of a young man who, according to her own words of the previous night, had impressed her favourably. Yet so marked had been the developments of the night that Norah chose rather to altogether forego her morning outing. She made her first appearance in the breakfast-room, and only a few minutes before the family sat down to breakfast. Doubtless with the idea of in some way occupying the time she usually spent in the garden, she had dressed her rippling hair no less than three times that morning, and had tentatively exhausted the resources of her wardrobe before deciding upon a costume for the day.

And yet the management of her toilette showed signs of extreme carelessness—signs made clear by what happened when, on entering the breakfast-room, Norah found its sole occupant to be Harold Foster, who stood loungingly in one of the open French windows.

The morning had so far been to Harold Foster golden and joyous as the bird's song which, floating in at his open bedroom window, had waked him to the consciousness of life and sunshine. For an hour he had strolled about in sunlight, drinking in the scented sweetness of the breath of flowers, newly waked and glistening from their baths of dew. He had stolen from the basket of a passing gardener a bunch of hot-house grapes, heavy with purple-gray bloom. These he had eaten with childish delight, strolling under leafy trellises the while, like Alkibiades in Sokrates' garden.

Now he stood leaning on one side of the breakfast-room window, which opened on to the verandah. The fragrance of summer morning was in his nostrils, the silky wine of the great purple grapes clung still to his palate, and his mind was a-tremble with imaginings of beauty to be discovered, joy to be found, and mysteries to be unfolded to him. No spurious glitter had been apparent to him in Leo Tarne or in Leo Tarne's words; and, in this morning sunlight, at all events, the self-revelation inspired by the young writer meant to Harold Foster nothing save beauty and delight. Henceforth his life was to be one of tasting, thrilling—the drinking in of colour and music, the discovering and feasting upon hitherto hidden beauty.

He raised his head, his lips being parted smilingly, and he saw Norah. It seemed to him rather that some soft, creamy material floated round her, than that she was dressed in any particular way. And her face—its perfect Tuscan oval—had light and colour in it which on the previous day had not been there. Where her hair dipped into a little valley there flamed a single poppy, vivid as the season which gave it birth. Her lips, too, were parted. Harold Foster sighed from pure pleasure. She was simply the crown and soul and emblem of his morning-time imaginings; the sun and stars and spirit-light of his new life that was to be. His parted lips set themselves involuntarily to articulate his wonder and delight:

"Oh!"

He made no further sound, and, in any case, another moment must have brought a wave of reality to drench him with confusion. But the girl was the first to waken, the feminine mind being, perhaps, more accessible to reality than is that of the man. Norah did not wait to hear more. The young man's exclamation had been sufficiently luminous.

"There! I have come down without a handkerchief. Good-morning, Mr. Foster!"

And the girl passed out of the man's range of vision as swiftly as she had flashed into it. Harold Foster blushed crimson to the roots of his yellow hair, and, turning, walked quickly into the garden, as Mr. Morley Fenton entered the breakfast-room.

CHAPTER VII.

A MATTER FOR MR. FENTON TO DECIDE.

" The beggar begs by God's command,
 And gifts awake when givers sleep ;
 Swords cannot cut the giving hand
 Nor stab the love that orphans keep."
Life.

DURING the three weeks which followed that queer Sunday morning meeting of Mr. Morley Fenton's protégé and his adopted daughter, Harold Foster paid six separate visits to Weir Lodge, and of these, two were stays over the week-end. True, in the case of the other four the medical student went down to Sunbury as the guest of Leo Tarne, and appeared with his host at the white house where Norah was. True was it also, and a little strange, that whether these visits to Weir Lodge led to boating, or lounging in the pretty garden, or chatting and listening to music in the many-windowed drawing-room—whatever the circumstances under which the two young men met Norah Fenton chanced to be, it was Leo Tarne who held the girl in conversation, and Harold Foster who occupied her thoughts and gave direction to her glances.

To Norah, Leo Tarne was an accident and a useful background, the environment in which she met Harold Foster.

To Leo Tarne, so far as his attitude to Norah was concerned, Harold Foster, despite his interest outside Weir Lodge as a study and a cultivation, was the veriest accident, and a piece of machinery the exist-

A MATTER FOR MR. FENTON TO DECIDE. 53

ence of which made more natural and easy than it might otherwise have been his—Tarne's—access to the girl whose eyes were like smooth-surfaced water in twin moorland pools.

And to Harold Foster, in the first flush of all the lately-revealed possibilities within him, Leo Tarne was the light and guide by whose aid he obtained vistas of his new life; and Norah was the emblem and embodiment of that new life's beauty. The neophyte is not at first jealous, perhaps not even envious, of his devout superior's advanced position in the path of flesh-subduing spirituality. And one may imagine circumstances under which the veteran superior's religious vanity might debar him from recognition of greater spiritual strength in the wondering-eyed neophyte than he, with his zeal grown hoary, had attained.

Harold Foster was by no means at this time in love with Norah Fenton. He was merely in love with his new life, or with his new conception of what his life might be. But if at that time Norah had disappeared from within the limits of his mind's horizon, as she had disappeared from out his range of wondering vision on the morning following Molesey Regatta, then the summit and the crown of things would have been lacking in the beauty vistas before him.

One of the few remarks which, coming from Leo Tarne, had crossed Harold Foster's tight-strung understanding, as crosses a ship's rigging one of those sudden gusts of chill wind near the Equator herald in the balmiest atmosphere the approach of a squall— one of the few things the writer had said which had caused a shiver, transient as thought itself, to pass through the younger man, was: " I make a point of never falling in love. It is so far to fall; so much trouble to get up again. And it is demoralizing, without the excuse of being immoral—according to Society's standards. So I confine myself to being either charmed or bored by people. That involves no narrowing of vision, and has the advantage of leaving one unsatisfied. The other merely dissatisfies."

Thus the two men in this curiously-situated trio. And Norah? But who shall venture, or desire, to probe into and analyze, on paper, that thing whose dainty, world-untouched simplicity is more complex than is the beauty of a daisy, dew-jewelled and blooming in a morning-sun-kissed meadow? Who would seek to pry into the heart of a maiden of nineteen? Norah, breathing soft happiness behind her white veil of only half-realized womanhood, was ready to stretch out a helping hand to Harold Foster, should he fall. And Harold Foster was drinking in deep draughts of new insight into new worlds. And Leo Tarne, in writing to one in London whom he addressed as "Carissima," spoke of being dominated by a "growing desire to carry a shepherd's crook and take lessons in playing upon a reed."

Then a thing happened.

Mrs. Fenton and the three girls were chatting, and drawing out the anti-climax of the family reunion at the breakfast-table. The lighting of Mr. Morley Fenton's cheroot was invariably the climax of the morning gatherings. Maud was in unusually high spirits even for her. In conversationally trotting about the universe she had happened across Leo Tarne and her father's protégé.

"Not that I know anything about them, of course, but I've met them casually when you have been otherwise occupied for a moment, my dear." This to Norah, over whose creamy face blushes scudded, like torn cloudlets in an October sky.

"Maud! How absurd!"

"Oh! I think it's worse—it's wicked. Poor things! They don't know which is which."

"What *do* you mean?"

"But I wouldn't so much mind your enslaving Mr. Tarne, though the poor man is dying to keep his promise about telling me how people write books, if you would only let Mr. Foster off."

"Maud—please!"

Mrs. Morley Fenton looked up quickly, like a bird, from a letter she was skimming, and saw the blushes die suddenly, leaving pallor behind them, in Norah's face.

"Because he's much more interesting," continued Maud mercilessly, "and much less enslaved."

"Don't be foolish, Maud dear," said her mother, with wakening thoughtfulness.

"He is, little mother—much more interesting. In fact, he's perfectly insane in some things."

Again Mrs. Fenton's eyes turned, bird-like, towards Norah. Norah's eyes flashed ominously, while her colour returned quickly.

"But even then," concluded Maud, with a little *moue* expressive of resignation, "I don't mind very much, as long as you leave me my dear Mr. Barnard."

This was the thing that happened, and it only occupied a few seconds; but its results were considerable. With Maud's last word came back to her Norah's momentarily-lost girlish diplomacy, and she laughed lightly, rallying Maud upon her devotion to the big barrister.

But her mother was wiser than Maud, or, at least, knew more. Leo Tarne and Harold Foster had promised to dine at Weir Lodge that evening. They did so, and when they left, after an hour or two spent in the drawing-room and in the conservatory opening out of it, Mrs. Fenton knew even more. Armed with her knowledge gained that day, and her impressions as to the tendencies of the last few weeks, Mrs. Fenton sat down to chat with her husband, after the girls had retired for the night.

Mr. Morley Fenton was a little worried that evening. But he was not given to showing his worries to his wife, nor often to anyone else. He had looked in at Bartholomew's during the day, but had not found Harold Foster there. Meeting the resident surgeon, whom he knew well, as he was leaving the building, he had been told that during the last few weeks young Foster's place—he was "clerking" at the time—had had to be filled by another student.

"Pity, you know," said the surgeon, "because this is an important time to him. He has been getting frightfully irregular in his attendance here lately. I expect he's reading too much, you know, and missing practice for theory. Great mistake—great mistake, because he's a very clever fellow, when he likes."

Mr. Morley Fenton had assented, with apparent unconcern, and walked away. He did not share the surgeon's inference about Harold Foster's devotion to reading. He was wiser than the surgeon, and knew more; just as his wife knew more of certain other matters than did Maud.

"My dear," began Mrs. Fenton, "what is the exact nature of your relation to young Mr. Foster?"

It was not in the nature of things that Mr. Morley Fenton, with all his restraint and impassive self-control, should have been able to avoid some slight token of the shock with which this question came to him. A very slight tremor passed over his spare frame. The muscles of his face contracted ever so little, and the skin over his high cheek-bones whitened.

"I don't quite follow you, dear," he said, with quiet precision, and after a luminously comprehensive pause.

A MATTER FOR MR. FENTON TO DECIDE. 57

"I mean, I don't know anything about his position. He is an orphan, I think you said, and I am in doubt as to how far your interest in him would carry you in a matter bearing upon one of ourselves."

"I am afraid my density leaves me still in the dark."

Mr. Morley Fenton was feeling his way cautiously —as behoves a man in the dark.

"Well, Morley, there is, of course, no very serious question involved—at present. But there is a very distinct inclination on Mr. Foster's part to develop love-making tendencies where our Norah is concerned, and—well, as a matter of fact, there is a stronger tendency on Norah's side to invite them. That is really what makes the situation pronounced, and were it not for that I should scarcely anticipate any result, because there are two of the young men. Mr. Tarne pays her pointed attentions. But I am sure I am not mistaken in thinking that she is absolutely indifferent to them, because of her inclination towards Mr. Foster."

"This is very unfortunate, and very surprising."

"Hardly surprising, my dear. It is a way young men and young women have. Of course, as I think I said, there is no serious question involved at present; but I am quite sure that you should decide at once whether or no you would care for it to become serious. That is why I wanted to know how far your interest in this young man went."

"You are sure the impression you have formed is correct, I suppose?" queried Mr. Morley Fenton, thoughtfully.

"Quite, dear. You see, we women learn to know something of the stages in such matters—though, to be frank, I must confess that my eyes were considerably opened by some joking of Maud's this morning."

"Oh! it has gone so far?"

"Well, yes; but Maud took quite a mistaken view, and did not for a moment regard the thing seriously. She had been more impressed by Mr. Tarne's attentions to Norah."

"H'm! Perhaps it is fortunate Mr. Tarne has been here so much lately."

"Yes; he is a charming man."

"Ah!"

Mr. Morley Fenton rose slowly from his chair, and said he had a couple of letters to write in his study before going to bed.

"You had better not wait, my dear; and—don't let this matter worry you. You are not expecting Harold Foster to-morrow, are you?"

"No! If he comes it can be only to call. He has not been asked."

"Yes! Good-night, dear. I shall not stay up late."

So the head of the house left the room slowly, and, with head erect and face impassive, walked across the hall, pausing to lower one of the lamps at the foot of the stairs, and stepping quietly then into his private room. Years had passed since the days in which Mr. Morley Fenton had been wont to decide impulsively, and at once, upon a course of action relating to any one set of circumstances. His wife could not remember those days, and may possibly have never known them.

Mr. Fenton wrote his two letters—even in the matter of excuses, he preferred always that his remarks should have a foundation of truth—and very able, lucid business letters they were. He did this in the way, and with the motives, which induce some men to cough, or to brush their hair, or to mix themselves glasses of brandy and soda-water, under similar circumstances. Then he leaned back in his chair to think

A MATTER FOR MR. FENTON TO DECIDE. 59

calmly, clearly, and with perfect freedom from emotional bias.

Next morning, when Mr. Fenton was shaving, his wife asked him naïvely if he had been late in coming upstairs on the previous night.

"No, dear; not very, I think."

But the Sunbury stationmaster thought Mr. Morley Fenton looked a little weary and over-worked that morning. And on the strength of it the good man told his wife that the Liberal Government was making "times worse and worse for people of position." The stationmaster was regarded by his own circle as being a warm man, whose fingers were more or less always on the great financial pulse of England. On the evening of this same day, the stationmaster's worst fears were borne out by the arrival of the 4.30 from Waterloo without Mr. Morley Fenton.

"Like as not there's been a run on some of the banks to-day," he said to Mrs. Johnson, as he sat down to drink a cup of tea before the arrival of the "forty-seven up."

At a quarter to four that afternoon Mr. Morley Fenton knocked at the outer door of George Barnard's chambers. He had only twice entered these chambers during the years which had elapsed since his days of part-proprietorship of them.

"Come!" shouted the barrister. "Door's ajar, isn't it?"

Mr. Morley Fenton entered the dark little lobby, closed the outer door behind him, and stepped forward into the barrister's working den.

He was welcomed at the outset by a curly brown dog, whose expression and general air of chuckling confidence suggested that he was on the verge of telling a ludicrously funny story. With a transparent pretence at recollection of having met Mr. Fenton on a previous occasion, this utterly undignified animal rolled leeringly on its back at the feet of the newcomer, declining altogether to consider the possibility of being trodden upon by any friend of its master.

The room was so consistently and excessively untidy as to produce at first an impression of careful arrangement. It seemed, for example, impossible to Mr. Morley Fenton that a man could reach without forethought that inspired contrariety which would lead to the hanging of hats on picture-brackets, whilst pictures stood leaning against the wainscoting, and a hat-rack supported an array of fishing-rods and tackle, surmounted by a pile of dust-coated magazines.

This was merely one slight example, however, of the curious "looking-glass land" effects which confronted one at every turn in George Barnard's chambers. The curly brown dog, the preposterous familiarity of whose welcome to Mr. Morley Fenton had almost disconcerted that gentleman, slept every night on an elaborate plush foot-warmer, which a maiden relative had designed and constructed as a receptacle for George Barnard's feet when he sat writing at night. The floor of the working den was somewhat draughty, and so beside the plush foot-warmer lay an open and dilapidated Gladstone bag, in which, on chilly nights, George Barnard was wont to rest his feet.

"Good-evening, George!"

"Hullo, old man! By Jove! is it really you? Well, I am glad to see you in the old room."

"Thank you, George. I looked in on my way home because I wanted to have a chat with you. Could you come down and sleep at Sunbury to-night?"

"I'm sorry, but I couldn't possibly this evening. I have to take some work to the *Budget* folk before eleven. They go to press in the morning, you know. But sit down, old man. Half a second! Not that

A MATTER FOR MR. FENTON TO DECIDE. 61

chair. Would you mind taking the couch? Yes, the same old couch. I'm going to buy another—er—shortly. Will you have some coffee, or—or some whisky? My housekeeper is out. You know her way. No, not dear old Mrs. Mugby. Quite a young thing—with a hare-lip and spasms."

Mr. Fenton deposited his hat, with some hesitation, on the couch beside him.

"That's a curious dog, George."

"Yes, poor thing, she is peculiar. She was being drowned when I first met her, and the man wanted to go on drowning her, so I gave him sixpence and a cigar—I thought of punching his head at first—and brought her home here. I think it rather affected her brain, you know—the drowning, I mean—but she's quite harmless, and very affectionate."

"Yes, it seems affectionate. A—— But I ought not to interrupt you."

"Oh, it's all right, my dear fellow, only I can't come down to Sunbury, that's all. Let's have a chat now. I can spare any amount of time, you know, and perhaps Mrs. Greet will come in by-and-by and give us some tea. What's the nature of the case?"

The briefless barrister's lips curled smilingly over the mouthpiece of the pipe he had lighted. He was all attention.

"Well, the fact is, George, I have some grounds for believing that there is a likelihood of Harold Foster and my adopted daughter, Norah, falling in love with each other."

The barrister smiled again at the end of a long puff of cool smoke.

"Well, Morley, and why shouldn't they fall in love with each other?" he said.

Mr. Morley Fenton stroked his moustache gently, and sighed.

CHAPTER VIII.

MR. MORLEY FENTON'S DECISION.

"When a man, aping Providence, fingers the reins of Destiny, then Heaven echoes the sighs of angels, God's frown makes darkness, and Hell is filled with the sound of mocking laughter."—CLUNY's *Reflections*.

MR. MORLEY FENTON did not make any verbal reply to George Barnard's question. Perhaps the barrister expected none. At all events, when his friend had sighed a second time, George Barnard continued speaking as though his first question had met with its answer, an answer which required parrying.

"Exactly," he said. "I have not forgotten all that. But, my friend, people are not such hidebound blockheads nowadays—in some matters—as they were. Hal is simply Harold Foster, a young man without family or relatives, but with a guardian whose —well, Morley Fenton is not a bad name to-day, is it? A pretty good name, in the most pharisaical circles, I think."

Mr. Morley Fenton's firmly-set lips, richly suggestive of that strength in a man which goes to place his name on an unassailable pinnacle—these firm, retentive lips gave no sign of acquiescence or dissent. Yet, between these two men, their strangely-linked lives and widely-divided positions and personalities, the compliment implied was a high one. Mr. Fenton's lips parted abruptly.

"And at any moment some unforeseen chance might fling in his teeth——"

MR. MORLEY FENTON'S DECISION. 63

"The fact that by an unfortunate train of circumstances, his mother died before his father was able to become her legal husband."

The little veins in Mr. Morley Fenton's temples throbbed and writhed. He crossed his legs with a movement peculiarly spasmodic in a man so precise and deft.

"My dear fellow," continued the barrister, "that is just what I referred to a moment ago. People are not such hide-bound idiots to-day, in some respects, as they were in our younger days. A man is judged and esteemed by his own manhood."

"And a gentleman, to a large extent, now, as ever, by his birth, and his 'people.'" The owner of Weir Lodge spoke with quiet bitterness. "No, George. You judge the world—the section of it which I live in—as you always did, by the standards of your work-a-day Bohemia. I spent last night—I spent a considerable time last night—in thinking this matter out. In the world I want Harold Foster to live in, the only world it is safe for him to live in, I know what such a discovery would mean. It would mean a slur being cast on an innocent man, and, if he had a wife, on an innocent woman, and later, on innocent children. That slur could never be lived down—unless by a very strong man in a life containing no mistake, no slightest deviation. And, George, the girl is my dead brother's child."

"Yes, yes, I know. But, believe me, you are over-sensitive in the matter. You exaggerate the view which people take of such things—you do indeed. And then you know, old man, he—well, you may be sure Hal will marry someone."

"But not necessarily my adopted daughter, for whose life I am responsible. No. And that is not all, George. Here are two young lives, both of which I know. My care of Norah must needs be even more watchful than if she were my own daughter. Would it be just or fair in me to leave her to judge and form her decision in a matter affecting her whole life, when she really knows nothing of the possibilities involved? I know all the possibilities, everything that can be known from birth to manhood, about the young man who, to her, is simply Harold Foster, your friend, and one in whom I am interested."

"Well"—George Barnard's blue eyes widened—"that is the same old question which we spoke of before, and the importance of which your over-scrupulous sense of honour, as I think, makes you exaggerate."

"Can you see nothing further in it than that same question, George? I thought there would have been no need for me to explain further. It—the subject is not a pleasant one to me, as you may guess."

"My dear old chap, don't tell me anything that hurts you in the telling."

"It is nothing you don't know well enough already, George. I said that, to Norah, he is simply Harold Foster, your friend and mine, a young medical student in whom we both show unusual interest. To me, to you, putting aside that first question which the world would never forget or put aside, Harold Foster is far more, far less, than that. We know that phrase of life of which the culminating point was Harold Foster's birth into the world. His birth—born of beauty and weakness, by selfish recklessness and lurid abandon, child of a wave of yielding to an all-absorbing hunger, by a storm of gratified passion, a gust of desire, dishonour, greed of lust."

"No, no; you slander a——"

"Dead man, George. His memory is dead except to us: its very foulness killed it."

MR. MORLEY FENTON'S DECISION. 65

The barrister had risen to his feet, and now stretched out one hand toward his old friend.

"You are over-just to others," he said.

"And this dead, dishonoured man, George, I knew him better than anyone else did. Where another human life has been influenced, reparation is impossible, atonement only a comparative thing. But, knowing all I know, George, the little reflections of the turgid storm in which he was born which have shown in Harold Foster's life, the growth of which you, in your goodness, stand beside me in the endeavour to stem and choke—knowing of all these things, can I let my dead brother's child link her life to his? Can I allow her to innocently risk—God, George! think of the risk."

Mr. Morley Fenton paused, recognising, perhaps, how strangely unlike himself, his usual sober calm, his words and tone had become. The man's self may have looked with cold disapproval at the man. His hand rose firmly to the silver-pointed brown moustache, his lips and limbs reset themselves, and with lowered and expressionless voice he continued:

"No, that must not be countenanced, at all events. Remember, nothing has happened so far. A tendency has been inspired by chance access. That chance access removed, the tendency will disappear. There is no question here of undoing, but only of refraining from encouraging."

"You mean that you will close your doors to Harold?"

"I mean that I will not for the present ask him to open my doors. When he makes any casual calls, I shall look to my wife to see that Norah is engaged in some way. The weather of this week has practically brought the summer, as far as the river is concerned, to an end. Mrs. Fenton will be going down to Ventnor for three weeks or a month in a few days. The girls will go with her. That will help to bring the visits to a natural end. For the rest—er——"

"And yourself—your attitude to Harold?"

"That is where I rely on your help, George. I want you, without even hinting at the real state of affairs, to smooth over this—the ending of the visits to Weir Lodge. It was indiscreet of me, no doubt, to begin them. Of course, I want to see Harold Foster when possible, and to continue in every way I can the influence which I hoped visiting at Weir Lodge would have had, of adding interest to his life, or enabling him to find interest in the kind of life he must lead."

"H'm! Well, of course you could meet him here."

"Yes; that is good of you. Or we could arrange to lunch together on Saturdays at my club."

"At the Constitutional? H'm! yes. Harold is seeing a great deal of Mr. Leo Tarne just now, you know."

"Ah, well, he has made few friends enough. But I forgot, you don't like Mr. Tarne."

"Oh, it doesn't matter about my not liking him, so long as he does Hal no harm."

"Well—but, my dear George, have you any reason for thinking that his influence would harm Harold?"

"H'm! No, I suppose I haven't any reason."

"But 'I do not like thee, Dr. Fell,' eh?"

"Ye-es—yes, I suppose that's it. However, I'll try and smooth over the finish-up of Harold's visits to Weir Lodge, as you say; but—well, I can't help feeling that it is a mistake. You will lose a great deal of close touch, and he will lose—yes, he will lose."

The set serenity of Mr. Morley Fenton's face relaxed momentarily, distress showing itself in twitches.

"My dear George, how can you think that remark

necessary—to me? Do you suppose I act on inclination—now?"

"Forgive me, old man. I'm a brute, I know, but I wish you—I wish you were less of a marvel."

Mr. Morley Fenton rose and picked up his hat. The curly brown dog rose, too, her expression and attitude saying clearly, and with ridiculous effusiveness: "What! going already? Well, be sure and look in again soon."

"Good-bye, George," said Mr. Fenton. "I shall expect you both at the club at two o'clock on Saturday."

"Good-bye, old man—good-bye! I'll let you know if there's any news between this and then. Sorry Mrs. Greet didn't turn up. My kind regards to all at Sunbury. Good-bye."

And Mr. Morley Fenton walked slowly down the narrow, sharply-turning staircase, which, a score and more of years before, had been so familiar to young Morley Fenton, the law student.

And when, a full hour behind his time, Mr. Morley Fenton stepped on to the platform of Sunbury station, the worthy stationmaster told himself definitely that at least one bank must have closed that day.

"Looked just like I felt on the morning after the Hampton collision," said Johnson to his wife some time afterwards.

CHAPTER IX.

CROSS-CURRENTS AND CARISSIMA.

"'Which things must—*why* be?'
Vain our endeavour'
So shall things aye be
As they were ever.
'Such things should *so* be!'
Sage our desistance!
Rough smooth let globe be,
Mixed—man's existence!"
Pisgah-Sights.

GEORGE BARNARD had not overstated the case when he said that Harold Foster was seeing a great deal of Mr. Leo Tarne. He might even have said that Harold Foster was practically seeing with Leo Tarne's eyes, and living in the life of the man whose creed was to never say what he thought, and to never act in opposition to a thought.

That this was no more than a phase in young Foster's life, was made clear to Tarne by the fact that in conversation he was sometimes checkmated and overwhelmed by the superior weight of the younger man's mental strength—strength artistic, intuitive, and reasoning. That he, Tarne, must exercise considerable diplomacy if the phase were to be prolonged was shown him clearly when, on more than one occasion, a light of something like horror woke in Harold's eyes, a flicker suggesting revulsion passed over his sensitive lips, and he ended a dissertation of the writer's by saying:

"Hush, Tarne! Your cynicism positively frightens me, though I know you don't mean it. Why should you, who sees so much of the world's beauty, say bitter things?"

"The man who sees little beauty, my dear fellow, feels no ugliness, and has nothing to be bitter about."

Once, in quite the early days of the writer's influence over the medical student, he was mistaken enough to make a slurring remark anent the "Stock Exchange nonconformity of the Weir Lodge man."

Harold Foster's face had flushed to the edges of his white forehead.

"For God's sake, don't ever say anything like that again!" he had said, more pleadingly than in anger, "or I shall lose you. You had forgotten—I owe almost everything to Mr. Fenton."

Leo Tarne had allowed the raw edge of the atmospheric tension between them to wear off while he thought for a few moments. Then, with tactful wisdom, worthy a better cause, he had replied lightly:

"My dear boy, I am very sorry if I jarred on your nerves; but really, you know, I did not contract any of your debts to Mr. Morley Fenton, and I don't know that they can reasonably be expected to seal my lips against any expression of such casual thought about the gentleman as may happen to enter my head. All my own male relatives, with the single exception, I think, of Lord Crossley, who is a coal-heaver, or a coal-miner, or something, are outstanding corner-stones of city and suburban ten-to-four nonconformity."

"Well, he is my friend, and I have intense respect for him. Let that seal your lips, Tarne, for my sake."

"Ah, that is another matter. For your sake, amigo, I will exercise a soul-rotting discretion, and be as dumb as—as Mr. Morley Fenton himself generally is."

On the afternoon following that of Mr. Fenton's talk with George Barnard in the latter's chambers, Leo Tarne and Harold Foster strolled down the winding drive which led to the porch of Weir Lodge, to call on their friends there. Mrs. Fenton, with her girlish face and queenly figure, looking fresh and birdlike as ever, welcomed the young men in the drawing-room which had become familiar to them both. She volunteered trilling little remarks about the prematurely dying summer; made tea for her guests with dainty hospitality; heard, with expressions of regret, Leo Tarne's announcement of his intention to vacate the pagoda and return to town almost immediately; deftly manipulated the inevitable pause which led to the young men's rising to take their leave; and was in every way as charming as callers were accustomed to find the hostess of Weir Lodge.

Then, as she followed her husband's protégé and his friend across the hall, she suddenly bethought herself of a matter which had obviously escaped her recollection.

"Oh, I quite forgot to make the girls' excuses. But I know you will forgive them. We are packing, you know, and but for my incorrigible laziness I should not have been visible myself. Yes, one must go somewhere, and we all like the Isle of Wight. No, not more than a month, I think; and then, of course, Sunbury is a wilderness till summer comes again. So kind of you to call. And you will excuse the girls, will you not? Good-bye, Mr. Foster! Good-bye, Mr. Tarne!"

Leo Tarne whistled softly as the two reached the garden-gate.

"How sharper than a what's-his-name it is to— and then you revile me for a cynic. By Jove! but it was frigid, and a trifle sudden, was it not?"

"She was a little odd," admitted Harold Foster.

"'A little odd, quotha!' Ye gods and little iron'es! And I saw someone suspiciously like Norah Fenton looking over the banisters as we crossed the hall. By gad! of course; that's it, depend upon it."

"What is—which?"

"Why, our ejection just now by the swan with the jenny-wren's voice."

"I say, steady, Leo. And, 'ejection'! Nonsense!"

"Eh? Well, a lady can't throw one out, you know. And, depend upon it, it's something to do with dark-eyed Norah. They don't like my innocent attentions, or your dangerous fascination, or something."

"Nonsense, Leo! What quaint ideas you do have! And I wish you wouldn't talk about Nor—about Mrs. Fenton and the others as though they were the merest casual acquaintances."

Harold Foster had coloured violently, and his face was full of resentment, but of another kind to that which it had shown on the occasion of Tarne's sneering remark about Mr. Morley Fenton.

"Casual acquaintances, my dear fellow, represent the one class about whom I speak with unvarying respect. One lives in hopes of finding respectable enemies among them. Satire I reserve for people whose houses I visit. And my friends I allow to criticise me, and inflict explanations upon, if I am very fond of them."

"Yes, I know, it is like my impudence to lecture you."

"On the contrary, it's like my sublime cheek to force you on to the plane of those I allow to criticise me. But look here, my dear fellow, the weather is too autumnal to permit of our spending the evening in Sunbury after so Arctic an afternoon. I will wire to the Carissima—that is, to Lisè Vecci—and we'll dine together in town, and go somewhere."

"But—who is——"

"Lisè Vecci? Is it possible that you have known me through all these countless weeks and have not yet come within the circle of the Carissima's fascinations? How I envy you what is to come! By Jove! it's as though one had never tasted caviare or fallen in love."

"And supposing I had never done either?"

"Away, base deceiver! Where is the nearest place to send telegrams from? Lisè Vecci—— Well, really, I cannot attempt to describe Lisè Vecci."

"Is she beautiful?"

"She is not Greek. She is Byzantine, and ravishing. She is less beautiful than charming, less charming than adorable, less adorable than fascinating. She is simply the Carissima—an incarnate temptation, a sin set to the music of a can-can movement. She is Paradise and the other place, Paris, Florence, Monte Carlo, Naples, Brussels, and the Orient, condensed into five feet of femininity; the seven deadly sins and all the cardinal virtues, with others; the voice of an angel, the only really purple head of hair in the universe, and a lisp with which she might govern Europe—all that, and more, set in a bewildering maze of froufrou, and christened Lisè Vecci for lack of a name. But come, let us find this telegraph-place, for the Carissima is a creature who makes countless engagements, and affects a method in the order in which she breaks them."

Harold Foster's lips moved responsively, and his face lighted up a good deal, while he listened to Leo Tarne's lavishly-thrown-out word-colouring; for this personality, thought he, must be the embodiment of a new kind of beauty. And he was to meet this won-

derful Carissima! That was part of his new life—
the discovering and admiring of fresh beauty, of colour
hitherto unseen. So his fair face, with its weak mouth
—the key to the senses—and its strong, bold forehead
—finger-post to the mind—lighted up and brightened,
as he walked beside his friend to the little telegraph-
office. But this added light in his face shone through,
rather than took the place of, the cloud which had settled there after the visit to Weir Lodge.

In leaving Weir Lodge a sense of loneliness had
oppressed Harold Foster, and the construction placed
by Leo Tarne upon their ejection had made this feeling of loneliness and isolation acute. He had felt
suddenly deprived of something the very existence of
which would never have been recognised by George
Barnard, in his breezy, incorrigible bachelordom, or
by Leo Tarne, with his undisguised selfishness, his
wordy cynicism, and his genuinely anti-domestic tastes
and ideals.

In Weir Lodge George Barnard had been appealed
to by Maud's comrade-like banter, and by the tobacco
and *tête-à-tête* comfort of Mr. Morley Fenton's study.
Leo Tarne had been interested in " dark-eyed Norah."
Harold Foster had been strongly drawn towards Weir
Lodge as a home. Norah's personality had charmed
him; but apart from that, a tenderness had been inspired in him towards the inner life, the family circle
of the house. The expression, " Mr. Foster's place,"
used by Maud Fenton in reference to the dinner-table,
had caused smiles of pleasure to chase one another
over his lips. The general air of suggestion that he
had his corner in that home circle had afforded him
food for soothing, pleasing reflection, which had extended over hours of time. The softening, refining
influences of home, and the womenkind of home, had
heretofore had little or no place in his life.

And now, suddenly, he had been made to feel that, after all, this was no home of his. He was merely a casual visitor there, to be received or denied admission, like any other chance caller, according to circumstances. And in all the world was no place where he, Harold Foster, had his own niche in one of these invisibly-walled magic circles of light and tenderness called homes. He told himself, a little bitterly, that he had been a fool, who had mistaken hospitality for affection, and girlish politeness for a warmer interest. Men friends were the best the world had to offer him, after all; and he ought to be very thankful for a friend like Leo Tarne.

So he eagerly accepted the writer's invitation, and surprised Tarne by a sudden access of interest and devotion. When he met the Carissima he was flushed and handsomer than usual; and during the evening, and over the late supper in Leo Tarne's Kensington flat, he displayed a conversational readiness, and even brilliancy, at which his friend smiled approvingly, as a new development. And the cloud which had settled on his face after the Weir Lodge visit was not visible whilst he was in the presence of the Carissima —in touch with her dazzling vivacity, her daring *esprit*. He had quite lost his aching feeling of isolation, that dull longing for the soft lights and dainty fellowship of the inner home circle.

But alone, in the bedroom which Leo Tarne assigned to him, and when the small hours were dying into the hush of the day's awakening, the cloud of empty loneliness crept over his handsome face again, and the corners of young Foster's sensitive mouth drooped almost childishly.

" Oh, d——n! " he muttered wearily. And then he sank on to his knees beside the bed and prayed. The man was a curious mixture at this period. His early training, though far too isolating in its tendencies, too lonely in itself to have been wholesome, had been devout and careful; and now he was living and moving in a maze of conflicting influences, half-formed tastes, and rudimentary theories.

"But I don't want the outside, wastrel life," he murmured to himself, as he lay down and closed his eyes; "and I won't have it! I'll win the other, where the responsibility is, and I'll hold it; for that's where there's love—it must be. And I'll have beauty, too. I—yes, I'll go down to the hospital in the morning, and I'll go and see George Barnard. He's not in the drifting life, yet he is not—I don't know! I'll go and see him, though, and——"

A good deal had happened him that day. Harold Foster fell asleep; then a very clean, and, in a way, noble expression crept over his face, with its fringe of gold-gloss hair, its effeminately perfect chin, and its heroic upper half. And he did not dream of the Carissima, nor yet of Leo Tarne.

CHAPTER X.

FROM NORWOOD TO TROUVILLE.

> " The burden of much gladness. Life and lust
>   Forsake thee, and the face of thy delight ;
> And underfoot the heavy hour strews dust,
>   And overhead strange weathers burn and bite ;
>   And where the red was, lo the bloodless white,
> And where truth was, the likeness of a liar,
>   And where day was, the likeness of the night—
> This is the end of every man's desire."
> SWINBURNE.

"HULLO, Harold, my son! You are the very man I wanted to see. Come back here, you idiot dog! Sit down, Hal. I was just writing to you, and you know how I hate writing letters."

"What were you writing to me about, George?"

"Well, I've a surprise for you for Saturday. In place of our plebeian chop and beer, I want you to partake of lunch in gilded splendour——"

"I thought your phrase was 'gilded misery,' George."

"Don't interrupt. Well, in palatial grandeur, at a terra-cotta club, where we shall probably hob-nob with several Prime Ministers and small gentry of that sort. Mr. Fenton wants us to lunch with him at his club."

"Oh! it's awfully kind of him. We shall miss our matinée, George."

"Ungrateful toad! Think of the magnificence—and, I say, mind those screeds on your left, Hal.

They'll be sat on sufficiently by envious editors, without being disciplined into it at this early stage."

"H'm! I called at Weir Lodge yesterday, George, with Leo Tarne. But we only saw Mrs. Fenton."

"Ah!"

"And—well, she didn't seem very glad we had come."

"Nonsense, Hal! That's your fancy, man. I'm always telling you you're far more sensitive than a medical student has any right to be. Wait till you're a leading light in Harley Street."

"But really, George. And Leo Tarne noticed the same thing."

"Oh, Leo Tarne! Fashionable novelists have the privilege of being faddy and fanciful—like swell doctors. Of course, people don't always want you pottering about their places. And you have been there a good bit lately, haven't you? A good deal more often than you've been here, for instance, eh?"

"Yes; I suppose I have. But still——"

"And the women-folk there are going away, too, I believe; a condition of things which makes womenkind as busy as coming home makes us."

"Yes; I gathered that. And perhaps you are right. Anyhow, I suppose it doesn't matter. Perhaps I wore my welcome a bit thin."

"Well, that's always a mistake, you know. Not that I suppose you did it; but—— Well, you have had a pretty fair share of Sunbury hospitality since Molesey Regatta day, have you not?"

"Yes. I say, George, I want to talk to you."

"Our present conversation being deemed mere frivole, eh? Well, go ahead!"

"I want to leave the Vicarage at Norwood."

"A-ha!"

"And have lodgings somewhere near the hospital —well, somewhere in town, anyhow."

"And"—George Barnard struck a match, and puffed vigorously at his almost smoked-out briar— "might I ask why?"

"Well, it's so awkward getting in and out at night, you know, for one thing. They are always wanting to know where I've been, and why I went there."

"That's reasonable enough."

"Do you think so? And they expect me to take the same minute interest in them and in their doings, and—they are so uninteresting."

"The Winthrops are very good people, you know, Hal," protested the barrister feebly. He was quoting Mr. Morley Fenton, without that gentleman's conviction or power to convince. "They are interested in you and your welfare, of course, and—theirs is the best kind of home life, you know."

"No, no, George, don't say that, even if you think it! You will destroy my most cherished illusions; and, as Leo Tarne says, excepting our bad habits, our illusions are the only things we have worth respecting."

"Pooh! that's a quote from one of his own boneless stories. You take my word for it, Hal, you'd much better stay where you are. It's—er—you will be better looked after there, you know; and I know Mr. Fenton wants you to be there."

"George, I don't believe you are saying what you think a bit. Oh, I wish you would try to understand! But you can't, you don't, living here as you do"— Harold looked round at the shapeless disorder of the barrister's den—"in Bohemia. You cannot conceive of the ineffable dulness of a household like the Vicarage. Yes, yes, I know; they are most estimable people, and I'm an unappreciative beast! But oh, George, the deadly evenness of it, the chilly sameness, the hushed sanctity, the suffocating earnestness of that atmosphere! The whole family was upset and the house in confusion the other night, because I smoked a cigarette in my bedroom."

"H'm! deuced bad practice! Doesn't the par— Mr. Winthrop smoke in his room?"

"Heavens, no! He doesn't smoke anywhere. The smell of smoke's a red rag to Mrs. Winthrop, and the girls have noses like—like pointers. But it isn't that, George; that's only an indication. But after I've spent an evening anywhere else, an evening there puts me in a cold sweat of repressed irritation; it makes me vicious, George. The air of their drawing-room makes me want to howl and use beastly language; their conversation makes me want to sing low songs; their awful games and puzzles produce mania in me, and fill me with a lust to smash the ornaments on the mantleshelf. And then they read aloud. They've been reading for months now, about an exasperating girl with red hair who has religious difficulties, and brags of 'em, and a curate who thrashes out her difficulties in an Aberdeen dialect. And that makes me lie about headaches, and go to bed when I'm not sleepy, and get up when I am—tired out."

"H-m! ye-es; I'm afraid you're rather far gone."

"Oh, I can't stay there any longer, George; it's giving me G. P. I."

"What in the world's that?"

"General paralysis of the insane."

"Great Scott!"

"Other fellows don't do it, George. Nearly all the men at the hospital live in lodgings."

"And are probably horribly uncomfortable and uncared for. Look at me!"

Harold Foster looked, and the barrister, lying back

in his swing-chair, pipe in mouth, was such a picture of healthy, good-natured content, that the humour of his self-commiseration struck through the younger man's seriousness, and the two shouted with laughter. The curly brown dog, fearful of missing some good thing, rose on its hind-legs, and, resting its front paws on Barnard's waistband, laughed as heartily and distinctly as a dog may.

"Idiot thing!" exclaimed the barrister explosively. And the dog grovelled indecently on its back between the two men. "I haven't the remotest idea what you are laughing at." The barrister wiped his eyes, and addressed Harold.

"Nor I. Oh, if only Mrs. Greet could have heard you!"

"H'm! Well, it's all very fine, but if I ever do have a meal here, I invariably have to sneak out to a restaurant and have another immediately afterwards. And—hush! she's in the kitchen now—even that imbecile dog can't eat the steak she cooks; she pretends to think its meant to lie on. But, however, there's no teacher like experience. I'll see what can be done, and I'll write to Mr. Fenton to pave your way with him in the matter before Saturday."

"Thank you, George; but——"

"Well?"

"Well, it will be much more difficult to explain to him, you know. I mean the Winthrops are very good and kind, of course, and Mr. Fenton will think I'm horribly ungrateful."

"Eh? Oh no! Anyhow, I'll explain to him."

"You are a brick, George. I say, you know. Leo Tarne has asked me to live with him. I wouldn't mind that a bit, or lodgings alone, whichever you thought best."

"H'm! I should advise the lodgings. You're not

through your final at the hospital yet, you know, and I should not think—er—Leo Tarne was conducive to reading—much, is he?"

"Perhaps not. But he's an awfully good fellow in some ways, George. I mean he's so interesting, and he knows such a lot of interesting people. He has suggested a tremendous deal to me. He sees such a lot in the world that ordinary people don't seem to see, and I don't want to miss the beauty and the colour of life, George, wherever I may live. He has realized such a lot of the things I have always longed for and never been able to explain, and he—he always seems able to understand me."

"H'm!"

"Yes, I know. I wish you *did* like him. I'm sure you would if you knew him as I do, George. I have often heard you say you don't get on well with conventional people. Well, no one could say Leo Tarne was conventional, could they?"

"No, no, I don't suppose anybody would accuse him of being conventional. But because I don't get on with conventional folk, that doesn't mean that I always admire unconventional people. However, I haven't said anything against Leo Tarne; only don't let him influence you too much, Harold. I don't believe it's a good thing to be very strongly influenced by anyone. I would rather see you lead your own life, subject to advice, you know, of course—Mr. Morley Fenton's, for instance."

"Yes. That's a curious thing about Leo Tarne. He always seems to me to be showing me myself and my own life, rather than anything from outside."

"Ah—hullo! By Jove! do you know it is after five o'clock, Hal? I must do some work."

A few minutes later the two had parted, and Harold Foster was making his way towards Victoria.

And when the question of living in town was brought up in the smoking-room of Mr. Morley Fenton's club, after the Saturday luncheon, the young man was delighted to find that very little opposition was raised to the carrying out of his plan. Mr. Fenton had talked the matter over on the previous evening with the barrister, and had arrived at the conclusion that the change was inevitable.

"You had better choose a pretty good place while you are about it," said the owner of Weir Lodge. He had a vague desire to make up in some way for having closed the doors of his own house to the young man. "George, will you try to spare a day to go round and buy furniture with Harold?"

"Certainly; yes. I'm free on Tuesday. I don't know how I stand after that."

"But that would do splendidly," said Harold. "I can find a place on Monday; in fact—well, I know a place now, in Kensington, and we could have the furniture sent straight there."

"H'm! Kensington? Let's see, where does Mr. Tarne live?"

Harold coloured slightly under the barrister's scrutiny, and was annoyed to find it was so.

"Yes; he lives in West Kensington."

"Ah!"

"Well, it will be just as well, perhaps, to live near someone you know."

Harold looked gratefully at Mr. Morley Fenton. The barrister shrugged his shoulders. It seemed to him that Mr. Fenton and himself were rather changing places in their relation to Harold, and he did not realize how entirely unconscious of this his old friend must necessarily have been.

Mr. Leo Tarne lounged into Harold Foster's new quarters in Kensington while the younger man was in the throes of furnishing. Harold was intent upon the adjustment of a workman-like little revolving bookcase, in order that it might be within easy reach of his reading and writing-desk. A man dressed in well-worn corduroy clothing was engaged in taking measurements for the insertion of gas fixtures. Beside him, Leo Tarne looked like some rare and brilliant exotic. There were tiny beads of moisture on the orchid which drooped its curious head from Tarne's buttonhole. There were larger beads of moisture on Harold Foster's forehead. The stand of the bookcase had not lent itself readily to the young man's desire. A cloud of Tarne's yellow cigarette-smoke preceded him.

"Ah, my poor fellow!" he said with a smile, "I see you are in the hands of the Ishmaelites"—he looked round at the new correctness of the room, and at the unfitted gas brackets—"and of the Philistines. H'm! I fear me, Harold mio, you will yet live in the odour of success and die in the sanctity of Harley Street." The gas man drew back to allow the gentleman with the orchid to pass him. "Pray don't let me disturb you," said Tarne with a bow. And he crossed the room to where Harold stood.

Harold laughed. He had seen more of late of George Barnard than of Leo Tarne, and had been more busy than usual.

"Well, my dear fellow, success would surely be nicer than failure, and if one's to be a doctor, why not a Harley Street man—or even a Grosvenor Square man?"

"Ah, you are indeed in the hands of Philistia. But why, in the preliminary steps to the gaining of conventionality's hall-mark, need there be excessive ugliness? You are not in Harley Street yet, at all events."

"Why, Leo, I thought you'd like the place. What is there that jars on you?"

Leo Tarne was gazing with pained, sorrowful fixity at the walls of the room which was to serve his friend as living place and study. Folding doors divided it from the bedroom. The wall-paper was of a cheerful, harmless pattern, consisting of sprays of hitherto undiscovered flowers, on a background which Tarne subsequently described as being "the colour of a Dorcas Society."

"Oh, I don't know of any particular thing that jars on me, Harold, unless, possibly, your apparent intentions in the matter of illumination. I was looking round with a view to discovering something which produced an impression of any kind upon me. The—er—flowers in your wall-paper almost roused me, but—their background has an absorbent tendency, a peculiarly colour-covering property, don't you think?"

"You are a merciless critic, Leo."

"A critic? You flatter me, Harold. I am only a writer. A critic is a man who has never sunk low enough to be a writer, and has not been gifted by nature with the ability to read. So he criticises."

"But, regarding the room?"

"The room? Yes. Why this severely patriotic absence of colour, Harold. I had no idea you prided yourself so much on your nationality. The true Englishman loves, I know, to treat colour as he regards wine and fruit, or beauty of any kind—as a powerful liqueur, to be sipped in tiny doses, and with self-denying circumspection. Why not colour the lower part of those walls in warm terra-cotta, and fresco the upper part in something pale? Why place that writing-table and chair like a T-square on an architect's drawing-board? Why not make it a thing of beauty set slanting-wise, on a square of brick-coloured felt which should be a joy for ever? Why an almanack to face you, when days and months are inevitable and never interesting, and Paris prints are irresponsible and sometimes charming? Yes, that is it. It is the inevitability of this room which numbs one's senses, Harold. I am thinking only of your health, you know. Who knows but this may lead—with the projected scheme of illumination "—Tarne glanced at the gas-fittings—" to colour blindness, and—er—moral decay?"

Harold Foster forsook the bookcase, and went out to lunch with Leo Tarne. Tarne said he objected on principle to breaking anything, particularly anything so personal as his fast. So he ate fruit in bed with his letters at a comparatively early hour, and lunched shortly after noon.

Harold subsequently altered his mind about the lighting of his new rooms, and compromised with the gasfitter by having a gas lamp in the passage outside, contenting himself with lamps, covered by deliriously-coloured shades, in his two rooms. He devoted more time, too, than he had intended, to the fitting-up of his working-room. He changed its wall-coverings, and revolutionized the adjustment of his furniture. The almanack he hung in his bedroom, in order that when he retired for the night he might always be sure of the date, and time of year.

Then Harold Foster began to work hard in his new quarters, and at the hospital. Mr. Morley Fenton took him to visit some very pleasant people who lived at Queen's Gate. Leo Tarne was in Paris. For almost three weeks Harold Foster was the most hard-working student at St. Bartholomew's. And during that time there floated constantly before him visions of ideal life in ideal home circles, where was music, and simple, flowing draperies, soft lights and innocent camaraderie.

Then, one afternoon, he heard that Leo Tarne had been in London for three days. Carlos, the Spanish servant, delivered a little note at the hospital, in which the writer said: "Have I in a moment of inadvertence given you good advice, or is thy friend a relative, that he should be shunned in this way? Don't leave Carlos to find his way back to me alone from Bartholomew's. He is young, and may be led astray, or anywhere else in a light like this."

The day was a dull one, and sky and air in London mingled in a sad greyness. Harold Foster excused himself at the hospital—his work at the time was very uninteresting—and drove in a hansom, with Rembrandt-faced Carlos, to Leo Tarne's flat.

The writer had just finished his work on a story. He had been at his table all night. His room was cloudy with opium-tainted tobacco smoke. The view from its windows was unmitigated greyness. Two or three letters in feminine handwriting lay beside his manuscript on the table. Tarne was in his dressing-gown, and a tall glass of yellow wine stood beside him on a little Turkish stool. He was turning over a folio of daringly-coloured French prints, and as Harold entered the room he said:

"I knew you would come, *mon ami*. Isn't this weather demoralizing? I have been up all night. You must excuse my frowsy appearance. Come over here, where there's a pretence of light, and look at these sunny little silhouettes of Trouville. Look at this of the Casino at eleven o'clock. That one is the supper hall after midnight. See; here's the sands at mid-day, and—— Yes, that's one of the cercles—mostly baccarat, you know."

Harold Foster admired the prints, and tasted some

of Tarne's Rüdesheimer. The influence of Leo Tarne's particular atmosphere was filtering into him.

"Yes," he said, his hand resting on a brilliant little picture of the promenade and its open cafés; "it suggests something rather different to that, does it not?"

Harold nodded in the direction of the window, and the misty colourlessness beyond.

"It does." Tarne shivered as he glanced at the window. "Do you know Trouville, Harold?"

"No; I have never been there."

"What's to-day?—Wednesday. Look here! Let us go to Trouville to-night, Harold; there's plenty of time to put things in a bag and catch the Southampton boat to Havre. We will spend the rest of the week there, and you shall be back at the hospital on Monday. I will just send a wire to the Carissima, she was to have dined with me to-night. What do you say, Harold? Get a hansom, Carlos"—Tarne had touched a bell beside him. "Run round in the cab and put some things together, Harold—Carlos will fetch them; and then come back here; we'll dine together. You will come, won't you?"

Harold sighed and glanced towards the window. Then he looked at the folio of prints.

"Oh yes; we might as well," he said. And then he followed Carlos out of the room.

CHAPTER XI.

SOME REMINISCENCES, AND A BIG MAN CALLED CARROLL.

> " As afternoon forgets the dew,
> As time in time forgets all men,
> As our old place forgets us two,
> Who might have turned to one thing then,
> But not again."
> *Felise.*

"WELL, sir, as I was sayin'——" It was Saturday morning in Furnival's Inn and other places, and the arrival of the mid-day post had interrupted Mrs. Greet, and provided welcome subject-matter for George Barnard's attention. "As I was sayin', sir, if you will let me speak just a word, I hev no desire to afflict myself where I'm not wanted, Mr. Barnard."

Mrs. Greet's bony hands rested on either side of that angular portion of her virtuous frame which the lamented Mr. Greet of pious memory must, at some period of his overshadowed life, have regarded as a waist. She glared, with reproach in the corners of her eyes, at the letters which George Barnard was surreptitiously opening, and, in a stealthy and deprecating manner, reading.

"But, in leaving your service, sir, where I defy the world, Mr. Barnard, to say I have not done my duty, even you, sir, while you're findin' fault and—and unbraidin' me, Mr. Barnard, must allow me to say a word in defence of my own character and good name, an' me a woman, sir, who has been doin' for gents in chambers for nigh on twenty year now, since my poor 'usband passed away, an' 'as never had a word said against me till I came to you, Mr. Barnard, though there was Mr. Thurlow who was a lord's son, an' my cookin' pleased 'im; but of course, as I says, every person 'as his own tastes, an' what's one gent's meat is another gent's poison; though if the steak did 'appen—me bein' ill at th' time an' worried 'alf out o' my life wi' work—to be a little overdone, sir, there is gents, Mr. Barnard, what would scorn to throw good meat to—to a mad dog, sir, askin' your pardon, an' slam out of th' 'ouse like—like a whirlpool, sir, to go to a common resterong. But I'm not a woman to afflict myself, Mr. Barnard, where I—where a person——"

"Trouville! Why—confound it! and with Leo Tarne! That is—quite so, Mrs. Greet; and I'm very sorry indeed that you should have been given trouble by my upsetting the coal."

"Oh, please don't demiliate yourself by apologizing to me, sir. I can't expect you to leave a letter for a minute to 'ear a word from me, I'm sure; and perhaps when I'm gone, you'll find a better 'ousekeeper, who 'asn't done cookin' for persons with dif'rent tastes. I'm sure I hopes you will, sir, for, as I says——"

"Yes; I had forgotten for a moment, Mrs. Greet. I have some rather important letters here. Believe me, I didn't mean to be rude at all about the steak. In fact—er—it was really a very superior steak; but I was obliged—er—to go out in a hurry, and rather than waste a good steak, I—that is, as you say, I gave it to the dog. But I think you might try things a little longer, Mrs. Greet. It seems a pity for us to part now. Just think it over, will you? And—er—I am very busy just now, Mrs. Greet. If you—er——"

"Oh, I won't obtain you, sir. Don't let *me* disturb you, Mr. Barnard. And I hope you'll look out for some person, sir, as *can* cook, an' I'm sure I——"

"That's all right then, Mrs. Greet. I knew we shouldn't quarrel. Yes, thank you. And you must have some medicine for those spasms, Mrs. Greet. Perhaps you could get something with that half-crown change from the money for the gas. And I sha'n't be wanting anything before this afternoon, thank you. Oh Lord! she gets more trying every month, and her steaks get worse with the spasms."

George Barnard had at last succeeded in bowing his irate housekeeper out of the room, as the curtain to her usual monthly performance of the giving notice tragedy. And now the barrister sat down to read again the short note headed, "Hotel de Casino, Trouville," in which Harold Foster explained the cause of his inability to spend that Saturday afternoon, as his custom was, with George Barnard in London. The letter was very brief, and said that Harold would be back at his work on Monday. It was dated "Thursday night," but, having been written at four o'clock on Friday morning, and posted towards noon of the same day, it had not reached the barrister until that hour on Saturday at which its writer was accustomed to make his appearance in the Furnival's Inn chambers.

"I'm sorry he went there," muttered the barrister, as he mechanically allowed the note to fall on the floor beside his waste-paper basket. George Barnard generally deposited his rubbish round about the sides of this basket, or, as Mrs. Greet had more than once remarked, "anywhere but in it." "Yes, I'm sorry; and I'm sorry he ever met Leo Tarne. I wonder what Fenton will say. H'm! And I thought Hal had got into a good working vein, too. Gad! I'd never say as much to Morley Fenton, but the youngster is weirdly reminiscent in some ways of his mother. And—yes, more reminiscent of his father in that mad phase of—— Heigho! It seems for some there is no path between. It must be rigid Methodism and the conventional fireside, or else—ah! and yet I don't know but what they have the best of it. Those firesides, they—— But then, there's the eternal meeting over the coffee-pot, and—— Come in! Drat the woman!"

The barrister bent low over his papers whilst breathing out his last exclamation, in the hope that Mrs. Greet might be touched by his air of absorption in business. The worthy housekeeper, however, having invested the change from the gas account in a flat bottle of medicine, which she had purchased at a grocer's in Holborn, was at that moment engaged in discussing her employer, and various other afflictions, with a spinster friend in Pump Court.

"Do you want to see me, Mrs. Greet?" The barrister lingeringly raised his head, and looking round saw Mr. Morley Fenton in the act of softly closing the outer door of the den. "I beg your pardon, old chap!" said Barnard, rising to greet his friend. "Come in and sit down. The fact is, Mrs. Greet has been handling me rather severely this morning, and I thought—— But how are you, Morley? You seem to me to be growing thinner. You really look quite run down. Ought to take a holiday, you know—eh?"

"Oh, I think I am all right, George, thanks. We business men cannot keep quite so fresh as you, you know. It is a wearing place, the City. I see you haven't Harold with you. I half expected to find you together, and thought you might come and lunch with me. I am not expected at Sunbury before this evening."

"Ah, well, I'm a poor substitute for Hal, but I shall be most happy to join you, if you won't mind giving me about ten minutes to write two or three notes in. I want to have a chat about Hal, too."

The barrister felt quite nervous about telling his friend of Harold Foster's absence. His reflections had been so curiously broken in upon by the arrival of the subject of them. Mr. Morley Fenton sat down and opened a newspaper. George Barnard scribbled a few short notes, and then, having made some slight change in his attire, went out with his friend.

The barrister, having claimed the position of host on this occasion, led Mr. Morley Fenton to the dining-room of a somewhat famous hostelry in Fleet Street.

"By the way," he said, as they took their seats in this establishment, "I don't know why I have not mentioned it before, but the reason you did not find Harold with me is that he has gone over to Trouville for a few days with Mr. Leo Tarne."

"To Trouville? Really! I had no idea of that."

"Yes, I had a letter from him this morning, written there, and saying that he would be back at work again on Monday."

"H'm! Trouville. I am sorry."

"Yes, I knew it would be unpleasant, by association, to you. But, after all, he knows nothing of the happenings of five-and-twenty years ago; and as far as Trouville itself is concerned——"

"Yes, of course, we mustn't grudge him a holiday. But—— However, it is absurd of me to be prejudiced against any particular place. Atmosphere is the product of action, rather than action of atmosphere —eh, George?"

"There's no doubt about that."

The barrister's confirmation was as emphatic as though it had been a denial; it was spoken with the assurance of a man who has no belief in what he says.

"How do you think he has been getting on since leaving the Vicarage, George?"

"Oh, very well, very well. He has been working very hard during the last few weeks."

"That is good. This trip to—er—it is not a reaction, I hope. He is not growing spasmodic?"

"No; oh no, I think not. Why?"

"I only asked, because I think the life of phases a fearfully dangerous one for—for Harold Foster; that is all."

"Yes; perhaps it is. I regard Mr. Leo Tarne as a phase in Hal's life, you know. But Hal has a great deal more strength than Tarne."

"Ah! well, he must have friends, you know. I often feel doubtful as to whether it was wise or kind to have practically brought his visits to my house to an end. But you know the feeling I had in the matter."

The barrister nodded, and the business of lunch was proceeded with, when Mr. Morley Fenton had remarked casually that he had not, until that afternoon, entered the room they sat in since the old days when the friends had together rioted and studied, feasted and starved, in the Furnival's Inn chambers.

"Ah," said Barnard, "the glory of this place has departed since then. I very seldom see any of the old faces now."

"Selfishly speaking, I am not altogether sorry for that, George, since you—since I have come here with you."

"H'm! That's one of your fathomless speeches, old man—one of the things that make you a marvel. I wish, sometimes, you wouldn't be quite so rigid."

"Do you, George? But perhaps I am not strong enough to be less than rigid. Only giants and George Barnards can with safety walk the hair-line between ways."

Whilst Mr. Morley Fenton was speaking, two men

entered the room by the door facing him, and took seats in a position which left both visible to the owner of Weir Lodge, though hidden by a Japanese screen from George Barnard. These men took no notice of the barrister or his friend, but as Mr. Fenton's eyes fell upon the foremost of them a little muscular shiver passed over his face, its lines seemed to deepen sharply, and the curious network of veins in his temples stood out and made visible their movements. He continued speaking, however, in low, even tones, to George Barnard.

The two new-comers were of that class whose disappearance from the restaurant the barrister had referred to in speaking of its departed glories. One of them was an old actor, who, whilst Bohemian to the backbone, had never over-stepped that curious, indefinable yet inflexible limit, which separates society generally from society's outcasts—that pale which is bounded on one side by the world, and on the other by the world's beaches. Then, too, he had been successful in his profession, and was possessed of a private income—that sheet-anchor to the shore of respectability.

The other man was one of London's characters, and one of the best known. He was a giant among vagabonds, a prince of outlaws, and a Bohemian ostracized from Prague itself. Originally a brilliant younger member of the profession which gave George Barnard the right to wear wig and gown, if he so chose, Carroll, who was never spoken of save by this one name, had for years been regarded as a privileged rioter, an accepted drifter about the sea of London cosmopolitanism. It was said that no man knew where Carroll lived—certainly no man knew how he lived. But Carroll knew and was known by most professional men who had attained middle age in the capital. He had been found sleeping on the Covent Garden piazza, and given shelter in artistic clubhouses. He had been bailed out, at West End police-stations, by men he had never seen, but whom tradition had taught to know him. In appearance Carroll suggested a very fine but decaying elm, or a lightning-blasted oak—a magnificent-looking man, upon whose noble features dissipation's hot fingers had been pressed till they had seared him to the bone, honeycombing and networking a face which might have been heroic, and was ruggedly fine.

Carroll reeled slightly as he sat down in the grey light which filtered through a grimy ceiling-window, and at that early hour his eyes were glazed, and his lips tremuolus, as the immediate result of heavy drinking. The other man called for "a long soda, with a very little dash," for Carroll, and immediately began to speak of a certain very Bohemian reunion fixed for that evening. Carroll had promised to accompany him, as his guest, to this function. Mr. Morley Fenton, whose eyes were fixed on his plate, heard every word which passed between these two, whilst himself talking to George Barnard. George Barnard, whose eyes wandered from his friend's face over all the room, heard only Mr. Morley Fenton's words, and answered them as occasion required.

Suddenly Carroll's friend, looking round sharply, saw and recognised the owner of Weir Lodge. He leaned across to Carroll, who was staring fixedly at Mr. Fenton, and whispered:

"I say, Carroll, there's Morley Fenton. You remember Morley Fenton, don't you? 'Sent down' from Oxford. Had a flare up of some sort."

"Ah!" A light of understanding flashed through the filmy coating of the older man's eyes. "Morley Fenton? of course! I couldn't think who it was. H'm!

Morley Fenton, Furnival's Inn; disappeared—found religion, or a wife with money, or both—or something. Ah, well!"

"Ssh!" murmured Carroll's friend. "He'll hear. Look here, I'll go and speak to him, and ask him to come to the W—— with us to-night."

At that moment the stem of Mr. Morley Fenton's claret-glass shivered and snapped between his thumb and finger, so that the bowl of the glass rolled without noise on to the back of his hand, and rested against his cuff. The glass was empty. When Carroll's friend had first whispered his name, every vestige of colour had left Mr. Fenton's face, and a spot of blood had risen through the skin of his lower lip, the while he paused with apparent deliberation in an expression of opinion regarding a bye-election then being decided in Lancashire.

"Hullo!" said the barrister, "you've broken your glass, old man."

"So I have. Waiter! Thank you! And bring me another, please." Mr. Morley Fenton spoke almost languidly, looking the while at George Barnard, and yet watching, with that curious tensity and breadth of vision which comes to a man at times, the faces of Carroll, and Carroll's friend. George Barnard had plunged with enthusiasm into the subject which he believed to be of absorbing interest to Mr. Fenton— the bye-election in the North. He even endeavoured to make clear his contentions by the aid of diagrams in breadcrumbs on the table-cloth. Mr. Morley Fenton's most attentive and most inscrutable smile hung over the firm lines of his mouth. His eyes, blind to that which was near, saw only the two men, who were hidden by the Japanese screen from the barrister. The expression in these eyes, however, was one of listening repose. The little veins above his white-skinned cheek-bones throbbed and quivered.

The actor behind the screen rose to his feet to carry out his promise to speak to Mr. Fenton. At the same time Carroll rose unsteadily, looking Mr. Fenton full in the face. The vagabond's eyes seemed to be gazing through George Barnard's friend, down the many coloured vista of his own curious past; piecing together disconnected links, and filling up long-forgotten gaps; seeing with the understanding which is picked up in the by-ways of outlying Bohemia, and of which nothing ever altogether robs the man who has found it.

"Excuse me a moment, George."

Mr. Morley Fenton had risen to his feet, his back to his friend, and between his friend and the Japanese screen. So, for a moment of time, Carroll, conventionality's outcast, and Morley Fenton, a pillar of conventionality, the man whose orthodoxy admitted of no question, stood looking into each other's souls, seeing and knowing.

Then into Carroll's eyes came a light which said: "All's well." He had apparently found that in search of which he had been mistily reviewing his past. Perhaps Mr. Morley Fenton's eyes had given it to his eyes. Perhaps the veriest vagabond may have in him, somewhere, a vein of sterling goodness. The actor had taken one step from his seat towards the carrying out of his expressed intention. Carroll's tremulous right hand gripped him almost fiercely by the shoulder.

"Sit down," whispered the vagabond hoarsely. And then he added: "No; we won't ask Morley Fenton. I—I don't want to meet him."

The whole thing had occupied no more than a few seconds, and as Mr. Morley Fenton, calm and impassive as ever, resumed his seat—there had been no appeal in his eyes when he had looked into Carroll's, but only understanding and self-revelation—George Barnard said carelessly: "What's the attraction, old man?"

"Nothing, George," replied Mr. Fenton, sipping his wine. "I thought for a moment I had recognised someone—that is all. You were speaking, when I interrupted you, of the split in the Liberal vote which J. C. Menzie's candidature would cause."

And a few minutes afterwards, having settled their bill, the barrister and his friend walked out of the room. Mr. Morley Fenton carried his hat in his hand as he passed the Japanese screen. His shoulders were set squarely; his figure was, even for him, unusually erect; and he did not turn his head as he reached the door, but stepped quickly into the street.

CHAPTER XII.

AFTERNOON TEA AND SCANDAL.

> "But you don't know music ! Wherefore
>   Keep on casting pearls
> To a—poet ! All I care for
>   Is—to tell him that a girl's
> 'Love' comes aptly in when gruff
> Grows his singing. (There, enough !)"
> *A Tale.*

THERE could be no doubt that from Mrs. Fenton's point of view, and in the light of what her husband subsequently conceived to be his duty, the time for making an end of Harold Foster's visits to Weir Lodge had been well chosen. Also, so far as Harold was concerned, the break had entailed no great sense of loss, beyond the feeling of being cut off from the softening influences of that home atmosphere, the beauty of which he had only so recently begun to realize. Norah he had hardly thought of as an individuality, but rather as the embodied type of this passive beauty.

Like many another young man whose own fleeting experiences of home life have been inharmonious, over the threshold of whose life circumstances have admitted but little tenderness, Harold Foster's instinctive appreciation of the ideal and beautiful in domesticity, was strong and keen; far stronger and keener than he himself would ever guess. Harold's contact with Norah had been too much diffused over the breadth of his appreciation of that atmosphere which Norah embodied, too much over-ruled by the sudden, new influence of Leo Tarne, to allow of its again resolving itself, during the short period over which the young man's visits to Weir Lodge had extended, into any such close and personal touch as was theirs on the Sunday morning which had followed Molesey Regatta.

And the girl herself, Norah, had to all intents and purposes been absolutely untouched by the influence of Leo Tarne. And, probably for that reason, she had roused in him an unusual degree of interest. She had had no consideration or appreciation of a new atmosphere to disintegrate and absorb the direct personal meaningness of her contact with Harold Foster. She had received her impression of the man, and not of any set of circumstances or framework of influences which the man brought within her range of vision. And this impression had made the girl lean strongly—sometimes with a strength which, regarded as it was by her as weakness, had frightened her—towards the young man whom Mr. Morley Fenton had requested his family to "be kind to."

Some day, perhaps, if the fates permit, scientists will make these matters clear for us, and by analysis of those chemical properties within us which, flying to their companion molecules, draw individuals of either sex each to each, will warn us against allowing our feet to stray in those of love's paths which have at their far ends danger or non-admittance notices. Then there will be no more unrequited attachments or forlorn loves. For the blind boy god will die, and ferret-eyed science will cremate him, and sit down then to compile learned memoirs of his life.

Meantime, Norah Fenton, who had no knowledge of the chemical key to such problems, hardly knew what could be tugging at her tender heart-strings when the family returned from Ventnor to Weir Lodge, or why, in the days which followed, she always caught her breath, the better to listen to Mary the housemaid's announcements of the names of afternoon callers.

Maud Fenton, warm-hearted and impulsive as she was flighty-minded and careless, never mentioned Harold Foster's name in Norah's hearing now. This dated from a certain evening in Ventnor, when a chance glance into a mirror before which Norah was sitting, in the girls' joint bedroom, brought an abrupt conclusion to a teasing remark in which Maud had deplored the hard fate which placed them beyond the range of Harold Foster's visiting list. The picture seen in the mirror had been a revelation to laughing, heart-whole Maud Fenton; for the glass had shown a face pale under its natural creamy bloom, and two wide-open eyes full of pain, and dimmed by heavy tears which hung between their lashes.

Maud had stepped forward impulsively, and, kissing Norah's pale cheek, had shown the loving understanding which formed the groundwork of her frivolous disposition, by leaving the room without a word, and not returning to it until a good hour had passed.

And now a whole month had elapsed since the family's return from Ventnor to Weir Lodge, and though Mr. Leo Tarne had paid one call of courtesy during that time, Norah had seen nothing of the man about whom she felt a natural disinclination to make any inquiry. Every evening, when Mr. Morley Fenton arrived home from town, Norah was in the hall —a pensive picture, framed in old oak, on a background of heavy rugs scattered over a polished floor —to welcome her adopted father. And, though at first sound of his footsteps on the gravel of the drive outside, Norah's great shadowy eyes would flash light rays from hidden depths to glistening surfaces, yet when Mr. Morley Fenton, alone, pushed aside the swing doors of the vestibule, these expectant gleams would sink back into the hidden places of their birth, and a little ring of loneliness and sadness would creep into the voice which greeted the head of the house.

"Your voice sounds sad, mavourneen," Mr. Fenton had said on one late autumn evening. "Aren't you happy, dear, or are you only a little tired?"

"Yes, father, that is all; I am a little tired." And then the girl's lithe arms had twined round the neck of the man whom she respected so deeply that she called him "Father," with a tenderness which had nothing to do with respect, and not much, perhaps, with the girl's affection for Mr. Morley Fenton.

Norah's childhood had been passed in her dead father's birthplace, which had also been Mr. Morley Fenton's home, a ruinous old country house in the west of Ireland. There were times at which Norah crept closer to the inner heart of her adopted father than either of his own daughters ever reached. There were bonds between them that had grown, perhaps, from out the man's protecting sympathy, which for years had stood between his weak elder brother—Norah's father—and the world into and out of which that brother had unresistingly drifted.

These bonds showed themselves, but only to the observant, in several curious small ways. Since receiving instructions as a lad of fourteen from his father, a devotee in music, Mr. Morley Fenton had played the violoncello, and played with a rare mastery of this instrument's subtle possibilities. But on no single occasion had Mr. Fenton been seen with his 'cello in any other part of Weir Lodge than his study, the one room in the house which no member of the family would have thought of entering without an invitation from its owner. And these invitations had never come when Mr. Morley Fenton intended taking the 'cello from its case. Yet, on the very evening of Norah's first arrival at the house of her adopted father, she had sat for more than an hour on a stool in the study, while Mr. Fenton made his instrument breathe comfort and sympathy into her heart. And since that evening, the master of the house had always played to an audience of one, and Norah had been grateful.

It happened that on a certain chilly afternoon some few weeks after Harold Foster's visit to Trouville, Mrs. Fenton forgot her diplomacy. On this occasion she left Weir Lodge with her two daughters to make a round of calls in the neighbourhood. Chance directed that on this same afternoon Norah should be suffering from a headache, and Mr. Leo Tarne from an acute attack of boredom. The resulting happenings were that Norah was left at home alone, and that, towards the hour of afternoon tea, Mr. Leo Tarne was announced by Mary the housemaid, and received by Norah in the long drawing-room.

Strung up by boredom to a high pitch of artificiality, Leo Tarne was conversationally more brilliant than usual. Then came to the man his pique-inspired desire to please Norah, and, acting under these combined forces, he exerted to the utmost his every power to interest. Norah responded with tea and polite attention. Tarne was puzzled and annoyed.

Then, with much girlish circumlocution and apparent indifference, Norah led up to a reference to Harold Foster; and Leo Tarne, who, with all his artificiality, was by no means lacking in intuitive perception, smarted under the light which shone out of her eyes at his, Tarne's, careless mention of his friend's mere name.

" Yes," he said, with a little wave of his hand, " I believe Mr. Foster is very well. We spent a few days in Trouville together last month."

Norah's indifference was the poorest piece of acting that even an innocent-minded, tender-hearted girl could have perpetrated.

"Ah," she said brightly, "Mr. Foster is studying at a hospital, is he not?"

"Ye-es!" Tarne smiled and his eyebrows were raised very slightly. "At all events, Mr. Foster is a medical student, Miss Fenton. The distinction, like all trifling distinctions, is not without a difference."

Norah's puckered mouth showed interested lack of comprehension. She made a little gesture of perplexity.

"I am sure that remark is like one of the books we used to get as prizes at school, Mr. Tarne, and 'will amply repay perusal.' But you know I can't peruse it."

"What a fearful condemnation to be pronounced on so harmless an observation. It merely meant that there is a wide difference, otherwise known as a trifling distinction, between studying and being a student. Everyone who studies is a student, and I believe there are some people who are students, and who, in spite of that, study. But the species is a rare one."

"Which means that Mr. Foster does not study?" Norah's eyes were a challenge.

"Well, I certainly don't think Mr. Foster has studied much in surgery or medicine of late, though I have no doubt that he has, on the other hand, been learning a good deal in connection with another interesting trifle, called life. The preservation of life is what one learns in the hospitals, you know, and preserved things are so much less interesting than the same things in a state of freshness."

"But if one is going to be a doctor?" protested Norah.

"Exactly." Mr. Tarne's tone was one of gentle

and acquiescent deprecation. " Mr. Foster is somewhat reckless in that respect. Really quite a dangerous companion for an easily-led man like myself. I assure you I was quite afraid in Trouville that my sense of duty would be overcome by his drifting seductiveness, and end in my indefinitely forsaking home and my beloved public, in order to waltz through an eternity of Trouville dissipations with Harold Foster. But I made a heroic effort, and brought him back to St. Bartholomew's and comparative virtue."

" Oh! "

There was serious wonder and distress in Norah's exclamation. Leo Tarne smiled slightly.

" But, joking apart," he continued, " Mr. Foster is a difficult man to act upon as a brake. His extremes are so whole-souled, his disregard of consequences is so bewilderingly consistent."

" But is not Mr. Barnard a friend of Mr. Foster's? I should have thought Mr. Barnard would—would be a brake."

" Ah! yes, I dare say he might. Yes, I think one can imagine him in the character of a drawback, certainly; but I fancy our friend finds drawbacks a nuisance, and is seeing very little of Mr. Barnard just now. Of course you know, Miss Fenton, every man understands his own affairs better than anyone else can—according to a popular superstition—and I don't mean for a moment that Mr. Foster is doing anything wrong. I think he is drifting, that is all—drifting. And, of course, he is not likely to drift beyond a certain point. That's the worst of being a gentleman, you know—or the best, or something: one cannot drift beyond a certain point. It simply is not done. But as far as my friend Foster is concerned, I am sorry his drift is so complete, because—well, you see, it will prevent his ever having any chances, professionally; and the business of prolonging life is, I think, about as good as any other—after that of living life. And that is not remunerative or respectable."

Mr. Leo Tarne rose, looking frankly into the girl's puzzled eyes.

"And now I really must run away. Thank you so much for giving me tea, and allowing me to stay. Will you give my regards to Mrs. Fenton? I am sorry to have missed seeing the others, and so glad they were out, and—you were not. Good-bye!"

Mr. Leo Tarne strolled out through the Weir Lodge garden, which was divested now alike of its summer vividness and its autumn glory. He was humming softly to himself, and the remedy he had chosen for his attack of boredom appeared to have most admirably answered its purpose.

Norah's headache had not been removed by her afternoon at home. So she did not come down to dinner that evening. But later on, when Mrs. Fenton and her two daughters were chatting together and working in the drawing-room, Norah walked slowly down to the hall, and, after standing for a moment in hesitation at the foot of the stairs, stepped forward and tapped at the door of Mr. Morley Fenton's study.

A few minutes afterwards Maud Fenton, in the drawing-room, raised her head listeningly, and said:

"There's father's 'cello: that's the first time this week that father's played. What a pity Norah isn't downstairs."

But Norah was sitting on the big hassock beside the study fire, and her eyes were full of tears. Mr. Morley Fenton's choice of music that evening favoured pathos, and there were sounds like a sorrowing woman's wailing in some of the notes he drew from his 'cello strings.

For a long while Norah sat thinking in her bedroom that night. The bedrooms at Weir Lodge were not conventual homes of chilly caution against slothfulness, but comfortable, firelit places, full of invitation to repose. At last Norah rose, and stepped across the room to where a little writing-table stood.

"I will," she murmured very softly. "I will write to Mr. Barnard. And he is not a 'drawback,' as Mr. Tarne said. I know he's not, and I am sure he is a good, kind man, else he wouldn't have such beautiful eyes."

Norah found her decision harder to carry out than it had been to make, and she tore in pieces and burned several quite long letters before finishing, as the hall clock was striking one, the short note which she posted next morning.

A few hours after this note had been posted in Sunbury, Mrs. Greet, having carefully read the address on its envelope, and sniffed suspiciously over its obviously feminine penmanship, handed the dainty thing to George Barnard, whom the good housekeeper discovered kneeling on the littered floor of his den, puffing tobacco smoke into the open mouth of his "idiot dog," and chuckling with delight at that animal's pretended appreciation of the process.

The barrister read and re-read the timidly daring little note, and leaned back in his pivot-chair to deliberate upon it.

"No," he muttered, after a few moments. "Good Lord, no! The boy's all right. But she's a dear, thoughtful little girl, by gad! she is. I remember now; I thought so before. But Hal's not drifting.

He can't be drifting. And yet—well, she must be a wonderful little girl. Only, Hal can't be drifting, you know—you imbecile, flap-eared dog!"

The dog turned over inanely, on its master's outstretched feet, and George Barnard sighed heavily.

CHAPTER XIII.

TWO MEETINGS AND A LITTLE SLEEP.

" And some are sulky, while some will plunge.
 [*So ho ! Steady ! Stand still, you !*]
 Some you must gentle, and some you must lunge.
 [*There ! There ! Who wants to kill you ?*]
 Some—there are losses in every trade—
 Will break their hearts ere bitted and made,
 Will fight like fiends as the rope cuts hard,
 And die dumb-mad in the breaking-yard."
 RUDYARD KIPLING.

THIS is all that was contained in the lavender-coloured note over which Mrs. Greet had sniffed, and in forming an opinion about which George Barnard had appealed for confirmation to his dog:

" DEAR MR. BARNARD: Mr. Leo Tarne called here this afternoon, and spoke about Mr. Foster. I think they are great friends, you know, and Mr. Tarne seemed quite distressed about him—about Mr. Foster, I mean. I am afraid you will think me rather mad and very stupid in writing and bothering you about it, but I know my father (that is, Uncle Morley, you know) takes a great interest in Mr. Foster, and Mr. Tarne says he is ' drifting,' and I am not quite sure what that means, but it sounds horrid, and Mr. Tarne is worried about it. So I thought I would write and tell you, because I know you understand things, and will go and help Mr. Foster not to ' drift ' any more. And I did not like to tell father, because—I don't

quite know why, but he does not seem to have anything to do with 'drifting,' does he?
"Yours sincerely,
"NORAH FENTON.

"P. S.—Please excuse this being so abominably written; it's better than I generally write."

George Barnard read this for the fifth time whilst arranging a fresh collar and tie, and then, changing his dressing-gown for a hardly less shabby walking coat, began to hunt about the room for his most presentable hat.

"She's a little brick, that's just what she is!" he murmured, as, having discovered his hat on a gas-bracket, he proceeded to blow off some of its loose dust. "And I'll go straight round and help him 'not to drift.' Drift indeed! Good-bye, lunatic poodle! No, you don't. Aha! go back!"

The animal retreated sadly from the closing outer door, and the barrister made his way out of the house.

"That's the worst of that dog," said George Barnard as he mounted the steps of a Kensington bus. "She's so horribly fastidious. If I take her out it means cab fares and loss of moral fibre."

Less than a minute later, an omnibus bearing on its side the legend "Waterloo Station," passed the vehicle upon which George Barnard had conferred his patronage.

"By Jove!" muttered the barrister, starting to his feet. "Why shouldn't I go down and answer that little brick's letter first. The afternoon is young."

He scrambled down the steps of the bus and careered wildly along the crowded street in pursuit of the Waterloo-bound vehicle.

Seated in a Thames Valley train, and meditating

behind his short briar pipe, the barrister more than half regretted the step which his enthusiasm about "the little brick" had induced him to take.

"What in the world excuse shall I make," he thought, "for arriving at Weir Lodge when the lord of the manor's not at home? And I don't suppose I shall have an opportunity of saying two words to her, anyhow. Maud wouldn't allow that. By gad! I believe I had better take Maud into my confidence. Little baggage, she'd chaff me so horribly; and then, the little brick mightn't like it. And she isn't very 'little' either. My word, I would sooner take Maud's chaff than get into the brick's black books. I don't know, but it's quite romantic. Eh, what a clown I am! And there's no fool like an old fool—an ancient imbecile, who might be her father, but he's not good enough, not by yards. Hullo, Sunbury! H'm! 'Pon my soul, I'm quite nervous. Old fool!"

But the fates were kind to George Barnard, in view, perhaps, of his age and foolishness. As he turned a bend in the quiet road from the station to Weir Lodge, he came face to face with the object of his visit. The "little brick" looked imperial, a flat-crowned scarlet toque surmounting the sweeping curves of her black hair, her creamy skin given a dusky bloom of warmth by exercise in a strong wind—so a Russian Botticelli might have pictured the head of a young empress.

George Barnard's cloth hat was in his hand, and the wind of young winter tossed the tawny hair back from his forehead. His foolishness must have more than balanced the barrister's vaunted age, for as he saluted Norah the colour in his face rose visibly. Such things as this, though one sees them seldom, make one forget for a time that our world has any ugliness.

"I am so glad I met you," began Barnard. "I had been thinking that when I came to Weir Lodge, I probably should hardly have two words with you. And then, I'm sure they would wonder why I had come without Mr. Fenton."

"It was kind of you to come, Mr. Barnard." If any colour, other than that which the wind brought, came into Norah's face, then the addition was trifling. "I did not think for a moment you would trouble to come and see me, and so soon."

"Oh, well, you know, as far as that goes, it isn't a trouble to come and see you. I am not quite so besotted a misanthrope as all that. And I didn't like the idea of your forming a wrong impression of Hal, you know. We are old friends, you see, Harold Foster and myself. May we turn down this lane, instead of going to the—— Oh, but I beg your pardon! You have a basket—you were going into the village?"

"No—that is, I was, but it doesn't matter in the least, and I would really rather go this way now, if you don't mind."

So they turned down the lane.

"I thought it was the very kindest thing I'd ever known, your writing to me like that, Miss Fenton—I did really. I didn't think a girl—that is, it was wonderfully kind and thoughtful of you."

There was no doubt now about Norah's added colour, and the barrister's stammering confusion made the two look like a pair of boy and girl sweethearts.

"And so Mr. Tarne was mistaken?" said Norah. "I am very glad. Perhaps he was only joking."

"I don't admire his sense of humour."

"It was very absurd of me to take it seriously, and I'm afraid it was very rude to interfere and to write to you. I—I have been wondering ever since how I dared!"

"My dear girl—forgive me! I am an old fogey, you know. But, please don't talk like that. You know what I thought of your writing, and some day that rascal of a Hal shall tell you how grateful he is."

"Oh no! Please, Mr. Barnard, don't tell anyone, least of—please don't think of telling Mr. Foster. It was so stupid of me. But, of course, I didn't really think—and it was no business of mine. Please say you won't tell anyone."

"Certainly I won't if you would rather not," replied Barnard. And then they reached the end of the lane, which was within sight of the Weir Lodge garden. "I expect Mr. Fenton will be home now, or very shortly," continued the barrister; "so they will naturally suppose I have come down to see him."

"But father went to Southampton to-day on business, and will not be back until to-morrow evening."

"Oh!" The barrister looked blank for a moment. "Well, do you know, I don't think I will come up to the house at all. You see, I have no—— Well, I really think it would be better under the circumstances; and I want to go and see Harold this evening."

George Barnard held out his hand.

"You know best, Mr. Barnard." He was still holding Norah's small hand. "You—you won't think me a very stupid girl for writing? And Mr. Foster is not 'drifting'?"

"I shall always think you a very sweet, kind girl for writing, and—and you mustn't ever believe anything against Hal—at least, not without writing to me. Good-bye—dear!"

"Good-bye, Mr. Barnard, and—I'm so glad."

A moment later and the girl was gliding, with long, rhythmical steps along the little path which led to the garden-gate at Weir Lodge; and George Barnard was watching her through a gap in the thin, wintry hedge which skirted the lane.

"Well," he muttered as he turned to walk to the station, "I'd no idea there were such girls. Drift! No, by gad! he *mustn't* drift! Lucky dog! If I were a painter—what a head!"

And hearing sounds as of a train in the distance, the barrister broke into a trot, and hurried on to the station.

When George Barnard arrived at Harold Foster's rooms in Kensington, he found that he had to all appearances made a journey for nothing. After knocking once or twice and receiving no answer, the barrister turned from the door which bore his friend's name, and stood a moment meditatively tapping his pipe against the banisters.

"H'm! I suppose he has gone out to feed. I wonder if Mrs. Greet is cooking a steak for me. Poor old lady! she is quite the worst cook in England. There used to be a rather good little Italian place somewhere near here. I might do worse than go out and have some dinner myself. Then I could come back here. Yes."

At that moment the housekeeper who had charge of Harold Foster's rooms and of other parts of the house, came slowly downstairs. She had met the barrister before; in fact, George Barnard had arranged with her in engaging Harold's rooms.

"Good-evening, sir," said the woman.

"Good-evening. Mr. Foster is out, I think?"

"No, sir; I think not. Mr. Foster has been out since yesterday afternoon, but he came in just after dark, about an hour ago, sir."

"Ah! I knocked two or three times, too."

The housekeeper stepped up to Harold's door and knocked loudly, but received no answer.

"Well, now," she said; "look at that! I'm sure I never thought he had gone out again. Mr. Foster don't waste much time at home, that's certain. I don't know whether he'll be back this evening, but if you'd like to go in and wait, sir, I can lend you my key."

"Well, I'm much obliged to you. I think I will. I particularly want to see him."

"Very good, sir; and if you'll just drop this key in the housekeeper's letter-box when you're leaving, I shall be able to get in in the morning."

So the housekeeper showed the barrister into Harold's sitting-room, and left him there.

A crumpled dress-tie was lying on Harold's desk, and its position and condition were peculiarly suggestive of hurry and of vehement language. Beside it lay two unopened letters, one of which was addressed in Mr. Morley Fenton's handwriting.

"H'm!" said the barrister, as his eyes fell on these objects. "H'm!" he repeated, as he walked round the room, taking in and noting its salient features with a journalist's swiftness of perception. "Place absolutely reeks of Mr. Leo Tarne. Leo Tarne walls, Leo Tarne floor, Leo Tarne pictures—— Hullo, begad! Here's a portrait of me! 'Pon my soul, I look quite decent, too!"

The barrister waited for an hour, and then went out to have a little dinner. Having ordered the meal in a restaurant near at hand, he suddenly bethought himself that Harold Foster might return home and go out again, without knowing that he, Barnard, was in the neighbourhood. So, much to the bewilderment of the waiter who had taken his order, the barrister rushed out of the restaurant, on his way back to Harold's rooms. Having left a note there, he returned to his chop and claret, thereby putting an end to an animated discussion between two waiters as to the probabilities of his being what one of them called a "bilker."

His dinner over, George Barnard lit a cheroot and strolled back to Harold's sitting-room, which he found had not been visited during his absence. The barrister picked up a novel written by Leo Tarne, which he found lying in a chair before the fire, and composed himself to read and to wait. Enforced idleness was as irksome to George Barnard as it is to most men of no fixed occupation; but he had sighed whilst assuring Norah that Harold was not drifting, and he was a good deal worried about the young man. The fire in Harold's sitting-room gave out a genial warmth. Leo Tarne's style of writing, as illustrated in the novel which the barrister had picked up, may have been soothing. At all events, George Barnard, after one or two long drawn-out yawns, nodded, woke, read another half page, rubbed his eyes, and finally slumbered peacefully and steadily, while the fire before him gradually dwindled down to a handful of glowering cinders, thickly coated in grey ash.

Then he woke, feeling stiff and cold, and wondering why the room was dark. The housekeeper had probably forgotten to trim Mr. Foster's lamps—the lamps with the lurid shades. They were out when George Barnard woke, in the chair before the dead fire, and a little crimson circle round the burner of one of them conveyed a suggestion of used-up vitality. "Dissipation on an empty stomach," was the thought which it sent across the barrister's mind, as, yawning and stretching himself, he rose from the low chair he had occupied.

Then he heard footsteps on the stairs outside, and realized that he had probably been wakened by the sound of the opening and shutting of the outer,

TWO MEETINGS AND A LITTLE SLEEP. 117

ground-floor, door. A moment later, and the sound of a key being turned in the lock of the sitting-room door, told the barrister that the period of his waiting was ended. He moved forward as the door opened, showing Harold Foster in evening dress, holding in one hand a candlestick with a lighted taper in it.

"Well, Hal!"

"Good heavens! Is that you, George? What in the world are you doing here? And in the dark!"

The young man's face was pale, and a little drawn and weary-looking. But his eyes were very bright, and he spoke quickly, with a suggestion of tension in his voice. There was a little wine-stain on one side of his shirt-front, and his hair, as he pushed his hat back, lay in little points on his forehead, as though its gold had been moist, and was now dry; as though Harold had been hot and was now cold.

"Like that confounded lamp-wick!" thought the barrister. Then he said aloud: "Well, I came round to see you, and the housekeeper let me in, and—I suppose I must have fallen asleep. What time is it?"

"Something after three," replied Harold, putting down his candlestick, with a little, dry laugh.

"Three? By gad! Nice hours, young man!"

Harold laughed again.

"Yes; I think one can live more in one of the small hours than in a dozen of the big ones. Leo Tarne wanted me to sleep at his place, but I thought I'd walk back here. I am glad I did. Hang it! these lamps have no oil in them."

"No; they've been living through the small hours, Hal."

"Ha! Yes; and you've been sleeping, George. Think what you have lost. You might have written an article which would have made Europe tremble; or been in bed, you know. One moment—I'll get a lamp from the bedroom, and then you shall tell me what you wanted to see me about."

Harold lighted his bedroom lamp, and returning presently, placed it on the writing-table before which the barrister stood. George Barnard picked up the lamp in his left hand, placing his right on the younger man's shoulder.

"Let's have a look at you, Hal," he said.

A wave of colour spread itself over the pale, tight-drawn skin of Harold's face. The weak lips twitched into a forced smile. The bright eyes flickered under the older man's gaze. Then the young man drew away, tossing back his fair head, and laughing nervously.

"Is that what you came to see me for?" he asked.

The barrister sighed.

"By gad, I believe it's true!" he said thoughtfully.

"What's true?"

"Eh? Why, someone said you were drifting, Hal, and I said you weren't; but I thought I'd come and see."

"Nonsense, George! Drifting? Who said so?"

"How does living in town affect work at the hospital, Hal?"

The younger man raised one hand impatiently.

"For God's sake, George, don't preach hospital to me at four o'clock in the morning! The hospital is not all the world, thank goodness, though some would have one think so. George, I have seen more of the beauty and colour of life since I came to live here, than in all my life before, and I cannot live as you would like me to—neither could you. When I have learned a little more of real things, lived a little more, I will work as hard as you like for the ends you want me to serve. But, George, don't ask me to close the eyes I never opened till a little while ago; don't ask me to shut out altogether the beauty which is outside professions and money-making! And who told you I was drifting, George? What made you come to—to find out?"

For a minute the barrister did not speak, but stood looking, with sad understanding, into the young man's face. And while he looked, his thoughts went back to the face of Harold's father, as it had been before Harold's birth; back along the lines of similarity to the voice and words, the phases of life, reflected there before him now. Then he took a step forward, and pushed his arm out to the elbow over Harold's shoulder.

"Dear old boy," he said, with a little break in his voice, "don't misunderstand me; don't, for Heaven's sake, think I came to spy on you! Never mind who said you were drifting. The—the man who said it lied, because we say you are not. Sonny, don't ever misunderstand me, because I—— Let's go to sleep, Hal. I shall walk all the weary way home if you don't let me sleep in here on this couch. Go to bed, old boy; you are—you're looking burnt out!"

And before many minutes had passed Harold was asleep. And George Barnard was thinking.

CHAPTER XIV.

IN THE MATTER OF A STRAIGHT LINE.

"These are the moments which mostly count in one's life, for from them spring those quaint denials of the theory of man's original and inherent badness, which we call 'good resolutions.'"—*Leeway.*

"TO-DAY'S Friday, George," said Harold Foster, as the two were parting after breakfast, when the sunlight of an early winter's morning had brushed into the past their conversation of the small hours, and other matters. "You'll let me come and have lunch with you to-morrow, won't you? We have missed our Saturdays for two or three weeks now."

Harold Foster spoke with some slight hesitation, as one who thought he deserved but little at the hands of the man to whom he spoke; but his tone, his attitude, his expression, and the man himself, in the light which one would expect a nerve specialist to consider a man, was as great a contrast to the Harold Foster of four o'clock that morning, as morning is to night, or as breezy moorland sunshine to the artificial warmth of a gambling hell at midnight.

"Why, of course, Hal, at the usual time, and I'll be waiting for you. Going to the hospital to-day?"

"Yes; I'm going in a few minutes."

"Good-bye, old boy, till to-morrow!"

"Good-bye, George. You—you are a brick!"

"It's that girl who's a brick," muttered the barrister, as he walked downstairs on his way home to Furnival's Inn, and the wrath of Mrs. Greet. The good housekeeper always treated George Barnard with unusual severity for some time after any occasion upon which, without due notice, he spent a night away from his chambers. "I must go and see Morley Fenton this afternoon," continued the barrister, talking to himself, and thereby scandalizing an old lady next to whom he had taken a seat on a Holborn bus. "I must go and see Fenton, and have a yarn with him about Hal. The boy means just as well as ever he can mean, but—— Well, there's something in Fenton's ideas about heredity, and the influences of a phase which precedes birth; and Hal oughtn't to live alone. Great mistake to have shut him out of Weir Lodge— and, by gad! what a girl she is! She'd do Hal a heap more good than Hal would ever do her harm. Ah, it's a big mistake to try and play at being Providence!"

Just as Harold Foster was preparing to leave his chambers for the hospital, and not more than ten minutes after George Barnard's departure, Leo Tarne walked into the little sitting-room, as though from an adjoining apartment. George Barnard had left open the outer door of the little lobby, and Leo Tarne never knocked at doors unless they were locked. He said it was a trying enough practice for postmen and other necessitous persons, who were paid for doing such things.

"Hullo, Leo!" exclaimed Harold, with a shade of brusqueness in his voice. "What are you doing out of bed in the middle of the night?"

"Ask of the publishers and other misguided enthusiasts who make night hideous with sounds of shoppy talk and unearthly appointments. I would not do it for anyone else, but I have an appointment for half-past ten this morning with the man who published my first book. I've always felt so sorry for him, poor man! that really I can deny him nothing. That is why I am so punctual. It is only twenty minutes past now, and in less than an hour I shall be at his office in Covent Garden. All publishers live in Covent Garden, and all maiden ladies live in Camberwell; it's most peculiar. The Carissima will probably go to Camberwell as soon as she is old enough to be a maiden lady, and missionaries from foreign lands will take tea with her, and say pretty things about her eyes. I believe the Carissima has fine eyes; I must ask a missionary——"

"Silence! Give peace in our time! Leo, you have a frightfully bad influence on me. Do you know that I am just starting for the hospital and the realities of life?"

"My dear fellow, at this hour London contains nothing else but realities, except, of course, in its morning papers. Did you see any of the reviews of my new book this morning?"

"No; I have only just breakfasted."

"Really! I wondered what had made you look so bucolic."

"Leo, you are poisoning me."

"Never! Moral I have been occasionally. For further particulars, see the reviews this morning. Melodramatic I have never been—I swear it, Harold! —it's too exhausting."

"My dear old man, think what this is for me, as preparation for a day at the hospital."

"I prefer to think of it as compensation, Harold. As a preparer I am less distinguished than as a compensator."

"I shall clear out, and leave you here."

"In pity, no! Your housekeeper will undermine my affections."

"I will lock you in."

IN THE MATTER OF A STRAIGHT LINE. 123

"I have a cab outside. Shall I lay bilkery upon my soul?"

"I am absolutely rigid in my determination to go to the hospital."

"In after years you will repent this youthful folly."

"I am armed with virtue, and clothed in righteous fixity of purpose."

"You have had a letter from your spiritual adviser at Weir Lodge?"

"I have had breakfast with my worldly adviser, George Barnard."

"Ah, I cry you mercy! As you are strong, be merciful. Come, I will prove my penitence by goodly deeds. You shall save ten precious minutes of hospital realities by sharing my cab."

"Thanks, Leo. I'm sorry to seem bearish "—they were already on the stairs—" but I really must keep hold of things, you know."

"Do, my dear fellow—St. Bartholomew's Hospital, cabby. My trouble is always to prevent things catching hold of me."

"You see," continued Harold as they stepped into Tarne's cab, " I have been rather—I have been drifting too far lately."

"By Jove! How quaint! Yet, now you mention it, I think you have; yes, I believe I have noticed that you've been drifting too much. And did Mr. Barnard tell you so?"

Harold Foster looked sharply at his friend.

"Well, oddly enough, I believe he did say something of the sort. Why?"

"Oh, merely that it is the kind of thing I should have expected he would say."

"George is a dear old chap, Leo, and I am very fond of him."

"I don't doubt it, my dear Harold; but don't

scold me because of that. I didn't make you fond of him, you know, or not consciously."

"You are incorrigible. But, really, he is an awfully good old sort, the oldest friend I have; and if only because it worries him, I mustn't drift too much."

"I am sure I cautioned you against it at Trouville, even before that fearful woman came and bored me."

"You did, and I was a beast. But I won't be any more. You know, Leo, I really do want to achieve something myself, apart from George Barnard."

"The worst of achievement is that it makes you so absolutely unable to do anything."

"Don't be cynical, Leo. I'm not strong enough—yet. And it seems to me, you know, that as far as I'm concerned, achievement lies at the end of a certain uninterestingly straight line—so." Harold drew the ferrule of his umbrella across the rubber mat at his feet.

"I thought the straight path was the one which led—— However, I interrupted you—yes?"

"Well, and colour and light and beauty—things which to me, alone, seem only to be reached by drift—lie out here, do you see, in curves on either side of my straight line."

"This grows upon me. Proceed, Euclid!"

"Well, when I take little dips into the curves, I can't pursue the curve to the extent of getting back to my straight line at a more advanced point by it."

"Why, my algebraic friend?"

"I don't know; but I can't. The ends of the curves have been cut off; they don't seem to rejoin the line. I always come up at the point from which I made the dip. So it follows that if, in anything like one little lifetime, I am to reach the end of the straight line—that's achievement, you know—my drifts along the curves must be neither frequent nor extensive."

IN THE MATTER OF A STRAIGHT LINE. 125

"You speak like a book—a library, in fact—of parables."

"Well—that's all. And here's the hospital. And as I want the straight line, or, at least, the end of it—I do, really, Leo, old man—I'm going to try and economize all I know in the matter of those curves. And you must help me. It was awfully good of you to bring me right down here out of your way. Good-bye, Leo."

"Good-bye, Harold. Come and dine with me on Sunday. They don't allow hospitals to keep open on Sundays, do they? Or is it public-houses? And—oh, I say, Harold!"

"Yes, old man."

"I say, you know, that straight line hasn't any end really, you know—outside the copy-books. It's been cut off, like the ends of the curves, if it ever existed, except as a mirage. Good-bye, Harold."

And then Mr. Leo Tarne told his cabman to drive to Covent Garden. And Harold Foster walked into the hospital, looking thoughtful.

CHAPTER XV.

"UP AT A VILLA, DOWN IN THE CITY."

"Myself have had hopes of converting
The foolish to wisdom, till, sober,
My life found its May grow October.
I talked and I wrote, but, one morning,
Life's autumn bore fruit in this warning:
*Let tongue rest and quiet thy quill be!
Earth is earth and not heaven and ne'er will be!*
Man's work is to labour and leaven—
As best he may—earth here with heaven."
Pacchiarotto.

THE occasions upon which George Barnard had crossed the threshold of Mr. Morley Fenton's counting-house in Lombard Street were not numerous. There was that about the man which made news-boys in the purlieus of the Stock Exchange forbear to press upon him journals which dealt in "Westralian" sensations or South African "slumps." Then mentally gauged the big man, with his viking head and his breezy gait, and half laughingly begged coppers of him, or proffered to him illustrated papers, or comicalities of the prize-competition variety.

Dazzling young clerks, with pale, lank faces and awe-inspiring collars, would eye George with languid superciliousness as being a bumpkin or "outsider" of some description. And, as the barrister yawed largely down narrow, silk-hat-thronged city alleys, grey-haired men, in whose faces feverish acuteness battled always with worn, flat weariness, would turn their heads to look after him, expand their lungs as the swing of his arms fanned them or a snatch of the tune he hummed reached them, and sigh heavily.

Towards half-past three on the afternoon of the day on which he had breakfasted with Harold Foster, George Barnard was wending his way through the city to the office of Messrs. Morley Fenton, Son and Co. At the corner of Lombard Street a small boy offered the barrister two oranges for three-halfpence. Barnard took the two oranges, gave the boy twopence, and then returning him one of the oranges, told the lad to eat that himself. Then he paused beside a lamppost, and began to suck the other orange with keen and evident enjoyment.

Just as the orange was half finished, and the barrister was in the full flood of his appreciation of the fruit, a man passed him, and then, turning round, stood quite still for some seconds watching Barnard. He was a red-bearded, grimy-skinned, tired-eyed man, dressed in shiny black, and carrying in one hand an old and shapeless brown bag. This was one of the hardest worked of London's city missionaries. As, at last, he turned from his contemplation of the big man with the orange, the missionary sighed, and said quietly:

"'And of such is the kingdom of heaven'—thank God!"

George Barnard wiped his lips and tawny moustache with a soft, old bandana, and passed on to the counting-house, where Mr. Morley Fenton held silent, methodical sway. Half an hour afterwards Mr. Fenton had persuaded the barrister to accompany him to Weir Lodge for the evening.

"You have great adaptability, George," said the man of business; "but you are not at home within a half-mile of the Bank. The setting is out of keeping, George. We can talk better down below."

And so when Norah, waiting and listening in the hall at Weir Lodge, heard steps on the drive outside, she turned away from the vestibule door with the indifferently preoccupied air of one uninterested in the matter of new arrivals. She had heard another step beside Mr. Morley Fenton's. When she did, with overacted nonchalance, step forward to greet the head of the house and his friend, she did so with a little sigh which, though she perhaps was not aware of the fact, meant: "Ah! it is not; no, but it is the next best to that."

Yet the girl was somewhat strained and nervous when she held out her hand to the barrister. George Barnard retained this little hand in his for perhaps a shade longer than he might have done before that walk in the lane behind Weir Lodge; but in doing so he looked frankly and assuringly into Norah's eyes, and her little twinge of nervous anxiety melted and disappeared, like hoar-frost in the light of an ardent spring sun.

For some reason similar to that which made Mr. Morley Fenton disinclined to talk to George Barnard in Lombard Street, the barrister, on the journey down to Sunbury that evening had chatted upon a variety of topics, but had said no word about the matter uppermost in his mind. Dinner over, however, and cheroots and coffee well under way in Mr. Fenton's study, he said:

"I went round to Harold's diggings last night, and fell asleep in his sitting-room while waiting for him to come home."

"Ah, and how do you think living in town suits him now? I felt a little uneasy about him when I met him after the return from Trouville."

"Yes, I felt a little uneasy about him yesterday. That's why I waited to see him last night."

"And——"

"I slept there, and left him this morning starting for the hospital very fit and full of work."

"Yes, and how had you found him?"

The barrister puffed thoughtfully at his cheroot, before saying, thoughtfully:

"Well you know, Morley, I am free to confess that I don't think Hal ought to live alone. You will think all my advice about him objective, because I fancy that even living alone in town, though not good for him, is better than living at the Vicarage in Norwood."

"And in what way do you think his present style of living bad for Harold, George?"

"Simply in so far as that I think it not actively good for him. And then I think his temperament demands an atmosphere which should be better for him, more strengthening and repose-giving than anything merely negative. After all, you know, it is a good deal to ask of any young man. He is put down, alone, in—well, in London, with no routine to steady him, and no incentive to work save such as may come from within, and—and doesn't come in a normal young man. The other life, at Norwood, of course, was an active influence on the other side; an irritant and direct incentive to the worst kind of frivole. So I think, at all events."

"And because of that—it was because of that, you know, George—we fell in with Harold's own wish to live in town."

"True; and for that reason my advice about him seems merely objective and not helpful."

"Not at all. Not at all, George. But what do you suggest? What do you consider lacking?"

"Well, I think Harold is lacking now, just that active influence which was shut out of his life by the bringing to an end of his visits here."

Mr. Morley Fenton's right hand rose to his moustache with a characteristic movement which suggested the attitude of a mesmerist whose will-power is being concentrated on the calming and controlling of a restive subject.

"That is what I have been waiting and fearing to hear from you, George," he said quietly. "From various causes, I am not able to see as much of Harold as you do, but yet, in some way, I feel most growths and changes in his life. Ever since his visit to—his little holiday in France, I have been filled by an uneasy consciousness, which has been strengthened by the little I have seen of him, that he was losing steering-way, and being affected to some extent by the kind of influences which I—the very influences from which we most wished to shield him. And now, old friend, I can see in your eyes that you are convinced of the same thing. Is he—has Harold committed himself in any way, George?"

"No, no, I don't think so for a moment; but I think what you say regarding steering-way is about right."

"Ah, it is very hard to know exactly what can be done, and you know the thought which made me remove whatever influence his visits here may have had. The circumstances have not changed, and there seems to me a risk of injustice involved."

"I can't agree with you, old man, and you know I couldn't at first. It seems to me that if the one course contains risks for your niece, the other entails injustice to—to Harold." George Barnard rose to his feet on the hearthrug. His mind was occupied by two pictures—Harold as he had appeared at the door of his own chambers at three o'clock that morning, and Norah Fenton as she had looked when receiving his, Barnard's, assurance that Harold Foster was not drifting. "Believe me, Morley, old man," continued the barrister, from his place before the fire, "when Providence brings two people together it's a risky thing to upset Providence's schemes; particularly if the two people are a young man and a young woman. I know you think that anything touching upon home life is beyond my grip, but yet I fancy I know, when I say that Norah could do Harold a lot of good—she might —but Harold could never do Norah any harm. We outsiders, old man, we sometimes see a little, you know."

Mr. Morley Fenton sighed, and uncrossed his outstretched legs.

"It is curious," he said, "that you should practically be pleading to me, for—on behalf of—Harold Foster. Believe me, George, I see with you eye to eye in Harold's interest; but then, you know, you have no feeling of moral responsibility for Norah's life, and—you don't know Norah, George, do you?"

The barrister coloured slightly.

"Not as you do, of course, but I have studied her pretty closely, and it was that study, and its result, which made me so firm in the belief I told you of just now. You think it over, old man, and credit me with some little knowledge of the good old gardener in us all. And believe me when I say that something—the *entrée* of this house, for choice—should be given Hal, for ballast."

"I do believe you, and I do credit you with knowledge, and wide knowledge. I must believe you, for I have told you of my own consciousness of the immediate need for some help in Harold's life. As a matter of fact, I wrote him a long letter on the subject only yesterday morning."

The barrister thought of the crumpled dress-tie and

the unopened letters on Harold Foster's desk, and he moved uneasily.

"Some time back," continued Mr. Fenton, "we introduced a new element into his life by bringing him here; and that with a hope of supplying some of the interest he seemed to lack. Then, to protect Norah from danger, the new element was withdrawn by me from Harold. Then, partly with a hope of filling the vacant place it left, we arranged the change in his way of living. And now, I see clearly that something must be done, and done at once, toward the supply of an incentive to work and to steady steering. I must think over what you have said, George; we must think it over, and do whatever can be done without injustice."

The barrister nodded his head slowly. He wished he dared say more. But he was thinking of "the little brick," and remembering her instant confusion when he had carelessly hinted at a possibility of his some day conveying to Harold an idea of her effort to have help extended in that "drift" of which Leo Tarne had spoken. No. In whatever cause, no light of pain must be brought into those great, shadowy eyes. The unspoken assurance with which he had answered her greeting in the hall that evening must be scrupulously lived up to. The barrister could say no more to his friend. But his thoughts in the matter were luminous, and widely comprehensive. And something of their light may have illumined and given meaning to his hand-shake, when he left Mr. Morley Fenton that evening, and repeated the expression of his opinion regarding interference in "Providence's schemes."

"By the way," he added, as the train in which he was returning to town began to move from the platform where Mr. Morley Fenton stood, "Harold lunches with me to-morrow, you know. Join us, if you can manage it, will you?"

Mr. Fenton nodded gravely as he walked beside the moving train.

"One o'clock at my rooms?" The barrister leaned far out of his carriage-window.

"One o'clock," assented Mr. Morley Fenton. And turning then, with a little wave of his hand, he slowly retraced his steps down the platform, responded with quiet courtesy to the stationmaster's salutation, and proceeded, with head bent thoughtfully, in the direction of Weir Lodge.

"I may be a little late to-night, dear," he said to Mrs. Fenton, before re-entering his study, and some ten minutes after parting with George Barnard at the station; "so you won't wait up, will you?"

Then he bade the girls "Good-night!" in his customarily grave way, and walked across the hall to the room in one corner of which stood his 'cello. But the 'cello was not on this particular evening to be disturbed.

Mr. Morley Fenton sat down in a wicker chair before the study fire. His limbs seemed to relax wearily, and as though in some way they were no longer amenable to any controlling sense. He sighed, and his hands shook slightly as he passed them slowly over his face, from which they seemed to remove, as a mask might be lowered, all its wonted impassive serenity, and much of its strength of purpose. Much there was which seemed taken from his face, and something there seemed added. The addition was age—sad, grey age, which sometimes has nothing to do with years. But it was the ageing of Morley Fenton, and the greyness of strength—tired strength.

CHAPTER XVI.

MATTERS OF EXPEDIENCY.

> " With faith it was friends bulwarked him about
> From infancy to boyhood ; so by youth
> He stood impenetrably circuited ;
> Heaven high and low as hell : what lacked he thus,
> Guarded against oppression, storm or sap?
> What foe would dare approach ? "
> *Red Cotton Nightcap Country.*

THE unquestioned authority over his own household held by Mr. Morley Fenton, resembled most things absolute, in that it was rarely asserted, seldom felt, and never overthrown.

Once during her married life Mrs. Fenton had expressed a strong desire to set up house in Belgravia. During an entire season Mrs. Fenton had urged her husband to terminate his active connection with the firm in Lombard Street. At different times during the year following a certain general election, Mr. Morley Fenton's wife had endeavoured to induce him to put himself forward as a candidate for political honours.

Throughout these phases Mr. Morley Fenton had, up to a certain point, been blandly, courteously deprecatory. The particular point which marked the end of his endurance being passed, he had in these matters allowed his authority to briefly, tersely, assert itself, making it to quickly disappear then behind the ramparts of its own immovability.

The owner of Weir Lodge remained the active ruler in the counting-house of Messrs. Morley Fenton,

MATTERS OF EXPEDIENCY. 135

Son and Co.; he continued to reside quietly at Sunbury; he refrained from any closer contact with the House of Commons than may be reached in the occasional perusal of the daily papers' leading columns; and these several subjects were struck out of the Fenton family's list of possible topics. But Mr. Morley Fenton's was not the hand which marked out these topics; and the head of the house was rarely known to say that anything must or must not be.

Whilst talking over the coffee partaken of abovestairs, on the morning following his conversation with George Barnard, Mr. Fenton said to his wife:

"Oh, by the way, dear, I am inclined to think, from one or two things I have heard this week, that we both exaggerated the importance of any feeling which may have existed between young Mr. Foster and our Norah."

"My dear Morley, I was quite sure of my ground so far as Norah was concerned."

"Ah! Well, in any case neither of them are children, and I don't know that we have any right to assume that our guidance is necessary to them, or to insist on their following it. I think it would be wiser, all things considered, to let events fall out naturally."

"That is, to allow these two to fall in love with each other."

"I do not agree with you, my dear, and I don't think you will find that such a thing follows. However, that remains to be seen. In the meantime, I think you know that I am more than ordinarily interested in Harold Foster's life. In fact, having been his father's closest friend, I have always felt towards him more as a guardian than a friend. He has no relatives living, and, with the exception of George Barnard, no other old friend except myself."

"Yes." Mrs. Fenton's tone and expression suggested expectant wonder and surprise. Her husband's voice reminded her in some vague way of the end which had been brought to those few phases in which she had endeavoured by persuasion to regulate according to a wish of her own, Mr. Morley Fenton's life. It was reminiscent of those rare occasions upon which she had been suddenly made to realize that her husband was a very strong man, who was master of his own life and his own house. "Yes, dear," she repeated.

"Well, Harold Foster has been living alone in town for some time past, and has had very few opportunities of enjoying any sort of home life. I want him to visit here again, and on a slightly different footing. I think you all liked the little you saw of him, and I think I may say that there will be no difficulty about Norah. I want you to set aside—let me see, suppose you set aside the little walnut room over my study, and let that be kept at Harold Foster's disposal, so that he may come down at any time, and spend his week ends here, you know. He will, of course, retain his town rooms, but I should like you to make him feel, as you so gracefully can, dear, that he may regard our home as his, and use it when he chooses. By the way, I think that was the second gong, was it not? I will be down in two minutes, if you and the girls care to begin breakfast."

Mrs. Fenton left her husband to the arrangement of his necktie, and went slowly downstairs, thinking over what had been said. There was, of course, nothing distasteful to her in this little family arrangement; but it surprised her somewhat, in view of the manner in which Mr. Fenton had received her intelligence of what she had observed between the young man in question and Norah. But tactful Mrs. Fenton promptly recognised that this wish of her husband's was one of the things which were to be.

She communicated the news in the wisest possible manner, and as an item of entirely pleasant information, to the three girls; and when the head of the house took his seat at the breakfast-table, he was promptly assailed with a running fire of questions, one in six of which he answered verbally, and all of which he responded to good-humouredly.

"Would you care to walk down to the station with me, Norah? The weather is beautifully bright and crisp, and you are not looking anything like so well as you might look."

If justified by expediency, Mr. Morley Fenton's comment on Norah's appearance was somewhat unfortunate when judged under reality's strong light. That the girl was unusually silent might well have been attributed to some other cause than depression, mental or physical, since Lucy and Maud left no gaps between their speeches and questions, and Norah's face was a beautiful and animated picture in ever-changing and, for her, brilliant colouring.

Norah was dressed for walking, and waiting in the vestibule for Mr. Morley Fenton when that gentleman lighted his cheroot and appeared, prepared for his day in town. On their way to the station he glanced once at the girl's changed face, her warmly-flushed cheeks and glowing eyes, which of late had contained little else than sadness. He said quietly, and as though touching lightly, *en passant*, upon a trivial subject:

"You are glad our friend Harold Foster is to bestow his society upon us a little more often in future, are you not, mavourneen?"

"Yes, father; I shall be glad to see him."

"Yes, I think we all shall. It is a pity for anyone young to live so much alone, and I think we have an opportunity of helping him a good deal by making Weir Lodge homelike to him. When a young man has no home he is so liable to make mistakes. With Harold Foster, now, who knows, if he lived alone much longer, whether he might not fall in love, or do some other foolish thing of that sort. I say 'foolish' because, at this particular stage of his work, such a thing would be fatal to his prospects. And then, again—that is one of the necessary evils of our social system—it is absolutely essential that Harold should marry someone of independent means, because of his own position and the particular career he has chosen —absolutely essential. What a beautiful piece of colour that strip of gorse makes, does it not?"

"Yes, beautiful."

"And, you see, I fancy that we can do a good deal towards saving Harold Foster from any such mistakes as that, even if he had any inclination to make them, by giving him a relief element of quiet interest in our home, as something to alternate with the hospital and town life. I am sure of your good offices in this, mavourneen, because I know he interested you. By the way, is it to-night that you and the girls are going to a dance?"

"Yes, father; at the Crossthwaites', you know."

"Ah, well, I will send down some flowers. I shall not be home much before dinner-time this evening myself, and I might bring Harold Foster. You will see that the little walnut room is snug, won't you, dear? And what sort of flowers would you like best?"

"Oh, I would much rather leave that to you, father; you always choose the nicest. I should like some violets, and—— Hark! Surely that's the train, father?"

"I believe it is; I must hurry. Perhaps you had

better not come into the station. I will send a boy down with the flowers. Good-bye, dear."

" Good-bye, father."

While it had lasted their little conversation had seemed to be a casual enough chat about flowers, and that evening's dance, and Harold Foster, and Sunbury scenery. But on her way back to Weir Lodge Norah began to realize that the talk had been one of import, great import to her, and of information—almost instruction—about Harold Foster. Norah looked very thoughtful when she reached the house. The effects of the draught of bright wine, which that morning's news had been to her, seemed to have passed off. But Norah, moving to and fro, and handling all things with dainty deftness of touch; Norah spent a good deal of time that morning, in the little walnut room over Mr. Morley Fenton's study.

When, shortly after one o'clock, the owner of Weir Lodge arrived at his friend's chambers in Furnival's Inn, he found George Barnard in pronounced dishabille, and scribbling hard at his littered writing-table. On the shabby old couch beside the fireplace, that couch which for at least fifteen years George Barnard had been threatening to make away with in favour of something new, Harold Foster lay stretched at full length and gazing at the smoky ceiling above him.

This was the end of Harold's first twenty-four hours of rigid adherence to his "straight line," that path which Leo Tarne had said was without any real end. The beginnings of most good things, like the ends of most bad things, are exhausting. The relative nearness of such beginnings and endings may have something to do with this family resemblance in their features. Social philosophy is lacking in observance of moral periodicity, and the phase life of the imaginative temperament.

Harold Foster had, since his visit to Trouville, been drifting more pronouncedly, perhaps, than even Leo Tarne had guessed—more, certainly, than himself of George Barnard had imagined. This was inevitable. It was part of Harold's character, and that part which marked the difference between his friend Leo Tarne's temperament and his own. His was in every way the more active, Leo Tarne's in all respects the more negative. Tarne's life was as nearly devoid of phases as his nature was of passion, or his writings of aught else beyond phases. Harold Foster's life, by reason of the vivid sensitiveness of all his perceptive faculties, was as full of phases as a tropical sunset.

"I live as I think," Leo Tarne had once said to Harold, "and you live as I write, which must be exhausting. And then, too, it produces resolutions and repentance, and—to avoid further alliteration—other things which interfere with one's appetite, and put one's liver out of order."

Leo Tarne led an "illustrated life," he being projected or reflected on to a series of canvases, himself a prominent figure in each picture. Harold Foster lived a dramatically-grouped life, himself stepping into the centre, the extreme point, of a series of "situations"; his the most outstanding personality in each *tableau vivant*.

As has been said, Harold Foster had been drifting almost unreservedly since his visit to Trouville. He had held only very loosely and listlessly the curb rein of his life's bridle. Then, with the chilly hour of his home-coming on Friday morning, had come the burnt-out lamps, and George Barnard's suggested likening of their condition to Harold's own state. That and the circumstances immediately following it, had been not simply a picture, no mere page in an "illustrated life," but a crucial situation, an important scene in a flesh and blood drama, and the living forerunner of "resolutions and repentance, and other things which interfere with one's appetite, and put one's liver out of order."

At the end of a hard day's work as his first in the "straight line" path, Harold had taken over another man's evening duty at the hospital, and then, after reading through the small hours, he had left Kensington at half-past eight to attend nine o'clock lecture on Saturday morning. And now, as he lay stretched on George Barnard's couch, his face contained no light of interest to relieve its overstrained weariness. And that inner voice of a man, which at times apologizes to the outer mind for what it says, was whispering to Harold that as a matter of courtesy he was bound to accept Leo Tarne's invitation to dine with the Carissima at his flat on Sunday. "And," added the small voice with deprecating modesty, "perhaps it is as well. It will be a great relief, a rest, a little rift of colour in the greyness, you know."

"Open that door, like a good fellow, Hal," said the barrister, looking up hurriedly through the cloud of blue smoke which surrounded him, as a knock fell on the outer door of the chambers. "I locked it to keep Mrs. Greet out. It's Mr. Fenton, I expect. Oh yes; I forgot to tell you Mr. Fenton's coming to lunch with us."

Down went the barrister's lion head once more, and up rose a dense addition to his smoke cloud, as murmuring, "By Jove! I wish I'd known," Harold Foster rose to answer a second brisk tap on the door.

"How are you, Harold? Thank you. It is quite a long while since I have seen you. You are not looking quite so well, I think, as when we last met."

"I am very well, thanks; but a little tired to-day," explained Harold.

"Good-morning, Morley," said the man under a cloud at the writing-table. "Sit down a minute and talk, and excuse me, will you? I want to finish this bit of work, so I can post it when we go to lunch. Mind the dog—oh, mind that unfortunate idiot dog! I won't be more than five minutes."

Mr. Morley Fenton had trodden on the over-trustful dog, and that animal had interjected a shrill and hurried remark.

"I see there is an afternoon concert at the Queen's Hall to-day," said Mr. Fenton, as he sat down facing Harold Foster. "I thought we might go there after lunch, but perhaps you are too tired."

"No, not at all," replied Harold quickly. "I should enjoy nothing better. I'm only a little fagged through—because I was up late last night."

"Ah! yes, living in town is conducive to late hours, I know, but you must be as careful as you can, you know, because a good deal depends on the next six or eight months, does it not?"

"Yes. My final at the hospital, you mean?"

"Exactly. And that entails so much in the way of consequences. By the way, I wanted you to come down to Sunbury this evening, and stay till Monday. What do you think? Mrs. Fenton expects you, and you have had a long spell of town life lately."

'Yes; I should have been delighted, really"— Harold hesitated. His face, being pale, 'showed instantly a very slight influx of colour—" but the fact is, I have promised to dine with Leo Tarne to-morrow evening, at his place, you know."

"Oh; I am sorry for that."

"Yes."

There was a slight addition to the suggestion of colour in the young man's face. He was silently arguing with that inner voice of his, and the inner voice was triumphing easily.

"They all expect you," continued Mr. Morley Fenton, adding then, with genuine and forgetful carelessness, "and I asked Norah to make the room over my study comfortable for you. They will be disappointed."

If at the end of this remark Mr. Morley Fenton had glanced at Harold's face, his subsequent conduct might have been a good deal influenced thereby. But George Barnard's dog, acting at the instance of, or in conjunction with, Providence, ordered matters otherwise. The discriminating animal had chosen this particular moment in which to rise on its hind-legs, and with tentatively wagging tail, announce to the best of its ability its willingness to forget and forgive the accident which had led to a too confiding canine nature and a too prominent right front paw, being trampled upon.

While Mr. Morley Fenton's attention was thus momentarily engaged by George Barnard's dog, a whole wave of recollection and of conflicting thoughts, was reflecting its vivid light upon Harold Foster's face. Norah, the beautiful, shadowy-eyed type and emblem of the short phase which in a few weeks had made Harold familiar with Leo Tarne, and dreamily, happily conscious of another atmosphere outside that of the novelist—an atmosphere of dainty white purity, soft music, and home tenderness—Norah expected him, and had prepared a room for him!

In an instant flash of fancy he saw the girl as she had appeared in the light of his awakening wonder, on the Sunday morning following Molesey Regatta, a scarlet poppy flaming out its colour from the hollow between her dark waves of hair, her little right hand raised, and her ripple-tipped lashes curving upward over a wide gaze of seeming wonder at his—Harold's —presence. He saw her in a dozen different garbs, and in the varying settings of a score of changing surroundings, all beautiful; and he remembered all she had embodied in that short phase, the end of which had come with rude abruptness, and yet he knew not exactly how or when or why. And Norah expected him!

When Mr. Morley Fenton looked up a moment later from George Barnard's aggressively forgiving dog, Harold Foster's face was pale and once more in repose. He was feeling in his pocket for a cigarette —an all-important conversational factor and refuge to the modern man—and his eyes were lowered, as he said quietly:

"Well, of course, I could send word round to Leo Tarne to explain that I cannot be with him to-morrow. I—I don't suppose he would mind."

"Ah, yes—that is better. After all, Mr. Tarne sees more of you than we do, I dare say; and I am sure an occasional change from town life is wholesome. Then we will regard that as settled?"

"Yes; thank you very much. I shall be very glad to come."

"Ah!—O-oh!" The long-drawn exclamation came from the smoke-curtained writing-table.

"What's the matter, George?" asked Harold.

"Oh, nothing—nothing, my dear boy! But I've finished my screed, that's all; and I'm the hungriest man in England—and the blithest. That's what's wrong with me."

CHAPTER XVII.

PROVIDENCE AND MR. MORLEY FENTON.

"No—'tis ungainly work, the ruling men, at best!
The graceful instinct's right : 'tis women stand confessed
Auxiliary, the gain that never goes away,
Takes nothing and gives all."
Fifine at the Fair.

GEORGE BARNARD'S appetite did not appear to be so startling when he sat down to lunch with Mr. Morley Fenton and Harold Foster at the Constitutional Club, as his own statement regarding it might have led one to think. He did justice to the meal, however, as he did to most meals in the preparing of which Mrs. Greet's peculiar talents had had no opportunity of asserting themselves; and he was obviously in the best of good spirits.

At Mr. Morley Fenton's suggestion, Harold Foster left his friends after luncheon, and proceeded alone to his rooms in Kensington, in order to despatch a note to Leo Tarne regarding the next day's engagement. At the same time he packed a small bag, and sent it to Waterloo to await him there. Hurrying back then to town, Harold met George Barnard and Mr. Fenton at the concert hall, where the three spent something like a couple of hours very pleasantly.

Later on, the barrister accompanied his friends to Waterloo, and stayed chatting for some minutes after Mr. Morley Fenton and Harold had taken their seats in the Sunbury train.

"Better come down with us, George, for the evening anyhow," suggested Mr. Fenton. He had made the same suggestion at an earlier stage in the afternoon.

"Thank you, old man, but I can't manage it. I must get through the work I'm on just now."

"Ah, well! you may be able to come down with Harold this time next week."

"Yes, I hope so. Good-bye, Morley. Good-bye, Harold. I suppose you will come up to town together on Monday?"

"Yes, pretty sure to, I expect. Good-bye."

And the Sunbury train moved out from the station, leaving George Barnard on the platform, looking after it half longingly. He had felt a strong desire to accept Mr. Morley Fenton's invitation, for, like most other bachelors, the barrister had his week-end phases of loneliness. But something had told him that Harold Foster might be made to feel the more at home in Weir Lodge on the occasion of this visit if he were Mr. Fenton's only guest. The barrister told himself that he represented town and bachelordom in Harold's life, and might therefore, without wishing it, stand between the latter and the home atmosphere at Sunbury—that atmosphere which was to serve Harold as ballast.

So George Barnard walked slowly down the station platform, and made the best of his journey back to Furnival's Inn alone.

"We shall have a very quiet evening, Harold," said Mr. Morley Fenton, when the train they were travelling in had placed some miles between itself and George Barnard; "but perhaps that will be quite as well, since you are tired. The girls are going to a dance this evening."

"Oh yes. Are they all well?"

"Yes, thanks; I think they are very well. Norah

has been rather pale and languid lately, but she was always a little delicate, you know. Constitutional on her mother's side, I fancy. And then I do not think she has ever been quite the same since her father died."

"No; she does give one the impression of having been saddened."

"Yes. They were great friends, you see, she and her father. He was a sweet-natured man, who suffered all his life through not having been born with an independence of some sort. He was not qualified for forcing one out of the world, poor fellow; and so Norah was left really without anything."

"Ah! yet she has a good deal which one does not see in all girls."

"Oh yes; she has her beauty, and a very sweet nature. I think she will make some man very happy by-and-by. And I think when that time comes it will do Norah herself a great deal of good. Hers is the kind of nature which I think is rounded off and greatly benefited by marriage."

"Yes."

Leo Tarne and all that he represented in Harold Foster's life, was fading fast now from out the young man's immediate mental environment, and all sorts of misty, delicate fancies and ideas were blending, in place of this, round the anticipatory influences of the Weir Lodge home circle. But these fancies were as yet vague, formless things, aerial shapes, to which meaning had not given outline.

"In fact," continued Norah's adopted father, "to let you into a little parental confidence, I may tell you that one of my ideas in bringing Norah to Weir Lodge was that we might be able to find the right husband for her. You see, when the child does marry, it is absolutely essential that she should marry a man of some means. Then, I think, she would benefit by marriage; but she must never be a poor man's wife. A country life is what I think Norah should have, and a well-to-do husband, with very few, if any, professional ties. But this is domesticity with a vengeance, and must be very uninteresting to you."

" Not at all "—the younger man coloured slightly, and smiled in a constrained way—" not at all. But I was wondering how you would manage if—if I call her 'Miss Fenton,' you see, I have no name left for your eldest daughter."

" Exactly. Call her Norah. You will be seeing a good deal of each other now, you know."

" Well, I was going to say, I was wondering how you would manage if Norah fixed upon the wrong man?"

" Ah, but I don't think she will. I don't think she is much inclined to fix upon any man. She feels at home where she is, and when she leaves us I shall miss her just as much as though she were really my own daughter. No, I don't think she will choose the wrong man. And then, you know, that is just where we fathers have to exercise our diplomacy, and look ahead with eyes which see more than our children's eyes can see. I am practically able to see that if that child—she is a very womanly child, by the way —were to marry anyone other than a man of leisure and of considerable means, she would be unhappy. Consequently, don't you see, I keep a sharp look-out along the rim of her horizon. Mrs. Fenton shares my look-out, and if we sighted any piratical-looking craft bearing down towards this particular schooner-yacht of ours, we should—er—range alongside to shield her, or even put her a few points off her course until the pirate was out of sight. Really, I had no idea I was so nautical—or so prosy."

"On the contrary, I am very much interested."

"A glimpse behind the scenes, eh?"

"Quite. And are all—all vessels without independent means, and the other things, you know, pirates?"

"In this case, yes, I think they would be. In most cases, no. But you follow my reasoning, do you not? You see why I feel that certain conditions are essential to Norah's happiness—a husband who should be thoroughly a home bird, amongst other things."

"Ye-es—yes, I see."

"Have you another of those cigarettes? Thanks. I don't know why my cheroot should have burned so badly to-day, I'm sure." (It was curious, in view of the casual vein in which Mr. Morley Fenton had been talking, that he should have so neglected his cheroot.) "Thanks, I was going to say, whilst still on this behind-the-curtain subject, that my wife, like most of her sex, has a way of jumping rather hastily at conclusions. In the looking-out process I fancy she was half inclined to regard you as a possible pirate, an unconscious one I believe she credited you with being, but a pirate. Well, of course I reassured her on that point, knowing you as I do. So for the future you will be a privileged cruiser, as it were, sailing under a flag of treaty in treaty waters, eh?"

"Just so; of course."

Thinking the matter over at a later stage, Harold Foster told himself that the manner in which he had become a party to this treaty was peculiar.

"Yes," continued Mr. Morley Fenton, as though in reply to some observation; "in this matter there is really a certain sort of similarity between your position and Norah's, except that it would be a rather dangerous thing for you to fall in love with even the most eligible of partis just now, because so much depends on your freedom from distraction during the coming year. Later on, of course—— But you are not a family man, and all this forecasting will bore you. I thought I might as well mention the matter, since it had cropped up between Mrs. Fenton and myself, and you are sure to be brought a good deal into contact, now, with my wife and the girls. At least, I hope you will. I want you to treat Weir Lodge as a home."

"That's very kind of you," murmured Harold.

"And, feeling sure, as I did, that you would readily grasp the situation, as affecting Norah and yourself, I had no hesitation in—er—in, as it were, giving peace guarantee for you, and asserting your privileges as a friend of the family."

"You are very good—very good."

It was one of those points in conversation at which one gropes in vacancy for an observation. Harold Foster's groping was unsuccessful. He had a curious feeling of having been absorbed and distributed along the lines of a stronger nature's desires. Mr. Morley Fenton lost no least fleeting change of expression in Harold's face, though he seemed to be studying contemplatively his cigarette. Only a very close observer would have noticed the slightest indication in Mr. Morley Fenton's fine face of any mental state other than restful, impassive serenity. But, then, this face had in it no tell-tale characteristics, unless, perhaps, in the network of fine veins, sometimes not discernible, but just now clearly visible, on either side of the high forehead.

"By the way," observed Mr. Fenton, with an inflection of casual interest in his voice, "are you still 'clerking' at the hospital, Harold?"

"No; I am dressing now, under Carrington. I think you know Carrington, do you not?"

"Yes." Mr. Fenton tossed his half-smoked cigarette under the seat facing him, with a little sigh which suggested relief of some sort. "Yes, I have known Carrington for some time. A very good man to be under I should think."

"Yes, he is counted amongst the first flight."

"Ah! and I suppose 'dressing' is more interesting work than the other, is it not?"

"Ye-es—yes, I think it is. There's more of it, anyhow."

"And, of course, it is more practical. Ah, here's Sunbury; this must have been a slow train. Don't forget your umbrella, Harold. Good-evening, Johnson. It is—very cold."

When Harold Foster and his host reached the Weir Lodge garden, they were chatting on the subject of singing in general, and the vocal items of that afternoon's concert in particular. There was a pleasant and satisfied ring in Mr. Fenton's voice, and Harold had forgotten, for the moment, both the conversation of the previous half-hour, and the little shadow of nervousness which he had felt about this visit to Weir Lodge.

"I suppose the girls are preparing for their evening's dissipation," said Mr. Morley Fenton, as he helped Harold to remove his overcoat, in the vestibule where Norah was wont to greet her adopted father on his home-coming. "If you will leave your bag there, I will—— Ah, here's Norah. Good-evening, dear. I'm afraid we are a little late."

Harold Foster had been facing the door at which Norah appeared, whilst Mr. Fenton had turned to place his gloves in a drawer. Consequently, the eyes of his two protégés had met before Mr. Morley Fenton was aware of Norah's presence. Norah was dressed for the evening, and heavy double violets nestled between delicate sprays of lily of the valley under her flowing girdle on one side, and in the bosom of her gown on the other.

Their eyes met, and were simultaneously lowered under one and the same impulse. Both were recollecting certain casual words of Mr. Morley Fenton's. Both were far more stirred by that suddenly averted look, each into the eyes of the other, than either would have been had either lacked that impulse of recollection. George Barnard would have called this the result of "playing at being Providence." But George Barnard was a bachelor and a Bohemian, two indisputable proofs, of course, of inability to judge correctly in matters connected with family life. As a matter of fact, all that happened was that Norah, who had been beautiful when she appeared at the vestibule door, became more beautiful while she stood there, with shaded eyes and rising fruit-like colour; and Harold Foster forgot to say "Good-evening" or anything else, when he took her hand in his.

But Mr Morley Fenton, being moved by no reminiscent impulse, chatted for both in calm and even tones, as the three walked into the circle of light and warmth round the hall fire.

CHAPTER XVIII.

THE WEARINESS OF HAROLD FOSTER.

" The common problem, yours, mine, everyone's,
Is—not to fancy what were fair in life
Provided it could be—but finding first
What may be, then find how to make it fair
Up to our means : a very different thing !
. . . . .
You see lads walk the street
Sixty the minute ; what's to note in that ?
You see one lad o'erstride a chimney-stack !
Him you must watch—he's sure to fall, yet stands !
Our interest's on the dangerous edge of things."
Bishop Blougram's Apology.

HAROLD FOSTER was more physically tired on this Saturday evening of his return to Weir Lodge than he himself was aware. He had been exhausted when, in the small hours of the previous day, he had found George Barnard waiting in his chambers, and since then he not only had been practically without sleep, but had been enduring a sudden and self-imposed strain—the strain of mechanical effort in an abruptly-changed mode of life. This is the keynote to the phase life, the bane and pathos of the extremist temperament: the price paid by the sanguine nature for its morbid reactions, by the morbid nature for its sanguine interludes.

Acting right through all this, Harold's meeting with Norah, and the instant sympathy evoked by their jointly-acted-upon impulse of reserve, had stirred the young man to his nature's deep places. Playing over and about the surface of all this, Maud Fenton's high-spirited effervescence during dinner spurred Harold on to responsiveness, almost to emulation, of her gaiety. Then, before the last stages of dinner were reached, came the warning sound of wheels on the drive outside, a vision of bright faces in cloudy settings of evening wraps, laughing excuses and hurried "Good-nights!" and Harold Foster found himself drinking his coffee alone with his host and hostess.

Then the young man's tiredness showed through the thin film of his reserve, a film which melted in the warm light of domesticity which the three girls had left in their wake. Harold became unguarded, naked almost, in his talk of himself. He spoke of all that he had found oppressive in his Norwood life; of that irksomeness which had wearied him in the hospital routine; of how he turned for relief from these things to Leo Tarne, and to ways and paths suggested by Leo Tarne's atmosphere; of how he had found some change in this way, but only a little relief; of how his own ideals pointed to a blend of much that Leo Tarne had shown him, with a softer, simpler life, the centrepiece and altar of which would be home.

Mrs. Fenton smiled sympathetically, eking out Harold's unguarded periods with encouraging commonplaces. Mr. Morley Fenton, with a feminine instinct of desire to shield and hide nakedness in one of his own sex, threw himself conversationally between his wife and his protégé. This he did repeatedly, without much success. Then he rose from his chair, and asked Harold Foster to join him in his study, where he wished to smoke.

"I shall be sitting up until after the girls come in, dear," he said to Mrs. Fenton; "so I hope you will not think of waiting for them. Harold, I know, is tired out, and will not be sorry to go early to bed."

"Not at all," protested Harold; "I feel beautifully rested now, really."

Harold had some time since passed that stage at which a young man's own opinion in this particular matter ceases to be of any great value.

Mrs. Fenton smiled as she walked past her husband to the door of the room.

"Ah well," she said, "I have a few letters to write and a little work to do, but in case I do not see you later on, in the drawing-room, I will say good-night, Mr. Foster."

"A wise precaution, believe me," said the head of the house; "there is such a thing as being too tired to feel tired, Harold."

So the three separated, Mrs. Fenton going to the drawing-room, and Harold accompanying his host to the room where the 'cello stood.

Most men are made to feel stronger by speaking unreservedly, and to a sympathetic audience, of their own weakness. Many men are made to feel comparatively well-to-do, by a little open talk about their own penury. He is refreshed and temporarily stimulated, who has with any degree of eloquence or lucidity given words to his weariness.

Arrived with Harold in his study, Mr. Morley Fenton sat down before his writing-table, and proceeded to fill a pipe. He motioned Harold to a very low, sloping-backed wicker-chair, which faced away from the only light in the room—a green-shaded lamp standing on the writing-table. Thus, Mr. Fenton saw the young man's face in profile, while Harold, except when his head was turned, saw nothing beyond a glowing wood fire, and warm, dull rays flickering from it in the surrounding shadows.

"Ah!" sighed Harold, as his gleaming head sank back into the cushion of the wicker-chair. "I feel wide awake and beautifully refreshed now. You are very good to me, and—there is the working den's sense of freedom about this charming room."

Mr. Morley Fenton smiled, and, leaning forward, lowered slightly the green-shaded lamp.

"I am afraid," continued the younger man, crossing his outstretched feet—"I'm afraid I shall never make a society man—a correct and useful member of the orthodox community."

"Why? Surely the presence of Mrs. Fenton does not mean any great conventional restraint to you?"

"Oh no!" Harold was in haste to redeem the sentiment his last words had implied. "No, you are all so kind to me here; you make light of my awkwardness, and hide from me my own sins against society's decalogue. But conscience, or something, opens my eyes at times, and I realize that I am never natural or really at ease, except in—except when hopelessly incorrect."

"I don't think you need be alarmed. It is not likely that these sins of yours against the proprieties are seen by anyone but yourself. They may be merely the creations of over-sensitiveness—and imagination."

"Hardly, I think; but it's true they don't weigh heavily upon me. May I be perfectly frank?"

"Please. You are at home, you know."

"Thank you. Well, it is not really that I reproach myself much for sinning against the canons, or for falling short of Mrs. Grundy's requirements, but rather that I cannot bring myself to try and refrain from these sins, or to endeavour to satisfy the requirements. They seem to me to entail so empty and deadly uninteresting a life. The standards seem so petty, the limits so narrow, their fulfilment so irksome, fruitless, and unsatisfying. The conventional state seems to me to represent so much pose and so little reality, such

THE WEARINESS OF HAROLD FOSTER. 157

endless process and such trivial attainment, such unceasing strain and quite colourless effects, so much wearisome existence and so very little life. So, if I am penitent for my shortcomings, I stand in dread —in positive dread—of the life without reproach on this score."

"Ah! I think I understand your feeling. But yet, I assure you, Harold, that conventionality has its uses, and respect for the canons you despise, brings its own reward—a liberal one."

"But it seems to me to render appreciation impossible—even the appreciation of its own reward. Of course, I don't mean that I think I am right and the rest of the world wrong. No; it is my want of understanding—something in me awry, some twist in my nature, which distorts my view of life and vitiates my taste. This seems inherent in me."

Mr. Morley Fenton sighed.

"There are very few inherent tendencies," he said, "so strong that they may not be bent and subdued into any channel one chooses. It is left to a lower creation to simply follow the surface dictates of its disposition."

"Yes; I suppose so. But is one right in assuming, as a matter of course, that one's inborn tendencies, when not in accord with all things established and accepted, should be subdued or forced to run along the recognised grooves?"

"That, of course, must be determined by the nature of the tendencies." Mr. Morley Fenton's voice lacked modulation. One might have almost fancied that of set purpose he spoke in a droning, or, at least, a restful key. "But as a general thing, I think, you would not be far wrong in that assumption. You see, you have the edicts, and presumably the wisdom, of all the ages to consider in juxtaposition with inclinations of your own, which may, after all, be merely the fruit of passing phases in your life. It is hard to be sure that any given tendency is really one of your nature's permanent needs. A poet whose work is fascinating in its wisdom has said:

> "'Grow old along with me !
> The best is yet to be,
> The last of life, for which the first was made.'"

"I see. Yes, of course, it is a sort of impudence for a young man to accept his own feelings as his guide and law, in place of the laws which conventionality has made and sanctioned."

Harold Foster's estimate of his own wakefulness appeared to be correct, for his eyes were shining now, his fingers moved nervously on the arms of the wicker-chair, and his voice was as full of unstudied animation as Mr. Fenton's was of restful evenness—natural or assumed. But the younger man's uncertainly moving lips and over-weighted diction, suggested rather the tenseness which comes of unstrung or too-highly-strung nerves, than the enthusiasm of healthy interest.

"No, not impudence," said Mr. Fenton quietly. "Say it is impolitic—a method which lacks diplomacy, and is likely to prove unprofitable."

"And yet, isn't there a kind of meanness about choking your own convictions, and living according to theories you—which you don't believe in, for the sake of possible, or even certain, gain? I mean when either course only affects yourself. Doesn't it seem a finer, cleaner sort of thing to say, 'Well, hit or miss, this is what I believe, and so I live accordingly'?"

"Ah! but the mere fact of yourself being the only person involved surely makes a pure matter of taste of the question of living according to your own convictions, or the convictions of those who have built up society. If either course involves meanness, then, in the light of your own view, it could only be a man's meanness to himself. As a matter of fact, I think it's not a fair statement of the case. You may be firmly convinced of the wisdom of eating without the use of a knife or fork. It is not meanness which causes you to refrain from acting on this theory. A man's method of dealing with the events of his daily life can never, in a civilized community, be a matter affecting only that man himself. Life as it is, the world as we find it, are, after all, the things one has to deal with; and believe me, ' it's wiser being good than bad—it's fitter being sane than mad.' Young folk sometimes speak contemptuously of conventional and worldly success, as though they themselves lived in the moon, or in some hitherto undiscovered planet. We have only one world to our hand, Harold, one world for one life—the life of the next will be made clear in the next —and granting that success is preferable to failure, and that ' worldly ' means ' of the world,' then what save worldly success should a man strive to win? And respect for the conventions is one of the conditions of the race; one of the things expected of those who want to be, by those who are, in the world which is— that world we know and feel, were born in and must die in."

Harold sighed, and Mr. Fenton continued, with a little upward movement of one hand, but with no change in his even tone:

"Am I preaching? Forgive me. But there are certain points in life, Harold, at which mistakes are more disastrous, indecision less permissible, than at others. Some tactics are made worth adopting by the goal they lead to, and—perhaps by the good in themselves, Harold."

Harold had not interrupted Mr. Fenton even by a

gesture, though, while the older man had been speaking with calm, gentle insistence, the young one's hands had been nervously clasping and unclasping on his knees, his head had ceased to rest on the cushioned chair-back, and his thoughts, tumbling one over the other, had evidently forced themselves to the extreme verge of articulation. Now that the tuneless flow of smooth words had ceased, Harold turned half round in his chair and faced Mr. Fenton, in the soft light of the green-shaded lamp. His eyes were filmy with physical fatigue, his chin out-thrust with nervous emphasis, his lips moving, as though the words they would give birth to were heralded by labour pains.

"I feel," he said, "as though the wisdom of the things you say would choke me. It is so pitiless and cruel—or else it is only untrue. But, right or wrong, I could not make it mine; and, if you think me mad, then please don't think me rude as well, for I don't mean to be; and I cannot even explain to you what I do mean. Only this, that in the kind of life you speak of—the world where people breathe by rote, and speak and eat and live according to policy—I have found nothing that has not been wearisome to me. I have seen no beauty in it, learned nothing, made no discoveries, experienced no single little thrill—unless, sometimes, of sadness. Outside that world, I have breathed freely and been glad to breathe. I have learned many things, seen much of what to me was beauty, been thrilled in a hundred ways, and made discovery on discovery. I have felt myself living—stood back and watched my heart beat, and my blood pulse. And for all of it I have been glad, and not weary. Yet that has been only from glimpses. I have lived always, really, in the world you speak of; but at times more entirely than at other times. And it seems to me, that at intervals, when my life has almost stopped, it was so empty, I have turned aside for one of these glimpses into the other world, and have started the blood in my veins again, by just one little look. It seems that against five-and-twenty years of existence in one world, I place five-and-twenty days of life in another, and that that forces the scale of me to balance in the centre of this moment—present."

Harold paused for an instant, and as though his mind half feared the launching into being of its own children. Then, with a little backward movement of his fair head, he continued:

"And I look at the lives of others round me and high above me in their assured states, and I say: 'Are we differently made, I and you, or is your life part hidden, or how, then, do you find something which looks like ease and content in the same kind of little narrow round that fills my lungs with fog? How do you pass so smoothly along the groove which for me seems lined with out-jutting spikes of impossibility?' That's when their eyes seem to me seeing and understanding eyes—eyes made to sweep the horizon outside. I don't want to ask that of the Norwood people. Some folk seem to me to hibernate in sanctity, to be cataleptics in conventionality, and to walk in a dream, drowsy with the fumes of rarefied respectability. But I—forgive me—I look in that way sometimes at you, and—and want to ask you. Please don't put this down as impertinence. I felt bound to tell you, after what you said. And when I watch you, coming and going, and here in this beautiful, still house, which seems to me like a great, magnificent place full of tiny separate cells; seeing how wise you are, and how strong you are, and how many lives you must know, I wonder—I, with my little tired life in one world, and my tiny, flash glimpses of another—I wonder how you have done it, how you go on doing it, whether you never want to shout, whether you never feel as though the restrained, perfectly-fitting, inevitable little round of things which knows no divergence, will—would choke you—you, who must have drawn so many breaths, and deep ones. I——"

Again Harold paused. This time his head reached its original resting-place against the chair-back. He began to speak again. But his mind had been delivered, and his body was left limp and listless. The jangling nerves hung loose and pulseless now. His eyes were half closed. The way of his weariness was undisputed by Harold. All he said was:

"I am afraid what I have said must seem like pure rudeness. I am very sorry; I did not wish to be rude, but only to try and explain myself in the light of what your words mean to me. My—my respect for you is as for my father."

Harold had leaned forward over his last words, with one hand outstretched. Mr. Morley Fenton rose to his feet, and took Harold's tremulous hand in his own, holding it for a moment; and a curiously inscrutable smile flickered under the heavy, silver-pointed brown moustache, as he said:

"Yes, yes, I know, my dear Harold. I don't misunderstand you."

There was something marvellously soothing in the older man's voice as he said these few words. Something there was, too, big with suggestion of restfulness in the slow, upward and forward movement of his hand, as, having released Harold's, Mr. Fenton raised and then gently lowered it to his side. So, and not in any other way, one may see a clever young doctor move his hand before a restive and nervously alert patient. With such a gesture, too, one may occasionally see a horse-breaker, who is an artist in his work, pass one firm hand over the forehead and quivering nostrils of a high-strung colt. Such men make no professions about hypnotism. Practice and profession are but distantly related; and this is well, in view of the value of the one and the amount of time requisite for proficiency in the other.

Mr. Morley Fenton, holding his long study pipe in one hand, turned from where Harold sat, and moved silently across the room to where a plethoric old bookcase stood. He drew out a book, with the touch of a man who loves books, and turned again then to his chair and the circle of soft light thrown out by the green-shaded lamp. A long-drawn sigh came from the low wicker-chair. There was nothing aggressive left now in Harold's immediate environment. The battling element in his nature was asleep; his eyelids drooped low; his position was recumbent; his hands lay still beside him; even the sensitive lips were in repose.

"Are you too tired to listen to something I should like read to you, Harold?" Mr. Fenton looked up from the open book on the table before him.

"No—please." Harold's eyes did not move as he spoke. Again that queer smile, which seemed to say so little and to mean so much, drew down the corners of Mr. Fenton's mouth.

"It is something written by a great-hearted man, Harold, whose loving wisdom is even more wonderful than his art. His work and—and my 'cello, have meant a great deal in my life. See! An elderly man, a 'potent grave and reverend seigneur,' is talking, over his wine, to a young, clever, literary man, presumably a Bohemian.

"'No more wine? Then we'll push back chairs and talk.'"

Harold listened, and, reading lovingly, interpreting lucidly, Mr. Morley Fenton pursued in low, full tones the pregnant English in which the subsequent lines were clothed glowingly. As these fell across Harold's passive intelligence, the effect produced on his senses seemed to him like that he would expect from the rustling of kingly robes.

> "'Now's the time :,
> Truth's break of day ! You do despise me, then ;
> And if I say, despise me—never fear !
> I know you do not in a certain sense—
> Not in my arm-chair, for example : here,
> I well imagine you respect my place
> (Status entourage, worldly circumstance)
> Quite to its value—very much indeed.'"

Harold was interested, deeply interested. Yet he was tasting the delights of abandon to completest languor. Looking up whilst turning a page, Mr. Morley Fenton smiled as he noticed that Harold's eyes were quite closed now. There was something of the nurse, a good deal of the mother, and all the kindness of the strong man, in Mr. Morley Fenton's smile.

> "'Your ideal of life
> Is not the bishop's : you would not be I.
> You would like better to be Goethe, now
> Or Buonaparte, or, bless me, lower still,
> Count D'Orsay.'" . . .

Harold's fair head inclined ever so little to one side, on the wicker-chair's cushion. The firm, even tones of the reader continued, without pause or change.

> "'So, drawing comfortable breath again,
> You weigh and find, whatever more or less
> I boast of my ideal realized,
> Is nothing in the balance when opposed
> To your ideal, your grand simple life,
> Of which you will not realize one jot.'"

With a sharp movement Harold's head reverted to its original position on the cushion. Mr. Morley Fenton did not raise his eyes. Harold's were opened widely.

THE WEARINESS OF HAROLD FOSTER. 165

"'Fool or knave?
Why needs a bishop be a fool or knave
When there's a thousand diamond weights between?'"

Once more Harold's head inclined sideways, slightly, on the chair-back.

"'Had I been born three hundred years ago
They'd say, "What's strange? Blougram, of course, believes;"
And, seventy years since, "disbelieves, of course."
But now, "He may believe; and yet, and yet
How can he?" All eyes turn with interest.'"

. . . .

Mr. Morley Fenton looked up quickly, and without pausing.

"'You disbelieve! Who wonders and who cares?'"

Again Harold's head moved sharply, and his eyes opened to the full.

"'But I, the man of sense and learning, too,
The able to think yet act, the this, the that,
I, to believe, at this late time of day!
Enough; you see I need not fear contempt.'"

And so on and on, "while the great bishop rolled him out a mind long crumpled, till creased consciousness lay smooth," read Mr. Morley Fenton, in a very slightly modulated voice, and in time as unvarying as the sweeping stroke of a piston-rod. And Harold, in his weariness losing control of himself, drooped again and again into momentary oblivion, his flagging senses careless of his willing brain's straining at the collar, till a sharper pull than usual startled him once more into wide-eyed understanding. Then, again, the droop. And then:

"'There, I hope,
By this time he has tested his first plough,
And studied his last chapter of St. John.'"

Mr. Morley Fenton rose slowly to his feet, closing the volume from which he had been reading, and walking with it towards the big open bookcase.

"And now, Harold," he said, as the young man leaned forward and uncrossed his legs; "I think you really must go to bed. I oughtn't to have kept you up so long. You must be worn out."

"Not at all, not at all, really." Harold's face was very grey, and his eyelids were swollen. He took Mr. Fenton's outstretched hand, and bade him "Good-night." "And," he added, as they parted in the hall, "thank you very much for reading—er——"

"The 'Apology,' Harold. It is always a pleasure to me to read some writers' works, even without a listener. Sleep well, my dear fellow, and don't get up till you feel inclined. Good-night!"

And Harold wandered loosely up the wide staircase, his head swaying forward as he walked.

Mr. Morley Fenton returned to his study and sat down by the table where the green lamp stood, to think.

"Ah!" he muttered; "the first step's taken, thank Heaven. And a night's sound sleep is a fine thing—a beautiful thing."

Just an hour later came girlish voices in the vestibule, and the owner of Weir Lodge stepped quickly into the hall to welcome his daughters. The night was crisp and cold, and even Norah's cheeks were glowing with rich colour. Lucy was sylph-like and in high spirits. Maud babbled and burbled, as her wont was. Norah was the first to kiss her adopted father, and, having done so, she drew back from him quickly, and looked questioningly into his face.

"Father, you are—— What is it, father dear?"

"Eh? Nothing, my dear—nothing. Do I look so very ugly and sleepy? I haven't been to a dance, you see. I am so glad you have all had a good time. And now you'd better each have a glass of wine and scurry off to bed. It's Sunday, already, you know, and you've a guest to entertain in the morning."

In a very few minutes the three girls were on their way upstairs. Turning round, when halfway up the staircase, Norah looked down at Mr. Fenton, where he stood in the hall, and said:

"Poor father! I'm so sorry—I mean, I hope there's nothing the matter, because—I have been so happy to-night."

A little tremor passed over the grey face of the man in the hall; and then, looking up with a smile at the pitying woman's face above him, he said almost gaily:

"Why, no, dear; there's nothing the matter. I'm always a little tired on Saturday nights, you know. Good-night, sweetheart!"

Then Mr. Morley Fenton returned to his study, and, closing its door, took down and opened the volume from which he had read to Harold. But Mr. Fenton found he was unable to read to himself that night. So he sat thinking before the dying fire in his room. There was a curious lifelessness in the position of his legs, bent at the knee and thrust to one side of his chair. His face, too, was strangely sunken, almost livid-looking. From time to time he raised one hand, with an uncertain sidelong movement, to his lips. The veins in his temples were unusually active, and outstandingly visible, on this Sunday morning.

Mary, the housemaid, rose unusually early that morning, and as she wended her way down the main staircase she heard her master's dressing-room door closed, softly.

"Well, I never!" said Mary; and passed on towards the kitchen.

CHAPTER XIX.

HOUSE.

" A soft and easy life these ladies lead :
Whiteness in us were wonderful indeed.
Oh, save that brow its virgin dimness,
Keep that foot its lady primness,
Let those ankles never swerve
From their exquisite reserve,
Yet have to trip along the streets like me,
All but naked to the knee !

. . . . .

Not envy, sure !—for if you gave me
Leave to take or to refuse,
In earnest, do you think I'd choose
That sort of new love to enslave me ? "
Pippa Passes.

WHEN Mary, the housemaid, was feeling that she had already accomplished a fair day's work, and a bright wintry sun—at this season a far later riser than Mary—was doing its best to announce the coming of noon; Harold Foster, in the little walnut room over Mr. Fenton's study, opened his eyes, ran the fingers of one hand through the fine gold of his hair, and said, " Ah! "

So, and not otherwise, would many a man like to wake on the morning of the Judgment Day.

Then Harold looked at his watch on a little table beside the bed.

" By Jove! " Harold flung both legs out of the warm bed into the still warm air of the bedroom. " Half-past eleven; and I came to bed soon after eleven last night! Gad, but I have slept! What a delightful house! No one called me, and no church-bells woke me. Oh, but I've had a lovely sleep! "

And then the young man betook himself to the next room—the "walnut bath room," as Mary called it—and bathed, with the whole-souled enthusiasm of a young grampus. And to Harold Foster, on that Sunday morning, there seemed no manner of doubt that all was well with the world—the world as it was. His thoughts, as he walked lightly downstairs and across the hall, had no bearing on a world which might be, less still on a world which might have been. It is such moments as this, no doubt, that give to great Nature's smiles their sweetness.

A maid-servant met Harold on the threshold of the breakfast-room, and informed him, with a smile, that his breakfast would be brought in immediately. "Dinner is at two o'clock on Sundays, sir; and Mrs. Fenton and the young ladies are away at church; and—and Mr. Fenton's in the conservatory, sir, and said he hoped you would join him there, when you'd had breakfast, sir; and—oh, here is breakfast, sir!"

Exit, with a curious little duck of the head, this well-intentioned, if slightly incoherent, maid; and enter, with some pride of place and a laden tray, Mary, leading lady in the servants' hall.

Whilst munching his toast, a function in itself highly provocative of retrospection, when gone through in solitude, Harold reviewed in his mind, carelessly enough at first, the events of the previous evening. Midway through his second egg, his reminiscences brought him to his talk with Mr. Morley Fenton in that gentleman's study.

"By Jove!" he muttered, whilst abstractedly dipping his eggspoon into his coffee, "I believe I must have been dozing part of the while he was reading. I wonder if he noticed it. Gad! I hope not; and—what was it he read? A magnificent thing, too; but I'd never heard of it before. H'm! and there was a bishop sort of defending himself, and scarifying an unfortunate literary man. Of course! Gigadibs—and he wrote for *Blackwood's*. The bishop was a bit of a —well, I don't know. He was rather rough on Gigadibs—a host to his guest. But, by gad, what a man— what a mountain, tossing back clouds of mist from its sides! It's—why, it's Mr. Morley Fenton himself!

"' You do despise me, then ;
And if I say "despise me"—never fear !'

Good heavens! and I must have implied that I—that I despised his way of living, and—gad, I must go and read that thing!"

Harold did not finish his second egg; but, walking across to Mr. Morley Fenton's room, found the well-worn volume of poems, in the place from which he had seen it taken in an overflowing bookcase, and sat down to search for the great bishop, and his " Apology." He found it, and read on through the forceful, vivid periods of the big mind uncreased—spread out, for such a one as he, Harold Foster. He was absorbed, glowing with a young man's new-wakened understanding; appreciation of the beauty of sheer bigness, of wide expanses, of rolling dales of human insight into human life.

Then, quietly, the study-door swung open, and Mr. Morley Fenton stepped into the room, glancing quickly as he entered at the volume in Harold's hands.

" Ah, good-morning, Harold! I needn't ask how you are this morning. I am so glad you were able to take a good long rest. I can see it's done you a world of good."

" Yes, yes, thank you. It has, as you say, done me a world of good, though I ought to apologize for not turning up to breakfast."

" Not at all. I'm very glad you did not."

"But," continued Harold, hesitatingly, and glancing as he spoke at the book in his hand; "I feel there are so many other apologies due from me that I—I——"

"My dear Harold, what nonsense!"

"No, it's true. I—I've been reading Blougram. It is magnificent."

"Yes. Yes, it is fine; and I am glad you enjoyed it. What do you say to a little stroll while the sun's out? We can meet Mrs. Fenton and the girls coming home from church—and we dine in the middle of the day on Sundays, you know."

"Yes. Thanks; I should like it very much."

So Harold replaced the book of poems in the bookcase, and walked out into the sunshine with Mr. Morley Fenton.

The owner of Weir Lodge had risen and been present at the family breakfast, to time, and as his custom was. His face, even when seen in the cold sunlight of the winter's morning, contained all its ordinary smooth impassivity; but his cheeks on either side the lines from lips to nostril, seemed flecked by a little shadow, his eyelids' rims were somewhat thicker and darker, the greyness of the fine face was a little more pronounced, than on the previous day. There was a strong touch of autumn in Mr. Morley Fenton—his voice, his movements, his slightly stooping gait—on this Sunday morning which found Harold Foster so young and so stored with vitality.

The Fenton family, strongly united as its members were by a quiescent kind of love, was not an observant one, in matters affecting itself as a household, or in the affairs of the outside world. The foundation of love which united the two girls and their parents, each to each, was a very passive bond. Their daily intercourse showed very little more than the polite good-fellowship of society. There were times when a mild and uncomprehended phase of boredom prevented even this being shown. Maud and Lucy Fenton were very good friends, and very rarely other than amiable and considerate to each other and to all comers. They were in no sense chums. In the presence of Mrs. Fenton they were two charming young women, with an equally charming and somewhat older lady-friend, whose interests were identical with their own. Every morning and every evening, the two girls kissed their lady-friend. Prior to Norah's arrival at Weir Lodge, an embrace was a positively unknown institution in the Fenton family. Even now, Lucy's delicate eyebrows were always unconsciously raised when she happened to see Norah place her hands on Mr. Fenton's shoulders.

A curiously illustrative comment on the Fentons' inner life was the fact—unobserved, of course, by members of the family—that the presence in the home of almost any guest, no matter how familiar or how little known, served temporarily and on the surface of things, to bring into closer communion the household's constituent parts. Parents and daughters, by tacit consent, held hands whilst facing and entertaining friend, acquaintance, or guest. There were times, too, when illness or emergency had rallied the four into closest possible compact. But the ordinary, daily life of the family had always been something which produced what Harold's sensibility had felt when he referred to Weir Lodge as, " this beautiful, still house, which seems to me like a great, magnificent place, full of tiny, separate cells."

Entering the house as an invisible presence, and when no guest was in it, one would, under average circumstances, have found Mr. Morley Fenton in his study, Mrs. Fenton in the drawing-room, Lucy Fenton writing letters, or otherwise occupied, in her boudoir, and Maud playing with her dog in the hall, or coiled up with a book on a couch in the library. In summer-time, the garden and the river brought the girls and the mother into somewhat closer contact. But, even on the river, Lucy preferred scarlet cushions and the punt, Maud was happier in her own dinghy than elsewhere, and Mrs. Fenton found a seat under the awning of the gondola more adapted to her tastes than was a place in either of the other boats. The presence of a near relative, or again, of the most casual acquaintance, was sufficient to alter all this.

Into this atmosphere dark-eyed Norah had crept, whilst her cheeks were yet stained by the first flood of tears which had followed her weak father's death. Instinctively she had groped her way to the side and heart of the strong, understanding man who during all his life had stood between her father and the world of busy conflict and rushing reality. Unconsciously she had to all intents and purposes ignored the mother and her two daughters. And, in the first loneliness of her sorrow, she had lain down her beautiful head on the shoulder of the big-minded man in whose life the smoothly executed duties, and easily-borne responsibilities of the Weir Lodge household, formed only one feature. She had asked nothing more than permission to sit at Mr. Morley Fenton's feet, in the little study where the 'cello stood, and, sometimes, to hear the 'cello's deep-bosomed voice.

For days, and without cessation, Mr. Morley Fenton had devoted himself entirely to his dead brother's child; holding her torn heart in his two firm white hands, whilst the edges of its wound drew together, draping her grief-shaken self, not in consolation or forgetfulness, but in quiet, ever-strengthening repose— great Nature's infallible specific, the earth's all-healing balm, less and less understood by her sons, perhaps, with every year which is added to the earth-mother's age. Mrs. Fenton, with her two daughters, had stood aside, pitying and waiting to help.

Later on, with Mr. Fenton's strength-giving repose written across the girlish forehead which sadness seemed to have ennobled, Norah had approached her new mother and sisters, holding gratitude in her outstretched arms. They had very graciously welcomed her, and quickly learned to love, though never to understand, this dark-eyed girl, in whose nature was much which resembled what clear-seeing eyes might have observed in the owner of Weir Lodge, more that all had seen in the man who was dead, and little which was part and parcel of the three who welcomed her. Afterwards, even without understanding, Norah became, perhaps, a closer friend to Lucy than was Maud, certainly a more loved friend to Maud than was Lucy, and possibly a better uniformly devoted daughter to Mrs. Fenton than were either of her own girls. Just how much she was to Mr. Morley Fenton, or he to her, only the two knew. Her influence upon the family as a whole had been to largely minimize and reduce that " tiny separate cells " element in the Weir Lodge atmosphere which, all unnoticed as it was by many people, had even at this period, chilled slightly the ultra-impressionable outer plates of Harold Foster's nature. Remove it she never could. Some parts of it were too strong. All of it was too many-headed and diffuse. Its mitigation even, would have quite exhausted the strongly loving girl, but for the rest to be found in the little study where she was always welcome, the relief which was embodied in the notes of the 'cello.

This was the family of which Harold Foster was practically to be made a member—this the household of united disintegration which Harold entered, with talk on his lips of " the restrained, perfectly-fitting, inevitable little round of things which knows no divergence." And between the outward personalities of Norah Fenton and Harold Foster Mr. Morley Fenton —wiser in most things than in matters affecting his deepest, inmost feelings—had been at some pains to erect a barrier which should be impassable to any closer relation than friendship.

But there is an impalpable something in us all more vital, more indestructible, and more essentially individual, than is any mere personality. Perhaps Mr. Morley Fenton relied on his palpable barrier even in dealing with the impalpable. Or, perhaps, consideration of the impalpable had no place in Mr. Morley Fenton's wisdom. A poet once said, in effect, that it was not the immensity of the scheme of Creation which filled him with admiring awe so much as its infinitesimal detail. But that poet was probably a man who never attempted, even in a small matter, to play the part of Providence; one who respected the seemingly trivial.

During the middle-day dinner at Weir Lodge, on this Sunday of Harold Foster's reinstatement, the conversation turned upon bachelors and the bachelor life.

" I always fancy the poor fellows must be so lonely," said Mrs. Fenton.

" I should think bachelors would miss a great deal in the way of music and the beautiful things," opined Lucy.

" I think it must be awfully jolly, and if I could have the river as well, you know, I should like to be a bachelor myself." Maud Fenton was not æsthetic.

" There are certain things which I think should be achieved before a man forsakes bachelordom," said the head of the house.

"I think a bachelor's greatest loss is the absence of any sense of community in his ordinary life. I mean, if he's living really alone—not in the kind of Quartier Latin colonies one reads about."

Norah looked swiftly across the table to Harold, who had spoken last.

"But I expect there are some homes, aren't there," she said, "where there is just as little community—less perhaps?" And then she lowered her eyes with a half-frightened look, as though regretting the impulse on which she had spoken.

"Norah means that a feeling of community makes home, but that home does not necessarily produce community. That depends on the individuals of the home. Is that what you thought, Norah?"

And the girl bent her head without risking further utterance of her thoughts.

"The river and the empty house-boats look very desolate and dreary at this time of year, don't you think so, Mr. Foster?"

Mrs. Fenton's bird-like head inclined interrogatively towards Harold.

CHAPTER XX.

COLD SUPPER, AND A BREATHING SPACE.

" Here's Spring come, and the nights one makes up bands
To roam the town and sing out carnival,
And I've been three weeks shut within my mew,
A-painting for the great man, saints and saints
And saints again. I could not paint all night—
Ouf! I leaned out of window for fresh air,
There came a hurry of feet and little feet,
A sweep of lute-strings, laughs, and whifts of song."
Fra Lippo Lippi.

"MR. FOSTER," said Maud Fenton, as the party filed out of the dining-room—Maud was gifted with a beautifully inexhaustible and varied curiosity—" I want you to tell me all about hospitals, will you?"

"Oh, I say, you know, you make me feel as though I were going up for my final to-morrow. However, where shall I begin?"

"Oh, in the drawing-room, or the conservatory if you like; it's beautifully warm there."

"No—but whereabouts in the matter of hospitals?"

"Norah," Mr. Morley Fenton stood at the foot of the stairs, addressing his adopted daughter, "I wish you would tell one of the maids to light the fire in the study."

"I lighted it before dinner, father dear. And you are going to have a rest, aren't you? Do; you are so dreadfully tired."

"Eh? Oh no; not dreadfully. But I am going into the study, and—it was like you to think of lighting the fire."

The head of the house touched Norah's shoulder lightly as he stepped past her. He was looking very grey and tired, but no one save Norah and, casually, Harold Foster had noticed the fact.

So Mr. Morley Fenton went alone to his study, and Norah joined the others in the drawing-room. After a little while Mrs. Fenton disappeared, seeming to fade away, so unobtrusively she left the room. It is possible that Mrs. Fenton understood and appreciated the value of the siesta. Family Sabbaths and mid-day dinners have a tendency toward that understanding appreciation; and perhaps at no other times are average men and women so curiously unobtrusive in their comings and goings, as in the early stages of sea-sickness, and in the steps preliminary and subsequent to the afternoon nap.

Harold Foster spent the afternoon pleasantly enough, in chatting with the girls in the drawing-room, with one short interval spent in the conservatory with Maud—and a cigarette. Maud did not notice the cigarette, but Harold was less unconscious of it.

Later on, matters were focussed a little by the serving of tea round the drawing-room fire. Mrs. and Mr. Fenton—the latter looking a little rested—were both present at this ceremony, over which Lucy presided, whilst Norah supplied everybody's needs, thereby suggesting the infinite superiority of ministering over ruling.

"You must excuse my having kept out of sight, Harold," said Mr. Fenton. "I've been feeling rather tired to-day, and I thought an hour or two alone would be better for me—and for the rest of you."

"My dear," said the mistress of the house, "if an apology is necessary from you, what shall I say for myself?"

"Nothing, my dear. Your correspondents—er—would suffer if you broke off your habit of Sunday afternoon letter-writing." Mr. Fenton's voice still sounded a little weary. His last remark may have suggested to him what Harold Foster had meant in speaking of the "perfectly-fitting little round of things."

When teacups were laid aside Harold asked Norah if she would play something. At Mr. Morley Fenton's suggestion the ringing for lights was tabooed, and Norah took her seat at the piano in darkness which was only relieved by the fire's warm glow. So everyone rested, and Norah, from her shadowy place at the piano, made the air of the room dreamily sweet by soft snatches from the work of great masters, and sweetly sad then by the low pathos of earthy little Irish airs. Later, lest minor clouds should prove too dominant, Norah called great Handel to her aid, and when at length a maid entered with lights, the room's occupants were barely cognizant of any change; so they were filled and thrilled by Mendelssohn's most beautiful wordless song.

Then Norah closed the piano, and seated herself on a stool beside Mr. Fenton. Small topics were made to furnish much talk. Some big subjects lent themselves to casual reference. The head of the house heroically cut down in their early life one or two yawns. There came a moment—it chanced to be at the usual dinner-hour, half-past seven—when Mrs. Fenton looked at her watch. A clock of genuine Sèvres ticked on a bracket above her head. The moment happened to be one of silence, when topics big and little seemed part of the day departed and the evening not begun. A sense of flatness and emptiness fell upon the party assembled before the fire, descended so suddenly as to be irritating to restful

Mrs. Fenton and to Maud and Lucy, painful to Norah, chilling and numbing to Harold's impressionism, and full of weariness to Mr. Morley Fenton.

Norah looked round her, and through this palpable flatness, pathetically. She could have been very fairly happy with Mr. Fenton and Harold, or alone with any member of the party; but with all five, and all choking in this painful silence, Norah felt helpless.

" Oh, mother, just fancy! We have none of us been to church this evening."

Maud's discovery was handled with feverish interest, and then with languid elaboration. But the crisis, the falling of the flatness, was passed.

At half-past eight the supper-gong sounded. With all that noble, if somewhat fruitless, sacrifice of comfort which distinguishes the orthodox British observance of the Sabbath, the hours for meals on the first day of the week were chosen at Weir Lodge on the principle that what is exceedingly ill-suited to the convenience of the family must needs be best suited to the requirements of the servants.

The cold baron of beef and flagon of ale style of repast is a relic of pre-railway days. As a refection it fails to entertain the modern man. It stiffens his mental joints, refuses to adapt itself to his physical economy, fills no vacuum, appeals to no tendency, and tires, but does not exhilarate.

Supper at Weir Lodge was a cold collation. The servants would have very much preferred preparing, and subsequently sharing, a hot meal—more particularly as the servants' hall was " at home " on Sunday evenings. But Mrs. Fenton was wont to deprecatingly remark, as she sat down to the collation, " One really must consider one's servants, you know. Sunday is as much Sunday to them as to us, and—— Thank you, Morley, a very little beef, please." And so, by

COLD SUPPER, AND A BREATHING SPACE. 181

some subtle train of reasoning on good Mrs. Fenton's part, it was ordained that on Sunday evenings Mary the housemaid's admirer should content himself with cold potluck, whilst in the dining-room ill-digested reminiscences were awakened of fishing parties on wet days.

After supper there was a little more music in the drawing-room, from Lucy Fenton this time, and a little more talk. But for Harold's presence, the party would have separated, drifting vaguely and in different directions from the dining-room door. In Harold's presence the members of the family remained together, by tacit consent. It was not done clumsily, but it lacked the ease of use and habit, though not obviously, and this produced a thinness of atmosphere which, coming after the collation and in conjunction with an absence of tobacco, was distinctly perceptible to Harold Foster.

Shortly after ten o'clock, Mr. Morley Fenton—his afternoon's rest had been very trifling—rose from his chair, looked at his watch, and yawned without disguise.

"Is the vestibule door locked, dear?" Mr. Fenton spoke with a tone of finality. Mrs. Fenton believed the door referred to had been locked. "Ah!" continued the head of the house. "Then I think—— Would you like a glass of wine, or anything, Harold?"

Harold rose to his feet, as an afternoon caller rises when he hears a door-bell ring, or steps crossing a hall.

"No, thanks," he said. "No—I suppose it's about bed-time?"

The girls had risen. It was not quite Harold's usual bed-time—not by some two or three hours.

"Well, yes; I think we are all pretty well ready for bed," said Mr. Fenton. "But, of course, you——"

"Oh, not at all—not at all. I—that is, I haven't been sleeping any too much lately."

Harold found it a little difficult to express his readiness to retire. Yet in sober truth he was not sorry for the opportunity. He had hastily pictured himself to himself, smoking in the arm-chair before the little walnut room fire.

"Good-night, father," said Lucy. Her sister followed suit. Mrs. Fenton trusted Mr. Foster would sleep well. Mr. Morley Fenton, looking extremely tired, was turning off the gas at two or three brackets.

"Good-night, Mr. Foster," said Norah, holding her little hand out to Harold.

"Good-night—er—do you mind my saying, 'Norah'? You see I have to think of you as 'Norah,' because—there is another Miss Fenton."

Lucy Fenton had already left the room. Norah coloured slightly whilst murmuring the necessary permission, with the necessary "of course." Mr. Morley Fenton's tired face lightened momentarily, as he stood with hand raised under a gas bracket. He smiled.

"And how do you think of poor me, Mr. Foster?" interposed Maud, who was standing near the open door of the room. Harold laughed lightly, and with an easier ring in his voice than had been there during the day.

"Oh," he said, "I think of you as George Barnard's Maud. Princesses and other autocrats are always called by their Christian names, you know."

"Then I think it's very disrespectful of you, not to—to be as respectful as Mr. Barnard."

So they all laughed, and at the foot of the stairs they exchanged a few slenderly-humorous remarks, which seemed to free the breathing passages and lighten the hearts of all concerned. In one brief but natural minute the effects of the cold collation and the evening's conversational gaps melted away, and the party separated—Mr. Fenton being still occupied with matters of bolts and gas taps—on a far friendlier footing than had been reached all day.

When Harold Foster and Mr. Morley Fenton were parting at Waterloo Station, after journeying up from Sunbury together on Monday morning, the latter said:

"Oh, by the way, Harold, I sent an order to the Stores on Saturday for some odds and ends which I thought it would be convenient for you to have at Weir Lodge. They will be down to-day—toilet things, you know, and sleeping suits, and linen, and so on. It will save the trouble of bringing things up and down. I would order a couple of suits to keep down there if I were you. The other things you must accept as a little present from me."

"It was awfully kind and thoughtful of you."

"No, no; not at all. Only I want you to feel perfectly free now to spend the night in your lodgings, if work requires it, or anything of that sort, or to run down to Weir Lodge. I shall always expect you, you know, and so, of course, will the others. Dinner at 7.30. How about this evening? Better make a good start. Come down if you can, will you? I shall catch the 4.30."

"Ye-es." Like most men of strong mentality and self-mastery, Mr. Morley Fenton managed to convey a good deal of command in his suggestions and requests. Then, too, Harold was very uncertain about his own wish in the matter. "Yes, very well," he continued, "I will try and catch the 4.30. Good-bye!"

So they parted, Mr. Morley Fenton, no trace of the previous day's relaxed air of weariness showing in his erect carriage or impassive face, proceeding to Lombard Street, whilst Harold started off for St. Bartholomew's.

During the previous day there had been for Harold moments, and longer periods, of thorough chill; phases of constraint and over-repression, as acute in their way as any he had experienced at the Norwood vicarage. Harold was not analytically inclined, and he had been at no pains to discover reasons or causes for this. He had experienced it, feeling it acutely, as he felt most experiences, and recovering from it readily as was natural in one of his temperament.

Sitting smoking before his bedroom fire on the previous night, he had reviewed the day's events, or lack of events, thinking of that in the little round which to him had been dreary, but seeing it in the light of those last few minutes of friendly chatter with Maud and Norah. Now, on his way to St. Bartholomew's, his reflections were focussed upon the chat at the foot of the staircase, seen under a vague light from the day's dreary interludes.

Two circumstances which had undoubtedly been factors in the constraint of the Weir Lodge atmosphere on Sunday, were, Mr. Morley Fenton's extreme weariness—the cost of bringing rest to Harold on Saturday night had not been trifling—and the tactfully arranged barrier which Mr. Morley Fenton had placed between Harold and Norah. The keynote of Weir Lodge, its dominating personality, had been quiescent from fatigue. The individuality in the Weir Lodge household, most naturally sympathetic to Harold's, had been separated from him by a distinct element of artificiality.

The porter at the hospital handed Harold two notes as he passed through the entrance hall. One was a few lines of piquant raillery and reproach for desertion, from the Carissima. Harold smiled, and coloured, and frowned and smiled again, as he read the dainty thing, redolent in its shape and scent of her who had written it. The other was from Leo Tarne, and said simply:

"I make no comment on your heartless indifference to my arrangements. Carissima will attend to that. In your presence it seems to me, I am becoming a detail of no importance to her highness. In your absence I am made your whipping-boy, which, were it not for the fact that I always was more interested in her rosy wrath than in her pale tenderness, would be very annoying. I will only say that you are to lunch with me at the Hereford, and that I believe we have to meet the Carissima after some chamber concert rehearsal, or something—somewhere. Seriously, Caro, don't let anything prevent your coming. You must have had a good deal of that weird 'straight line' of yours since Friday.
"Forgivingly yours,
"LEO TARNE.

"P. S.—One o'clock, the Hereford—déjeuner for me, you know."

"I must go," muttered Harold, as he walked down the corridor. "And that will mean an afternoon wasted. Bother! But I must go, I suppose—H'm!"
The young man's brows were drawn into a protesting frown. His tone implied annoyance and regret. His lips moved in a smile which denied itself. His eyes shone with a light of pleasurable anticipation.

CHAPTER XXI.

ON A WAYSIDE SLOPE.

"Therefore, no sooner does our candidate
For saintship spotlessly emerge soul-cleansed
From First Communion to mount guard at post,
Paris-proof, top to toe, than up there starts
The Spirit of the Boulevard—you know who."
ROBERT BROWNING.

WITHIN five minutes of one o'clock, Harold Foster, stepping springily and humming under his breath a little French melody of the Carissima's composition, walked into the entrance hall of the Hereford Hotel. He had left word at the hospital that he would be back soon—" as soon as I can, you know." And now, having glanced into the drawing-room of the Hereford —Leo Tarne said he always chose the drawing-room of an hotel to smoke a cigarette in, until he was interfered with, because smoking-rooms smelt so abominably of tobacco—Harold approached the gold-laced official in the entrance hall. Both Leo Tarne and himself were well-known at the Hereford.

" Have you seen Mr. Tarne, this morning?" Harold asked the man.

" No, sir; Mr. Tarne's not been here this morning."

" Up to the present, that is. How are you, Harold? Hope I haven't kept you waiting. I met a man named Tritton in Vere Street—an awfully well-intentioned nuisance, who persists in asking me to *tête-à-tête* dinners, and reading me dyspeptic passages from his own poetry. I once committed myself by saying at a club that some verses of Tritton's in an evening paper had opened my eyes to the existence of hitherto undiscovered organs in myself. I merely meant that the verses told me I had a liver susceptible to jaundice and things. But ever since then, I have been bullied by him as though I were an art patron, or a discoverer of genius, or some horrible vulgarity of that sort. However—No! Let us take this table, my dear Harold, if you don't mind. A window-table is almost as beautiful an institution as a hansom. It secures you a certain amount of privacy, and enables you to give people the pleasure of seeing you—people in the street, I mean, who, being less real, are always far more tolerable than people close at hand. Excuse me. Bring some olives, Gustave, will you, and a bottle of Reisling Berg, or would you rather begin with some fruit, Harold? No. That will do then, Gustave, thank you. And now, my poor Harold, tell me how you are. I need not ask how our friends at Weir Lodge are, because the suggestion in your own charming features, of exhaustion, tells me that Weir Lodge is in the full enjoyment of health and strength and faculties of absorption. Do say something, my dear Harold, to show me you are not utterly worn out. Unless you would rather wait for the Reisling Berg."

Leo Tarne paused at length. He had babbled on continuously from the time of his entering the hotel, when Harold was talking to the hall-porter. And he had done this because he was so thoroughly interested in watching the smiles quickly reinforcing each other on Harold's mobile lips, chasing away deprecation, smoothing out lines of resistance, and telling frankly of enjoyment, in the handsome, plastic face of the young man.

"I'm sorry to falsify your conclusions, Leo, but

truth compels me to remark here that I've had a very pleasant time indeed at Weir Lodge," said Harold brightly.

"Ah! how charming of you! The lamented Grandison might have said that very thing, with just your air—in his young days, I mean, when even a gentleman's swearing was delightful. Though the gentlemen themselves, by the way, must have been a fearful nuisance, taking themselves and their immorality so horribly seriously as they did. But, really though—lovely colour that Reisling has, has it not?—have you had a very dull time, Harold?"

"My dear fellow, I haven't had a dull time at all. I don't know what has given you that notion." Harold looked back at Weir Lodge now, over the yellow-rippled edge of his hock glass, through the colour with which, in his eyes, Leo Tarne always managed to saturate his immediate atmosphere. "On the contrary, I enjoyed it very much," he continued, lowering the slender Venetian glass from his lips, and lifting between thumb and finger an olive. "Quiet, of course. None of the Carissima's after-dinner ditties, you know."

"Hardly," murmured Tarne.

"But a very pleasant time, all the same; and good music, of another kind, too."

"Ah, 'Songs without Words,' or 'Hold the Fort.'"

"Leo, you are very rude."

"I do my best."

"And succeed—infamously. We had some Mendelssohn, and we had some deliciously plaintive little Irish airs."

"Oh yes. The Botticelli fairy, *n'est ce pas?*" Harold coloured slightly.

"She is a very charming girl," he said slowly.

"Very—very charming! Though why you should mention a delightful and undeniable fact so resentfully,

I don't know. Were you ever sufficiently strong-minded to dive far enough through Browning's prickly shell to reach his beautiful pearls, Harold?"

Harold looked up sharply.

"I know very little of his work but, curiously enough—— But why do you ask, Leo?"

"Oh, nothing of any importance. Tell me that 'curiously enough' thing. I was merely about to ask whether you knew 'Fifine,' and if so, whether the charming Botticelli study at Weir Lodge should be called Elvire. But I await the something 'curious.' There is so little that is curious, outside people's commonplaces."

Harold laughed quietly.

"You will probably find my curio the essence of commonplaceness. I shouldn't have mentioned it but for your question. It is merely that Mr. Morley Fenton read something of Browning's to me on Saturday night, when I was very tired."

"Ah, that straight line of yours! But I am much interested, my dear Harold. Mr. Morley Fenton—h'm! What did he read you—'Bishop Blougram'? or——"

"That's exactly what he did read. You are a most extraordinary man, Leo."

"Not at all. I did not suppose for a moment he had read 'Blougram' to you. I suspected him of the 'Pied Piper,' or 'Ghent to Aix.' I merely said 'Blougram' because I was just thinking that Mr. Morley Fenton might have a good deal of the 'great bishop' in himself."

"This is sheer clairvoyance."

"No. Did you think the same thing? My dear Harold, that is natural enough. If you wrote books, you would find that we should hit upon the same titles. You would use up all my best situations, while I worked on them, and then accuse me of barefaced plagiarism. That is why we are lunching together to-day. It will always be so. You live as I write, or I write as you live—as you like. The theory of opposites in friendship is a grotesque absurdity. In choosing a friend one really is feeling for a mouthpiece— a personality who gives expression to one's thoughts, or lives one's tastes: just as in forming acquaintances one looks for capacity to comprehend and admire one; just as in making enemies one's attention is directed towards those who are clever enough to see through one's little disguises, vulgar enough to show that they see, and inartistic enough not to admire what they see. But how about Mr. Fenton and the 'Apology'? Did it make you more tired?"

"I was too sleepy to appreciate; but I read it myself next morning——"

"And sympathized with Bohemia under orthodoxy's bludgeon?"

"No; but felt painfully like Gigadibs, and wanted to apologize to—to the Bishop."

"By Jove! Poor old chap! You must have been horribly bullied. After that, I don't know whether to tell you to read 'Fifine' or Balzac. I only feel safe in taking you at once to the Carissima. She is very good reading, and—in lovely voice just now. We will certainly dine at Carlo Varni's to-night. Poor Harold! Poor persecuted medico!"

"Don't be absurd, Leo."

"Absurd? I languish in sympathy."

"You revel in exaggeration."

"As you will. May I give you some Camembert, or—the Brie looks moderately tempting. No; ah well, the Carissima shall sing you her answer to the ponderous bishop this evening."

"But I am going down to Sunbury this evening."

"Nay—absurd! Consider the lilies and things, and the Carissima, how she is waiting. By the way, don't let me forget St. James's Hall at four o'clock."

"Or I my train—4.30 at Waterloo."

"I forgive you for reverting to that impossibly ridiculous topic, but—don't let it occur again."

"Ah, Leo," rejoined Harold with fine irrelevance, "I'm awfully glad to see you again, anyhow, and—you are very demoralizing."

So, sitting over his winter-sunlight-flecked Rüdesheimer, in the window corner at the Hereford, Harold Foster smiled at the past, draped rosily the future, and threw a careless main in pleasantry with Leo Tarne for the present. And Leo Tarne, lounging opposite Harold, smiled, and, in his own way, thoroughly enjoyed the moment as it passed. Of all our facial signs and expressions, this that we call a smile is surely the most comprehensive, embracing as it does the poles of pure delight and that exultation which is regarded as Mephistophelian.

There had been a period during which Leo Tarne was dominated by a passion for playing upon stringed instruments; queer sensitive things, of grotesque shape and strange shrill tones; odd Eastern lutes, and Moorish gimbris, picked up for Tarne by sailors and travellers in out-of-the-way Persian towns, and in Levantine ports; instruments the writer had never tried to master, but only to draw strange chords and eerie responses from. It was a very similar desire he gratified when he set himself to talk to, and listen to the talk of, Harold Foster. He had no deliberately evil intent, but he had been unable to resist telling Harold that the end of the "straight line" had no existence, because of the sudden desire which had come to him to see the quick flash of impressionistic pain, foretaste of readily-believed-in disillusion, which he knew would illumine Harold's sensitive face; to hear the curious ripple down from staccato C major to a lingering minor key of doubt, which he had known his careless flick of cynicism would surely bring into Harold's voice.

Harold surveyed the quiet bustle of a West End thoroughfare through one broad pane of the corner window. He erected ramparts of rusk crumbs round his wine-glass, tossing them idly aside with one finger then, as he raised the spiral-stemmed toy, and smiled over its edge at Tarne. He, as it were, coquetted with that side-slope of his life of which Leo Tarne was keynote and embodiment, whilst endeavouring not to altogether lose his grasp of the slope's antithesis, the straight line, the life exemplified by the "little round of things" at Weir Lodge. It was as though Harold Foster had said to the thing within himself which was himself:

"You see how pleasant it is here on this sun-suffused, flower-carpeted little slope; how the air is glad here, and the light laughs in one's face. So I am resting here, just resting, while an hour lives and dies. And then—the summit, of course. The narrow track above for me, where the mist envelopes one, and the wind calls for unceasing resistance. But I know it has its end, that grey-walled track; while, of course, the slope runs down to the river, on the banks of which the wild oats grow, and rank weeds flourish. And the narrow track has its glimpses, too, where the sun breaks through the crevice of a moment. That chat by the stairs last night; and, yes, there is Norah. But —just by the way, you know—a little hour's rest, my soul."

Harold had forgotten, probably, that a peculiarity of these slopes is that one is always slipping forward on them, and never sitting or standing still.

When at length the two men rose from their seat by the window, Harold looked at his watch, and said, with a slight inflection of annoyance in his voice:

"By Jove, Leo, it's positively three o'clock already!"

"Ah! Shall I say I am sorry, or delighted? I really don't know what is the correct feeling to have about your interesting discovery. Three o'clock in the day is one of those absurd hours which have no real existence. It is the time at which things are 'held,' things one subsequently reads about, if one is a student of topics current and reads the evening paper posters, as I, for instance, most religiously do. It is my chiefest tribute to institutions of which you know nothing; like 'the age we live in,' 'society' and 'the world of to-day.'"

"Institutions I know nothing of, indeed! My dear fellow, you ought to see me at the family board this evening."

"I shall."

"At Sunbury, I mean. I live in and of those institutions."

"Ah, you think so. Well, with regard to this question of three o'clock—good, serviceable old three o'clock! There is just time for us to stroll comfortably through the park, read the posters, smoke several cigarettes—it is a mistake to ever smoke less than several cigarettes, cigarette-smoking being essentially a pleasure of excess: moderation in it vitiates one's taste —smoke several cigarettes, as I said, and meet the Carissima. I wish she wouldn't go to St. James's though, because it makes one think of comic songs and the sadness of life."

"I must go to the hospital, Leo, I must really."

"Harold, the manner in which you flaunt that dismal charnel-house of yours in my face is positively indecent. In Regent Street there is a funny little place where messenger boys assemble for innocent recreation and conversation. There we will interview a gentleman who holds a pen between his lips all day, and thrives on it. He will despatch one of his aides-de-camp to the charnel-house, with a message, telling in guarded terms of the lamentable accident which robs you of the pleasure of further surgical amusement for to-day."

"This is not such a bad town, this little London of ours, Leo, after all. Look at that stream of carriages beyond the trees."

"Yes. Might be Unter den Linden—when some big funeral was taking place, eh! Then, as I was about to remark, when we have taken the Carissima home—she will probably like to have tea at Sartello's—I will go round with you to your rooms. Or, better still, I'll send round for your things, and you can dress at my place. The young man who eats pens will arrange that for us. Like Tritton, he is a well-intentioned young man, and, unlike Tritton, he is well worth knowing."

"I too, am like Tritton, in so far as that I was thoroughly well-intentioned this afternoon; but——"

"But don't do yourself an injustice, Harold. Where you differ materially from poor dear Tritton is in your capacity for lucid intervals. Tritton remains sunk in a chronic mire of good intentions. Wisdom comes to you occasionally, as now, and you rise almost to the level of the happily intentionless man."

"You cloak it charmingly. But I frankly confess that if I remain with you it is because I want to be with you, and don't want to be at the hospital. Only, don't forget, Leo, that if you always exert this sort of influence over me—— Why, hullo! there's George Barnard! How are you, George?"

"Harold, I'm so glad to see you. How do you do, Mr. Tarne?"

The barrister, looking more dishevelled than usual, had been staring into the window of a bookseller's shop in the street down which Harold and Tarne were walking from the park. This was the afternoon of the first Monday in the month, and Mrs. Greet's day for giving notice, a process which generally drove the barrister direct from his writing-table into the street. Mrs. Greet must have triumphed signally on this particular occasion, for George Barnard to have been driven into wandering so far afield as Regent Street, or its immediate neighbourhood.

The change of expression in Harold's face when he caught sight of the barrister's kindly features had been very curious. Colour had rushed into it, as though Harold had been detected in some misdemeanour. Then, quickly, had come a look of general awakening, recollection, and some regret. George Barnard was part, and the most generous, least constrained part, of all that Harold had clung to, whilst lunching at the corner window-table in the Hereford, and had relinquished, brushed aside, in his subsequent yielding to Leo Tarne's persuasions.

"Why, Harold," said George Barnard, "I fancied you would be on your way from Bart's to Waterloo by now."

"Our friend was kind enough to make lunch enjoyable for me to-day," explained Leo Tarne. "And we were arranging to dine together, this evening. If you would be induced to join us, Mr. Barnard, it would have the effect——"

"I'm sorry," interrupted the barrister, the lie coming from him with transparent want of ease, "but I have to put in a working evening to-night."

Leo Tarne bowed polite regret, and turning to Harold again, the barrister said:

"I met Mr. Morley Fenton outside a music-shop in Holborn. He had one or two little things to do, and then was going on to Waterloo. He told me he was to meet you there in time for the 4.30, and he spoke of some letter he had had about you. I know he expects you, and I fancy he will wait for you."

"I'm sorry," said Harold, "but I don't think Mr. Fenton will wait, George."

But Harold's tone was full of amenability, almost of penitence. The barrister's frank blue eyes flashed upward understanding and sidelong resentment. Leo Tarne stood at his side.

"Seems a shame to disappoint him, Harold. He certainly expects you. And—er—in view of to-day's lunch, I dare say Mr. Tarne will excuse you, won't you, Mr. Tarne?"

The barrister's endeavour to give a genial ring to his question made Leo Tarne smile—a smile which concerned his upper lip alone, and was not the most cordial kind of expression.

"I excuse my enemies, Mr. Barnard, and my acquaintances, I believe, for the most part excuse me. But I do not excuse my friends. Felicitations are the things to reserve for one's friends, I think—or condolences. In pleasing himself, Harold will, I am sure, delight me."

"H'm!" The barrister glanced at his watch. "It is only five minutes to four now, Harold. If you jump into this hansom, you'll get to Waterloo, with five minutes to spare. What do you say? Shall I hail it?"

"Well, you know, I left my bag at the hospital, George."

"But you have things down at Sunbury, haven't you."

Harold thought of Mr. Fenton's little present.

"Ye-es," he said with slight hesitation. "I have some things."

"And they don't dress for dinner as a general thing, I think. Let me call this cab. Don't disappoint—— Yes! Here you are, Cabby! Waterloo!"

Leo Tarne accepted the situation gracefully, and smilingly wished his friend a pleasant evening.

"My kindest regards to all at Weir Lodge," he said, as Harold leaned forward in the cab to shake his hand; "and to the Botticelli fairy," he added, lowering his voice. "Yours, of course, to the Carissima? Yes. Adio."

And as the cab moved away Leo Tarne turned, and stood facing George Barnard, where he stood on the pavement's edge. For a full and somewhat awkward moment these two men looked into each other's eyes. Then Leo Tarne made a little, half-laughing, inarticulate sound which might have been regarded as the clearing of his throat.

"Let me offer you a cigarette," he said, holding out his case to the barrister. "I am due at St. James's at four. I think I had better cab it. May I put you down anywhere?"

The barrister had mechanically taken one of Tarne's cigarettes, and was twisting it unconsciously between finger and thumb.

"No," he said at length slowly; "no, thanks, Mr. Tarne; I'm just meandering about—er—that is, for a few minutes, you know."

Leo Tarne smiled, whilst unobtrusively beckoning to the driver of a passing hansom. As the vehicle drew up beside the two men the barrister stepped aside to allow Tarne to enter it.

"I say, Mr. Tarne," he said hesitatingly, and whilst resting one hand on the splashboard of the cab, "you have a good deal of influence with Harold Foster, don't you think so?"

"It's very kind of you to say so." The sneer in Leo Tarne's voice was very thinly, if gracefully, disguised. "I like to think so."

"Yes, just so. Well, there are reasons, believe me, why parts of your world, even my shabby old world, are rather dangerous places for Harold just now. His examination at the hospital comes on soon, you know."

"Ah, yes." Leo Tarne flicked the ash from his cigarette, and looked all the polite interest of polite boredom.

"Well, forgive my boring you, but, for the sake of one or two people who've been watching that boy since he was a child, and—who love him, Mr. Tarne, don't exert any influence that is likely to keep him back in the world—more than you can help."

Again the eyes of the two men met for just one moment, and Leo Tarne's were the first to be lowered, though they were lowered carelessly enough.

Then the barrister stepped back from the cab and bowed, as Leo Tarne murmured:

"I am afraid I don't quite follow you, Mr. Barnard, but—yes, St. James's Hall, Cabby. Good-bye, Mr. Barnard."

The cab moved on in the direction taken by Harold's cab a few minutes before. The barrister turned slowly towards the bookseller's window.

"Hang! Damn your smooth face!" he muttered. And a gentleman in black cloth gaiters passing, at the moment, turned his irreproachable head, and gazed with horror at George Barnard.

The gentleman in gaiters was clean shaven.

CHAPTER XXII.

A QUESTION OF DIAGNOSIS.

"But try and, what you find wrong, remedy,
Accepting the conditions : never ask
'How came you to be born here with those lungs,
That liver?' But bid asthma smoke a pipe,
Stramonium, just as if no Tropics were,
And ply with calomel the sluggish duct,
Nor taunt 'The born Norwegian breeds no bile !'
And as with body, so proceed with soul."
Red Cotton Nightcap Country.

HAROLD FOSTER had both time and food for reflection during his drive to Waterloo, and during the five minutes which he spent there in waiting for Mr. Morley Fenton. He remembered a favourite saying of Leo Tarne's to the effect that "Virtue brings its own remorse."

"Hang it!" he muttered, looking about him in the crowded station, with half a frown and half a smile of amused perplexity. "I wonder what made me throw over Leo and his dinner so meekly. It seems to me that my best friends either bully or poison or exhaust me. Good old George; how disreputable he looked! And Leo must have thought it deuced unfriendly of me. Bother! I wonder if Norah—— Ah!"

Harold stepped forward slowly as he noticed Mr. Morley Fenton approaching him from the gates at the head of the platform.

"So you are here before me," said Mr. Fenton, holding out his hand. "I am very glad you came. Didn't you bring a bag?"

"Well, the fact is, I—I was going to dine with Leo Tarne, only I met George Barnard, and he said he thought you might wait for me, so I——"

"Exactly; it was good of you to put off Mr. Tarne, and I am glad you did. I have had a very interesting letter from Dr. Wainwright, in which he tells me a good deal about you and your work at Bartholomew's."

Harold and Mr. Fenton had taken their seats, and the Sunbury train was beginning to move slowly out from the station. Mr. Fenton drew a letter from his pocket, and held it in his hand as he leaned forward to talk to Harold. The carriage they had chosen had but one other occupant. Harold knew that the distinguished physician, behind whom he had frequently walked the wards of Bartholomew's, was an old acquaintance of Mr. Morley Fenton's. But he rather wondered what the great man could have to say about so insignificant a personage as himself. "Nothing flattering, certainly," reflected Harold, thinking of the extremely spasmodic nature of his recent work at the hospital.

"This letter is of course a confidential one," said Mr. Fenton; "but I don't think for a moment that Dr. Wainwright would mind my talking to you about it. In fact, I fancy it was with a view to something of that sort that he wrote it."

"Ah! Then I suppose he has nothing very pleasing to say about me," said Harold, with a rather strained smile.

"On the contrary, he says several very pleasant things—things almost too flattering for you to hear. Here is one. He says: 'If I am any judge, your young friend has all the material in him of which really brilliant doctors are made. He will never be a surgeon, but my firm belief is that he can, if he likes, be a cleverer physician than any one of the students now at Bart's will be. His diagnostic insight has startled me more than once, and he has all the really big doctors' sensitive, perceptive touch.' That's pleasant enough, Harold, is it not?"

The young man nodded. His face was aflame.

" It's very kind of Dr. Wainwright," he murmured.

" Then," continued Mr. Fenton, " he says that last Friday you positively upset the verdict of one of his own colleagues, re-diagnosed a case, and proved an able man to have been quite wrong in his judgment, thereby, in all probability, preventing so serious an accident as a useless operation."

Harold's colour deepened under this shower of *kudos*.

"Ah, that's nothing," he said hesitatingly. " Any man might have taken that hæmatoma for a cold abscess. That was mere chance."

"H'm! very creditable chance—very." Mr. Morley Fenton's brows straightened; his moustache was drawn inward slightly. " Well, then," he continued, "after all this, comes a little of a different flavour. He says you are more irregular in your attendance than 'the most roystering chuckle-head on the students' list.'"

Mr. Morley Fenton raised his eyes till they met Harold's like levelled lances. The young man's face had regained its natural colour. His expression implied nervous annoyance under a thin veil of polite indifference. Mr. Fenton resumed his extract from the eminent medico's letter.

"'He is as full of moods as a fashionable practitioner; as variable as a woman; as little inclined to steady effort as a young poet, and as nonchalant as a crack surgeon. These be trifles which, if not seen to, may prove sufficient to prevent one of the most possible, the most promising, students I ever gave a hint to, being able to write M. D. after his name, far less succeeding in his profession.'"

Again Mr. Fenton's eyes met those of his protégé, and this time the younger man flinched under the sharp attack. Then Mr. Fenton replaced the letter in his coat pocket, and leaned back, puffing thoughtfully at his cheroot.

"An interesting letter, is it not?" he asked quietly, after a silence of a full minute's duration.

"Very," said Harold, without raising his eyes. "And I dare say the latter part is very true. I have been—irregular. Regularity is the one thing most hard to me."

Then both were silent again. The train passed through Hampton.

"Yes. Regularity is a habit, like irregularity, but a little more difficult to cultivate, and a great deal more useful when one has it."

Harold nodded, and a few minutes later the two were walking together towards Weir Lodge.

As they were leaving their coats in the vestibule of the white house, Mr. Morley Fenton turned suddenly, and placed one hand on Harold's arm. Harold thought afterwards that there had been something curiously uncertain and undecided in the touch— something which suggested the touch of a man groping his way in a dark room.

"The first part of the letter must come true, Harold; the material must be used."

Mr. Fenton paused, and cleared his throat.

"Yes," assented Harold, rather vaguely. And then came light footsteps in the hall, and the two men stepped forward to meet Norah, who announced herself before Mr. Fenton pushed aside the swing-doors of the vestibule, by crying:

"Is that you, father dear?"

Norah had been running across the hall. Catching sight of Harold's fair head as the swing-doors opened, she dropped on the instant into a gliding walk, advancing demurely then to meet Mr. Morley Fenton and his guest.

CHAPTER XXIII.

INTERVENTION.

*" 'Tis an awkward thing to play with souls,
And matter enough to save one's own."*
ROBERT BROWNING.

NORAH advanced towards Harold, full of abruptly-recalled consciousness that a mystic ring surrounded that young man, with his glinting fair hair, and his eyes coloured like far-off mountain-sides seen in sunshine which has followed rain—a ring across the edges of which she might not allow her little feet to stray.

Harold addressed Norah by her Christian name in saluting her, and was surprised at the little thrill which the indulgence of this permitted familiarity sent through him, even there in Mr. Morley Fenton's presence.

A few moments afterwards Harold was in the little walnut room over Mr. Fenton's study. Whilst making some slight change in his dress, there floated insistently before Harold's eyes a picture, in which the figure was dark-eyed Norah, in the flowing creamy gown she wore that evening, the foreground was the great rug at the foot of the Weir Lodge staircase, and the background was an oak wainscoted wall, illumined by the uncertain, warm glow of the hall fire.

Harold sighed, and smiled, as he stood before the dressing-table in the little walnut room, a hair-brush in either hand, his head inclined sideways, as though he questioned his own reflection.

INTERVENTION. 205

" What was it that poet-sprite wrote? " he said:

> " ' Not content to dig with other men,
> Because of certain sudden sights and sounds
> (Bars of broke music ; furtive, fleeting glimpse
> Of angel faces 'thwart the grating seen)
> Perceived in Heaven. Yet when I approach
> To catch the sound's completeness, to absorb
> The faces' full perfection, Heaven's gate,
> Which then had stood ajar, sudden falls to,
> And I—I——'

I forget the rest, but it was something about 'men's mocking at the man who didn't care to dig.' H'm! and the gate falls to. No; it seems some kind soul always pushes it to—in my life. Ah, well, I'll go downstairs, and talk to George Barnard's Maud, about hospitals and theatres, and—things! "

There was half-amused bitterness in Harold's face as he left the little walnut room; but, perhaps, by reason of that " furtive, fleeting " picture he had seen in the hall, he had as yet given no thought to the Carissima, or to Leo Tarne, or to the evening he was to have spent with them.

Harold did not edify Maud Fenton when he went downstairs, with information about " theatres and hospitals." There were difficulties in the way which Harold had not anticipated in connection with his laudable design. Maud was in the breakfast-room, coiled all round a volume from a circulating library. To reach the breakfast-room the hall had to be crossed. In the hall, on a low shadowy couch, at one side of the fireplace, sat Norah, dreamily watching certain evening stars that were beginning to peer through the big hall-window, in the mauve light against which Harold's figure appeared silhouetted, as he descended the stairs.

Harold felt vaguely that he was on his honour in the matter of maintaining a certain reserve between

Norah and himself. He intended now to pass her, with a smile and, as chance directed, some casual remark, and then to find Maud, and talk to her. Suddenly, and as Harold's feet touched the floor of the hall, a brilliant wintry moon, new risen, sailed over the edge of a sullen snow-cloud, and poured down a broad stream of its beautifying light through the upper half of the hall-window. It glanced along the polished balustrade beside the stairs, shimmered, like sea-phosphorescence, across one side of a quaintly fretted Venetian lamp, and stretched at last slim fingers of purity over Norah's massed dark hair; giving to her sweet face a curiously saintly beauty, and circling her creamy throat, from where her ears crept out, under overhanging tendrils of hair, with a band like nacre— nacre bedded in the shadowy foam of laces on her breast. There the light melted into sepia indistinctness.

Regarded as a picture merely, a thing without life, Norah, under her silvery diadem, was calculated to appeal strongly to the admiration of any man, to fascinate some. Harold stood still, his head gleaming in the same moon-ray which gave Norah her crown, gazing at the girl in much the same ecstasy of appreciation which had been his on that Sunday morning of the previous summer that had followed the evening of his first meeting with her.

"Father has gone into the study. Were you looking for him, Mr. Foster?"

"No, thank you. I was—that is, I think I must have been looking for a cathedral organ, or—or for the other angels. But you are not a cathedral vision, or a dream of Corregio's painted on mother-o'-pearl, are you, Norah?"

The girl laughed cooingly, a warm glow creeping over the cream of her cheeks. Then she remembered the barrier, and bending forward out of reach of the moonlight, she said slowly:

"Aunty and Lucy are in the drawing-room, I think."

Harold's virtuous resolves anent theatre and hospital talk had melted away in the moonlight, as frost recedes from a March sun's advances. He sat down on a low stool within a yard of Norah's couch.

"I am glad to-day is not Sunday," he said, referring evidently to some subject as yet undiscussed.

"Why?" asked Norah, with fine impartiality.

"Well, really, I could hardly tell you why, unless it is because Sunday is a more correct day than the others, and I—I am less correct than most people, perhaps."

"Oh! Being correct is rather horrid, is it not? That is, I mean being very correct, you know."

"I'm awfully glad you think so. But you—you manage it much better than I do."

"Perhaps that is because I am more used to it. But I'm sure I am not correct at all."

"No, no, perhaps, all things considered, you are not more correct than is absolutely necessary, to avoid upsetting very correct people, you know, and thereby becoming less charming—well, I mean, of course you couldn't be like that, you know."

Harold seemed to be recklessly approaching dangerous ground.

"Oh, I have not asked after your friend, Mr. Tarne," said Norah. And, of course, she may have wished to hear something of Mr. Tarne.

"And I haven't told you that Leo asked to be remembered to you, just as I was leaving him this afternoon. He is very well, I think. The giving of those messages is just one of the correct things I am always forgetting. Of course, they are often sincere enough; but then, again, they are sometimes such palpable humbug. I—I wonder why I say all these things to you. You will think me a fearful barbarian."

"You don't think that, Mr. Foster; you know you don't."

"But somehow I always fancy that you understand; and so, I suppose, I am daring enough to expect sympathy."

So these two chatted while the moonlight gradually spread, penetrating every shadow, and trickling into every corner of the hall. Harold had, for the moment, forgotten the existence of any barrier between them. With each unimportant but much portending sentence which they exchanged, the barrier became more misty and unreal to Norah. Once there was a little rustling noise at the drawing-room door. Then, all being still again, the two in the moonlight babbled on. They were drawing nearer, nearer each to each, with every word that passed between them.

Then suddenly the drawing-room door swung back. Curiously enough, Norah felt quite convinced that the door had been shut; yet it opened noiselessly, and Mrs. Morley Fenton stepped briskly into the moonlight from out a flood of yellow light from the drawing-room.

"Norah dear, why didn't you ring for lights? Oh, Mr. Foster, this is too bad of you, not to have come in to see us all. We thought you must be in your room. Where's father, Norah?"

"In the study. I will run and tell him it's nearly dinner-time. I thought the hall looked so much prettier without gas."

So Norah, for whom the hall seemed to have lost some of its attractiveness, disappeared in the direction of Mr. Morley Fenton's room, whilst Harold, murmuring a lame apology to his hostess, walked with her to the drawing-room, where Lucy Fenton sat, working flowers in silk on a hand-screen. Mrs. Fenton's bright, keen eyes swept searchingly over Harold's face, as the rather glaring light from the drawing-room gasalier fell upon it. Mrs. Fenton had less faith in her husband's manipulation of some matters, at all events, than had that gentleman himself. And, curiously enough, the thought of her own daughter, Lucy, proving an attraction to Harold Foster was rather pleasant than otherwise to this good lady.

After dinner the family gathered in the drawing-room.

"I want everybody to excuse my being fearfully rude here," said Maud, "because there's no fire in the billiard-room, and the breakfast-room's horrid after dinner."

"What special form is your rudeness to take, Madcap?" asked the head of the house.

"Oh yes; I forgot. Why, I have four more chapters of 'The Gigantic Fragment' to read, and I must read them now, else I shall forget what the rest of it was about."

"Oh yes! Complimentary to the author, isn't it, Harold? Norah dear, do you feel like giving us a little music, if we are self-denying enough to postpone our smoke?"

Norah smiled and moved towards the piano. Harold stepped to her side. Mrs. Fenton raised her delicate eyebrows. Mr. Morley Fenton misunderstood his wife's expression.

"Yes, I know, my dear," he said; "you don't mind your curtains being spoiled in the least, and you are rather fond of the smell of smoke. But we won't take advantage of your goodness, all the same."

Mrs. Fenton shrugged her shoulders ever so slightly, and Harold stood at ease to turn the pages of

Norah's music. So Norah played from printed music, though she preferred playing from memory.

Later on in the evening, when Mr. Morley Fenton had perhaps forgotten the matter of his after-dinner smoke—he was staring rather fixedly into the fire, whilst Mrs. Fenton knitted, Lucy embroidered industriously, and Maud remained coiled round her " Gigantic Fragment "—Norah left the piano, and strolled to the open door of the conservatory. Harold followed her, drawing a cigarette from his pocket as he did so.

The atmosphere of the conservatory was warm and flower-fragrant. The light there was very beautiful. Neither Norah nor Harold Foster were slow to appreciate these facts, but Norah was severely general in her share of the conversation. Harold was guarded, and not forgetful—particularly during the first three minutes.

Ten minutes afterwards Mrs. Fenton laid aside her knitting, and her fair face showed that knitting had ceased to interest or charm her. She rose, and glanced at her husband.

" Why should you not have your cigar in the conservatory, dear, since you insist on sparing the drawing-room? "

" Ah, to be sure! Yes—thank you, dear; I'll go to my room. Yes, I think I will go to the study, thanks."

There was a distinct look of impatience on Mrs. Fenton's usually smiling face as she stepped towards the conservatory door. But her voice had all its wonted trilling sweetness when she said, whilst on the threshold of the conservatory, and immediately behind Norah:

" How pretty the moonlight makes these ferns under the glass. Don't you think so, Mr. Foster? "

Mr. Foster did think so, and moreover said as much, with some added comment about " tropical effect" and the branches of a certain palm. But he had been unable to restrain a movement of surprise, and, perhaps, of annoyance, when the first sounds of Mrs. Fenton's voice had reached him. He tossed the end of his cigarette into an empty flower-pot, and turned to speak to the lady of the house. The discarded cigarette-end was at least two inches in length. But then it was not alight.

Yet once again during that short evening, was the joint attention of Harold and Norah called to the barrier which had been carefully erected between them; this third time by its architect and builder. The party had separated for the night at the door of the drawing-room. The ladies had made their way upstairs, Mr. Morley Fenton had gone into his study to write a letter before going to bed, and Harold had paused beside the hall fire, dividing his attention between a cigarette and Maud Fenton's brown spaniel—a pampered animal with an exaggerated fondness for chocolate creams.

Norah came running downstairs alone, with a perfectly innocent desire to find a letter which she had left on the piano in the drawing-room with her handkerchief. Having found her property she lingered by the hall fire. Common courtesy forced her to do this, because Harold besieged her with small questions. The study door stood ajar. Just as Harold's questions were veering from Pompey, the spaniel, to Norah, whom Leo Tarne called "the Botticelli fairy," there issued from the study a sound as of the turning, in a hesitating way, of a revolving chair. One minute later and Mr. Morley Fenton appeared in the hall. There was a curious, half-reluctant, half-annoyed expression on his face, as he said:

"Aha! you two late ones; I thought I heard voices. You ought to be in bed, you know, Norah.

I was just going to put the lights out. Will that train we went by this morning suit you to-morrow, Harold?"

Norah kissed her adopted father somewhat hurriedly, and, with a funny little smile over one shoulder, and a " Good-night," which contained no suggestion of barriers, to Harold, she ran lightly upstairs, leaving the two men alone before the hall fire.

" Oh yes, thanks; it will suit me very well," said Harold, speaking with some little constraint. " Goodnight! I—I know it will relieve your mind to see me go to bed."

Mr. Morley Fenton looked up sharply; but Harold had turned, and was moving towards the staircase. Then the last vestige of annoyance faded from Mr. Fenton's face, leaving only regret, reluctance, and some weariness, in its place.

" Why yes," he said, as Harold paused with one hand on the balustrade—" yes, I like you to rest well, my dear boy, because I want Wainwright's prophecies to be fulfilled; and—and that must mean working well, mustn't it?"

" Yes—oh yes; it means working. Good-night!"

" Good-night, Harold!"

Something insistent and not happy, rang through the cheerfulness of Mr. Morley Fenton's voice.

" Well, of course, she is no more to me than any other girl," muttered Harold, whilst moodily poking the fire in the little walnut room. " And I'm no more to her—not so much," he added, with more emphasis than lucidity. " Only, it does seem a weird thing, rather, that I can't be allowed—oh, hang! Of course, it's part of the general impossibility of things. H'm— part of the whole eternal question. And, of course, Norah is no more to me than anyone else," he repeated, as he began listlessly to undress. " She—she can't be!"

CHAPTER XXIV.

REACTION.

*" I called the devil, and he came ;
To view him with wonder I began.
He is not ugly and is not lame ;
Far from it, he is a charming man.
A man in the vigour still of his years,
A man of the world and polite he appears."*

HEINE.

GUIDED by that general principle which, to him, seemed to underlie all the laws which governed Weir Lodge, the principle of acting always in direct opposition to the inclination of the moment, Harold Foster paid a good deal of polite attention to Lucy Fenton, when the family met at breakfast next morning. Perhaps this may have influenced Mrs. Fenton in her evident forgetfulness of all that which, on the previous evening, had more than once brought a look of impatience into her dainty face.

She inquired with almost effusive solicitude whether her husband's protégé had passed a good night. Actuated presumably by motives of courtesy to his hostess, certainly by no inherent love of truth, Harold replied in the affirmative, thereby leaving unexplained the dark semicircles under his eyes, and the weariness which, denied by his words, was made obvious by the flat ring in his voice.

As a matter of fact, Harold had passed an extremely tiring, if varied night, in the course of which he had read disconnected chapters from an uninteresting novel; smoked the first halves of five or six cigarettes; endeavoured to restore to life a hopelessly defunct fire, with the aid of leaves from a work on obstetric surgery; and, in broken snatches of restless unconsciousness, had dreamed persistently of being forced over the edge of a most forbidding precipice by Mr. Morley Fenton, who, presumably with a view to hiding his identity in this episode, had clothed himself in the vestments of a bishop of the Episcopal Church, gaiters, sleeves and shovel hat *en règle*.

"It's all very fine, Blougram," Harold had defiantly opined, during one of his tussles with the *soi-disant* Church dignitary. "Your *status entourage* and the rest of it may be very well for those who like to pay the price you pay for it. I don't. I prefer the heath here, with the gipsies; and——" And Harold had waked again, to find one leg in reality dangling over a precipice formed by the side of his bed.

The previous evening, with its suggestions of pleasant interludes inexorably nipped in the bud by his host and hostess, had, as a whole, been chilly and constraining in its impression upon Harold. The night, so far as its brief intervals of sleep were concerned, had been a grotesque exaggeration of the evening's worst points, plus that feeling of intense reality which actual life, it would seem, never yields in the same degree as do experiences in that mysterious land of the unexplained which one sometimes visits whilst sleeping.

"I shall look out for you at the usual time this afternoon," said Mr. Morley Fenton to Harold when the two were separating at Waterloo. "But if you cannot manage the 4.30, come on by a later train, won't you? I am half expecting a young fellow from

Ireland this evening, a very clever fellow, I believe. My poor brother took a great interest in him, and he knows Norah well."

"Oh yes! He is not a 'piratical craft,' I suppose?"

"Eh? Oh ah! Oh dear no! No; I believe he is one of the few rich landholders left in the West of Ireland. Anyhow, he is a very nice fellow. Well, I will look out for you at 4.30, then?"

"Yes, thanks. Good-bye."

So they parted on this dull February morning. And Harold made the best of his way through London's early-day rawness to the hospital, feeling thoroughly in keeping with his atmospheric surroundings of chill, clinging greyness.

The day dragged, to Harold, whilst doubtless tripping along gaily enough to many less fortunately placed. Noon passed, and Harold, feeling too dispirited to go out to lunch, took the place for an hour of a fellow-student " on the door."

The special destiny which overlooks such combinations as the short-sighted amongst us call "trifles," was not well disposed towards Harold Foster on this February morning. He made several small mistakes whilst on duty in the casualty ward, and was afforded a fine insight into the highly inflammable temperament and dictatorial fastidiousness of the average outdoor patient.

He was subsequently overcome by an altogether unaccountable attack of nausea in the operating theatre; and, finally, towards four o'clock, having been severely rebuked by two surgeons, wrathfully remonstrated with by a motherly nurse, whom, having forgotten in a fit of abstraction, he had left supporting a patient's half-bandaged leg, and unmercifully chafed by a number of his fellow-students; Harold took his hat and coat in despair, and decided to go home to his rooms in Kensington.

Whilst standing moodily in the doorway of the cloak-room, Harold was hailed by a passing porter, who said that a lady was inquiring for him in the waiting-room on the ground-floor.

"Oh, all right, Lawson—thank you!" said Harold, as though at this particular hour he was in the habit of entertaining his lady friends in the hospital. Then, hat in hand, and dressed for walking, Harold made his way to the room beside the main entrance.

In the waiting-room the friends of several poor patients, carrying, for the most part, babies, these in various stages of irritability, were comparing notes upon the disorders and ailments of their respective families, and upon other matters. Some carried quart medicine bottles, most carried baskets of allegedly edible treasures, and all carried that peculiar odour of combined illness and poverty which is so full of pathos, and unpleasantness.

Standing in the middle of the room, and bending over the by no means cleanly head of a small boy, whose mother was being treated in the casualty ward, Harold Foster saw the Carissima. He also heard her rippling, silvery voice as she spoke words of consolation to the grimy and temporarily motherless small boy, whose fingers clutched her gown. The other occupants of the room raised their eyes as the door was opened by Harold, and then lowered them with a curiously contemptuous deprecation, intended as a disclaimer, and an assurance of complete absence of connection with the couple who stood apart.

A blended fragrance of Parma violets, and of some perfume more subtle, hung between the Carissima and the good ladies who resented her presence. Her hat was a bewildering little bower of shimmering fragilities.

An outstanding cloud of sunset-tinted foam which clung about her shoulders, was probably, Harold thought, the Carissima's idea of a cloak. The curiously Arcadian-looking crook or wand upon which her white-gloved hand rested, like a snowflake, was doubtless regarded by its owner as an umbrella. Four stunted fingers of the temporary orphan's right hand were buried in the folds of a Parisian modiste's dreamy ideal, materialized to serve the Carissima as a gown. Whilst Harold Foster's mind absorbed and informed him of these things, the bewildering hat moved upward and backward, and the Carissima's violet eyes met those of the young man.

The whole thing was very simple from the Carissima's point of view. Leo Tarne was brutal, and had refused to be amusing that afternoon, pleading in a cowardly way, so the Carissima explained to Harold, that he suffered from neuralgia. It was obvious that someone must amuse the Carissima. Harold looked at the small boy, whose mother was in the casualty ward. It was also obvious that a second kidnapping of Harold by the gentleman from Sunbury, whom the Carissima thought of as being some kind of a tract-distributor, in goloshes and blue spectacles, was not to be permitted. Ergo, "Che, che!" exclaimed the lady, with a little wave of her Arcadian crook—a slightly unusual end to her afternoon drive, and here was the Carissima prepared to personally ensure for Harold immunity from tracts and kidnapping.

"The brougham is outside. You shall take me to Sartello's for tea; and then—then we will go and bastinado the infamous Leo."

"It's awfully good of you," murmured Harold, as the Carissima plucked a shilling out of her dainty silken purse, and bestowed it on the small boy who still clung to her skirt; "but, you know—well, you mustn't come to this place, you know; it's too absurd. They'll take you for—for an outdoor patient, you know, and want to examine you, or something."

The Carissima laughed trillingly, such a laugh as possibly had never before been heard within the precincts of St. Bartholomew's. Then she carried Harold off in triumph to her tiny waiting brougham, and hall-porters assembled about the entrance doors with affected nonchalance, looking over each other's shoulders to see the last of this dazzling vision from a world they knew but slightly. As the miniature brougham rolled away, the porters turned again to their duties, with many solemn winks and knowing shoulder-shrugs.

"Well," said one, "I've knowed a few gents in this 'orspital; I've knowed a few, but—well, I reck'n Mr. Foster takes it—yes, I reckin 'e takes it!"

After which lucid summing up of the situation the other porters realized that further comment would be a work of supererogation, and therefore a thing not to be thought of.

Harold drove with the Carissima to Sartello's, and there, over daintily-served gossip and tea, he allowed the cold greyness of his own atmosphere to gradually lose itself in, and become dominated by, the rosy light of piquancy which was part and parcel of Leo Tarne's "guardian," as that gentleman was fond of calling the beautiful Italian, who always persisted in regarding him as an erring child.

After three-quarters of an hour spent in this way, they rose from the æsthetic little alcove in which tea had been served, and Harold said:

"I'm awfully grateful to you for having cheered me up so; I was getting sordidly wretched. And now, if you'll let me put you in your carriage again,

I'm afraid I really must get away. I have promised——"

Harold paused. The Carissima's hat appeared to be in imminent danger of actual dissolution. The Carissima herself, an embodied ideal of carnival merriment, was laughing with charming and insolent frankness.

"Oh yes! yes!.yes!" she trilled out at last; "you have promised, Signor Dolorous—you have promised. Ha, ha! Come, come; it is true. I had forgotten. We have no time to waste. You must drive with me to disagreeable Leo's. I could not go alone. Che, che!—most improper, most improper! Come, Signor!"

Harold bowed, and for the moment said no more. So it happened that, presently, Leo Tarne's servant opened the door of the flat in West Kensington to admit his master's friends, Harold Foster and Lisè Vecci.

Leo Tarne welcomed his visitors with graceful cordiality. His neuralgia, he said, had worn itself out, and left him in high good-humour. The Carissima, without removing her sunset cloak or her bower of fragilities, sat down before the piano, and, accompanying herself with Southern verve and brilliancy, sang half a dozen verses of half a dozen roundelays, each more trilling and more joyous than its predecessor. Then, with no shadow of any decrease in her marvellous vivacity, the Carissima lighted a dainty Russian cigarette, and dashed off into the most recklessly irresponsible French dance-music, punctuated by odd snatches of song, and such quaintly thrown-out colloquialisms from three languages as one might expect to hear from the lips of a burlesque actress turned vivandière.

Meanwhile Leo Tarne, at his best just now, chatted brightly, and exerted to the full all that influence of which George Barnard had spoken on the previous afternoon—a very real force to Harold, and one the strength of which no one could realize more clearly than did Leo Tarne himself.

Later on, a messenger was despatched to Harold's rooms for his dress clothes, and the dinner which was to have been partaken of at Carlo Varni's on the previous evening, was on this evening made a pronounced success in another famous restaurant. The Carissima expressed herself as well content with the conduct and happiness of her "two children." Harold, growing brighter and more vivacious as the evening wore on, gave no further thought to Mr. Morley Fenton or to Weir Lodge. As Leo Tarne had said, he, Harold, lived as his friend wrote—in phases. He was living now through the reaction from the previous evening's repression, from that day's greyness; and he drank not in sips, but in gulps, from the cup of neurotic exhilaration.

It was not until a rather chaotic little supper was being discussed during the early morning hours, in the dining-room of Tarne's flat, that the Weir Lodge household was mentioned. Then the speaker was Leo Tarne himself, who mockingly raised a tall Nuremberger glass of Rhein wine, and drank to "the apotheosis of appearances, coupled with the name of the Lord Bishop of Weir Lodge."

The Carissima shook with unrestrained merriment, till purple drops fell from the Burgundy glass she had raised to her lips, on to the snowy cloud of lace which nestled over her bosom. And Harold, who had once almost quarrelled with his friend over a sneering reference to Mr. Morley Fenton, drank this toast with laughing enthusiasm; and, in mockingly giving thanks for the same, he said that the one thing which prevented his adopting the cult of conventionality was "the deadly nature of the advantages it offers, the chilly misery of its rewards to faithful adherents."

When Harold unlocked the outer door of his own chambers, which he had not visited for three or four days, the dawning of another raw February day was close at hand. And Harold's only comment as he climbed into bed was:

"Well, Dr. Wainwright may be right, and Mr. Fenton may be right, as regards themselves and their lives; but for me—by gad! they have to pay too big a price for the *status entourage*, and I don't like it when it's bought. Oh, the everlasting little round of things, and the smoke in the curtains, and the locks and bolts, and musts and must nots, and—— H'm! and the Irishman isn't a piratical craft, because of——"

If continued at all, Harold's reflections must have partaken of the nature of a dream. For at this point he fell asleep, and did not open his eyes until the housekeeper knocked at his door, and made a remark about "letters."

Two hours later Harold rose, picked up three letters which lay near the door, glanced at his watch, and realized that morning lecture-time at the hospital had passed. He hesitated a moment whilst looking at the outside of his letters. Then he yawned, and returned to bed to read the said letters, comforting himself with the threadbare shibboleth as to being hanged for a sheep, and reflecting that, in any case, the day was already a broken one.

If after leaving his bed Harold had proceeded to wash, shave and dress, his subsequent actions might have been considerably influenced thereby. He did not, however. Two of his letters contained tradesmen's bills, and found their way speedily to the floor by the bedside. The third was from George Barnard.

It was brief, as were most of the barrister's letters. It said:

"DEAR HAROLD: Come round to Furnival's Inn, like a good fellow, when you leave the hospital to-morrow. I want a yarn, and we can go somewhere and feed together, and do a theatre if you like. Anyhow, come.   Affectionately,
"GEORGE BARNARD."

It had been written on the previous afternoon, and was headed "Four o'clock."

"H'm, just about the time of the Carissima's appearance at the hospital," muttered Harold, lazily. "Great Scott! how she must have startled the porters! Good old George! Wonder what he wants to see me about! I suppose I'd better go, and yet, I don't feel much like it—h'm! But George is certainly part of that straight line. And what a wearisome line it is. Yes, I'd better go. Shall I? H'm, I don't—— Hullo! who's that? Come in!"

"I'm coming, my good sybarite; I'm coming, be not afraid. But you see, I stumbled over your boots. Very clumsy of me, I know; but I'm not used to coming in with the milk as it were. How are you?"

"Ah, Leo, old man! Glad to see you. You look verdant and daisy-like as ever."

"Don't feel like it, I assure you. I had to dress in a hurry, and interview the editor of the *Green Review* this morning. Heaven knows what time he rises. Indecent, I call it, positively. Our supper-table hadn't been cleared."

"What did the gentleman want—breakfast?"

"No—copy. It appears they begin publishing that Berlin story I told you of, as a serial, on Saturday. Well, you know, the fact is I have only written four chapters of it. I didn't tell the early-rising man that; but it is so. The story is all atmosphere and colour, you know; and I really don't feel as though I can go on with it, to order. But it appears they have advertised it all over the country; and—well, they gave me a very decent cheque beforehand. That's the worst of the evening paper posters. They don't tell you when a thing like that is being advertised."

"H'm! Well, what's your idea?"

"Don't talk like that. That is how the *Green Review* man put it. I must go on with the thing, and I must have the right colour. So I am going where the colour is; and I have come round here, at great cost of—er—vitality and things, in order that you might have plenty of time to pack your bag before we start."

"But, my dear Leo, I——"

"Oh, of course, you have promised to go to Sunbury this evening, or Margate, or somewhere! But you are coming to Berlin instead."

"No, I wasn't going to say anything about Sunbury. As a matter of fact, I believe I have to dine with George Barnard, to-night. But, the hospital, my dear Leo; consider——"

"No, I won't consider the charnel-house. It will jog along without you for a week or so. You want a holiday. Harold, there is more colour and movement in one street of Berlin, than in all London and Sunbury put together. We will go and bathe our eyes in that colour, and come back seeing, breathing, living. Come with me. You mustn't say 'No' to me, Harold. You cannot say 'No' to me in this thing. I want you. And I want to show you heaps of things. You don't understand, Harold. Alone, I shall not see the colour, as I shall in showing it to you. For my sake, Harold, you must come. You will, will you not?"

It was very seldom that Leo Tarne expressed himself so emphatically as this. With every word he said Harold's eyes had been growing brighter. Now the younger man sat up in bed with parted lips, and head thrown back.

"Yes, I'll come, Leo," he said. "I'll come and see this colour with you."

So Leo Tarne gained his point, as he had known very well that he would.

CHAPTER XXV.

PHASES.

" There was a graven image of Desire
Painted with red blood on a ground of gold,
Passing between the young men and the old,
And by him Pain, whose body shone like fire,
And Pleasure, with gaunt hands that grasped their hire.

. . . .

Death stood aloof behind a gaping grate,
Upon whose lock was written *Peradventure.*"

SWINBURNE.

DURING the afternoon of that day on the morning of which Leo Tarne had interviewed the editor of the *Green Review,* George Barnard received from the hands of the worthy Mrs. Greet a telegram which informed him that Harold Foster was unable to come to him that evening.

"Thanks to Mr. Leo Tarne, I suppose," said the barrister, addressing his dog. That canine absurdity promptly rose on its haunches, and assumed a begging attitude. This senseless formula was reserved by George Barnard's dog as a fixed answer to all questions the significance of which was not obviously apparent; and it was also adopted as a means of cloaking the evasion of all requests which, if acceded to, would involve any decrease in the animal's own comfort. In this way, and by the exercise of such simple diplomacy, the mongrel dog had proved that situations fraught with all the elements of serious discomfort might be resolved into the mere acceptance from George Barnard's hands of a stale sandwich, or a more or less uninteresting biscuit.

The first post on the following morning brought to the barrister, sandwiched between a returned manuscript, a bill for coal supplied, and an invitation to subscribe to a Hamburg lottery, a brief note from Harold Foster. The note said:

"Leo Tarne has been called away on business—business on the Continent. He begged me to go with him. I have been hungering for a change lately, so thought I would go for a few days—not more than a week, I think. I will write, giving you an address. We leave this evening for the Hook of Holland. Please tell Mr. Fenton. Affectionately yours,
"HAROLD."

Once more the barrister's dog was appealed to for an opinion on a subject outside the range of that animal's own immediate concerns. And once more the stereotyped diplomacy aforementioned proved an eminently satisfactory solution, and an appetizing foretaste of breakfast to come. But the barrister's language, in the soliloquy which usually formed part of his morning toilet, was of a kind unsuited to the hearing of a well-regulated dog, and by no means creditable to even a briefless young barrister of forty-five.

Towards noon, George Barnard was appealing to a superior young native of Brixton, newly engaged as comptroller of the enquiry desk in the counting-house of Messrs. Morley Fenton, Son and Co.

"Yes, I believe Mr. Morley Fenton is in," said the comptroller, with a glance of deprecating disapproval at Barnard's soft hat and irresponsible necktie. "But this is mail-day, and after eleven o'clock Mr. Fenton never sees anyone except by appointment. Er—perhaps I——"

"No, I think not, thanks; not this morning. But

if you could spare time to tell Mr. Fenton I want to see him I'd be obliged. My name is Barnard."

"Oh, I beg your pardon! Mr. Barnard, of Barnard, Schnell and Co."

"My young friend, your imagination is too vivid—much too vivid."

The big, kindly face of the barrister wore a rather heightened colour, as he strode past the enquiry-desk to the sanctum on the door of which was painted the name of the firm's principal. The wings of George Barnard's cape-coat created quite a little commotion among loose papers lying on the desks he passed. His footsteps echoed in the humming silence of that smoothly-working temple of finance. A brisk tap at the door marked, "Mr. Morley Fenton, Private," and the privacy of the apartment it protected was broken in upon. The barrister disappeared from the mildly-surprised view of the temple's beautifully appointed machinery.

The superior young gentleman from Brixton had not departed from the truth in implying that the day was a busy one for his employer. But Mr. Morley Fenton managed to spare a little more than half an hour of this busy day for conversation, in the lemon-coloured half-light which left the greater part of his sanctum in shadow, with the caller whose flapping coat-wings had disturbed the serenity of the counting-house atmosphere. And then, somewhat to the consternation of the gentleman at the enquiry desk, Mr. Morley Fenton walked out through the office, accompanying George Barnard to the swing-doors of the entrance.

"Well," said Mr. Fenton to the barrister, "I suppose it is one of those unfortunate things which cannot be altered or remedied. We must try and counteract the influence of it when Harold comes back."

"Yes—yes," assented the barrister reflectively, as they reached the entrance doors, and paused there, where the somewhat clearer light of the outer air fell across Mr. Fenton's face. "But I'm afraid it is rather a large order, that—to counteract Mr. Leo Tarne—er—confound him! By Jove! I say, old man, do you know you're looking horribly seedy. You are really."

"Oh, I am all right, George; a little tired, perhaps—nothing more."

"H'm! You ought to go away somewhere for a rest. I couldn't see you in that little clockwork den of yours, but, by gad! I can now. You look regularly run down. It's this place with its telephones and tubes and tapes and—cussedness. Ugh! aren't you rich enough to give it up, Morley?"

"Give it up? My dear Barnard, you talk as though I were an old man."

The financier's voice changed suddenly. It was lowered, and seemed to suggest a light on the inwardness of Mr. Morley Fenton, such as, perhaps, would never have been shown to other eyes than George Barnard's.

"I've heard of prisoners, George, who have been released after serving long sentences, and who have been killed by the change—couldn't stand without their fetters, as it were, you know. Dear me, what nonsense we're talking! I think I have said before that you have no place citywards of St. Paul's, my old friend. In Lombard Street you are really demoralizing. Good-bye, and thank you very much for coming down to tell me about Harold."

"Good-bye, old chap. But I—I wish you weren't such a marvel."

And presently George Barnard was looking over the heads alike of loiterers and of scurrying human ants of the city, for the bus which should take him from the Bank to a part of London slightly less foreign to his large and easy Bohemianism.

Mr. Morley Fenton returned briskly to his "little clockwork den." He took up his pen quickly, and laid it down again slowly. He raised the finger-tips of both hands to his smooth-shaven chin. He breathed a tired, thoughtful ejaculation, and allowed his mind's eyes to sweep away back, over five-and-twenty years of "telephones and tubes and tapes and—cussedness," with all that pertained to them, to that point in his life at which, as a young man of something like Harold's age, he had crossed over to the Continent for "two or three days," in the company of a beautiful capricious woman, and had remained there during the four most reckless months of his life. He thought of the immediately subsequent six months, spent in chilly regret over the ashes of the four months' abandon. And then had come Harold, and a beautiful woman's death.

Mr. Morley Fenton's correspondence of that day lacked its customary completeness, its lucid and detailed precision.

"I suppose I am a little run down," he admitted to himself, as he was preparing to leave the office that afternoon. "H'm! Well," he added grimly, whilst buttoning the trim Chesterfield which his tailor called "a Mr. Morley Fenton coat"—"well, I must climb up again, that is all—climb up again."

And he walked out into Lombard Street, bidding his employés good-night with grave courtesy as he passed through the outer office, and hailing a hansom with the very slightest inclination of his erect head, as he stepped on to the pavement.

A week passed, during which Mr. Morley Fenton called each afternoon at the barrister's chambers in Furnival's Inn, to ask if any word had come from

Harold. None came. Another week passed in the same way, and Norah Fenton, at Weir Lodge, grew sad and inclined to sit silently and for hours at a time in the room where the 'cello was. There were at least two reasons for Norah's growing sadness. One of them was the fact that Mr. Morley Fenton's face seemed each day to develop new lines of pain and worry and weariness. Norah spoke to him of this when they were alone, and showed very loving sympathy.

A third week passed, and brought no smallest sign from Harold Foster. Then Mrs. Fenton told her husband, whilst he sat one morning sipping his coffee and glancing through some letters in his dressing-room, that she thought he was not looking very well.

"I think you work too hard, my dear," she said, bending forward to remove a speck of fluff from her husband's coat-collar. "You are not looking at all bright this morning. Why not go up North for a few days' fishing?"

"Too early, dear, for one thing," said Mr. Fenton, looking up from his letters. "And, besides, there is really nothing the matter. I may have been doing a little too much reading or writing, because I have noticed lately that my eyes have been weak. Things have looked misty to me. A little indigestion, I expect. It will pass, dear—it will pass off in a day or two."

On the following morning, George Barnard at Furnival's Inn, and Mr. Morley at Weir Lodge, each received a note of some half-dozen lines hurriedly scribbled on paper headed with the name of a famous Berlin café.

"I must apologize for not having written before, but I don't seem to have had a minute to spare; and then, of course, you knew where I was. I have had an awfully good time, though I am not very well just now. Leo has finished his business, and we leave here for London the day after to-morrow.

" Yours affectionately,
" HAROLD."

There was practically no difference between the two notes, unless, possibly, that one had, if anything, been more carelessly scribbled than the other, the most legible being Mr. Morley Fenton's.

Mr. Fenton wrote at once to Harold at his Kensington chambers, asking him to come down to Weir Lodge as soon after his arrival as possible. Mr. Fenton was, not unnaturally, a little hurt by reason of what he considered want of courtesy and lack of frankness in Harold's treatment of him.

George Barnard hurried off to Harold's rooms at what he supposed would be the time of that young man's arrival in London. Harold had not returned, but the housekeeper had received written instructions to send his letters to Mr. Leo Tarne's flat. The barrister jumped into a cab, and drove to Leo Tarne's address. The writer's servant was suave, but reticent. Yes; his master had returned to town with Mr. Foster at an unheard of hour that morning. They had breakfasted in the flat with—the servant hesitated slightly—with a friend, and they had driven almost immediately afterwards to Victoria Station. No; the man could not say what the place of their destination might be. George Barnard risked half a sovereign. The servant was not accustomed to dealing with impecunious barristers. He accepted the coin with unconsciously humorous deprecation.

" I have been instructed, sir, to forward letters for both the gentlemen to the Hotel Central, Brighton, for the rest of the week. But, of course, I cannot say, sir, whether——"

"Quite so—quite so. I'm much obliged. Good-morning."

The barrister walked slowly out into the street again.

"Oh Lord!" he muttered, with the profanity of abstraction. "The bit's between his teeth—fairly. It's young Morley Fenton over again; and, by gad! it will send old Morley Fenton off his head." The barrister paused in a covered lobby to fill his pipe. "Oh, Harold, Harold! For God's sake, my son, simmer down and—and catch hold!"

There was moisture in the big man's blue eyes, and a little break in his deep voice. The words were not well-chosen, perhaps, but a child would have felt the purity and goodness of their intention.

Having filled and lighted his pipe, pausing once or twice in the process to cough and clear his throat, George Barnard mounted an omnibus, and started off for the counting-house in Lombard Street.

On the following day, whilst discussing a twelve o'clock breakfast with Leo Tarne and the Carissima, at a window overlooking the sea and the Brighton promenade, Harold Foster glanced through two letters received from London. One was brief, distinctly reproachful, and a little curt; the other was lengthy, slightly incoherent, and brimful of affectionate appeal. The first was from Mr. Morley Fenton, and the other was from George Barnard.

"It is sad," said Leo Tarne—he was peeling grapes for the Carissima—"very sad, because in most respects he is rather a treasure of a servant; but I shall be obliged to dismiss Castor when we get back to town."

"But, my dear fellow"—of late the morning-time

of each day had found Harold Foster very languid and susceptible to irritation—"why in the world should you? You did not forbid the man to tell anyone our address; and, besides, what does it matter?"

Tarne sipped his Rüdesheimer, and continued his grape-peeling.

"There is such a thing as principle, sir," he said solemnly. "The traditions of our order—er—er— Excuse me; I haven't seen the evening paper posters for so long, I lose my fluency. You see, had I forbidden Castor to be communicative, his giving our address to a moneyed inquirer would have been mere disobedience, with an eye to pecuniary gain—a kind of commercial transaction natural enough to a man of Castor's class. But I didn't forbid him. I trusted to his discretion, and he betrayed me; I dozed in the shadow of his acuteness, and he wandered off on business, leaving me in the glare of forced publicity—a man with an address. No; I am sorry, but Castor must go. Carissima, I beg you will keep a look-out for Pollux; I don't want to have to advertise, there has been sufficient publicity. Look at our poor friend with his letters."

Harold wrote two vaguely apologetic, mistily explanatory letters after breakfast, one to Weir Lodge, the other to Furnival's Inn. In each he said that he should be back in London and at the hospital on the following Monday. Then he went out for a drive with Leo Tarne, the Carissima, and a lady friend of the Carissima's. Then came evening, and at this period, evening meant gaiety to Harold Foster, and thought for the moment only.

Just a month before, being at that time very weary of what seemed to him the essential greyness, the irritating dulness and repression of the life of which he now always thought in connection with his "straight line";

Harold Foster had yielded to Leo Tarne's persuasions to join that artist, who wrote as he, Harold, lived, in the assimilation of the vivid colour and dancing movement in which, Leo Tarne said the atmosphere of Berlin was rich.

For more than three weeks the two men had lived in the German capital a life in which nothing they desired was lacking or denied. There are great possibilities in Berlin to the lover' of carnival gaiety. There is a nearness to Prague about the place, in other senses than the geographical, which, in this particular phase of his life, was very fascinating and very poisonous to Harold Foster.

Throughout a certain portion of each day in the Berlin life, Harold had been listlessly alive to the danger of his position. While these periods lasted he had been languid, depressed, and full of weak resolutions regarding the immediate future. During these daily interludes of depression in Harold, Leo Tarne, to whom times and seasons seemed to make little or no difference, had always worked steadily, only putting aside his papers when signs of returning energy and desire for pleasure and movement, in Harold, had told him that evening was approaching.

And now that the two were in England again, Leo Tarne was in more than usually good spirits. He was in the best of health, and his story was developing very satisfactorily from day to day.

Harold Foster was in a state of highly unnatural nervous tension. His daily life was one of sharply-defined and extreme phases. As a necessary consequence, his physical condition was poor. His health was very obviously affected by the unfair demands made upon it by his nervous system. His mental powers, tossed to and fro between his phases of depression and elation, were suffering with those of the body; and decision, even in small matters, was daily becoming more and more a difficulty to be avoided if possible.

"These grey hours of yours are a huge mistake, my susceptible friend," said Leo Tarne. "If only you would live more as—as the Carissima lives, *par example*, and less as I write—— Ah!"

But Harold could not.

CHAPTER XXVI.

AFTER MANY DAYS.

"Fool! all that is, at all,
Lasts ever past recall;
Earth changes, but thy soul and God stands sure."
Rabbi Ben Ezra.

LATE on an evening which came some two weeks after Harold Foster's return to England from Berlin, the owner of Weir Lodge sat writing by the light of the green-shaded lamp which stood on his study table.

Mr. Morley Fenton alone and in his study, was always, perhaps, a rather different man to Mr. Morley Fenton the head of the smoothly-working home of finance in Lombard Street. Assuredly he was a new rendering of the impassive, gravely good-humoured man who sat at the head of the Weir Lodge dining-table.

Now the light of the green lamp, falling softly over his face, whilst leaving the fine head in shadow, showed lines of nervous anxiety and naked weariness. All the natural hollows and indurations of the face seemed deepened and darkened. The heavy eyelids hung listlessly and low, over a livid crease which seemed to reach up and after them. The lower lip, crowning as it did a chin rich in suggestion of strength, massive and enduring, protruded slightly under the silver pointed moustache, while the chin itself drooped, like a Samson shorn of his locks, a corner-stone robbed of its buttress.

All this, however, spoke of power, strength wearied,

but strength. But over and beyond this, permeating every feature with its pathos, tainting the wearied strength with its morbidity, and clouding all else in a haze of the unexplained, the light from the green lamp showed a curious instability, a fleeting, shifting weakness, a muscular and mental uncertainty, sad to see in any setting, grotesque almost in such a face.

Mr. Morley Fenton was obviously very wearied, and, some would have thought, far from being at peace with himself. Yet his daily life was stainless in the eyes of those who knew it best. His was the standing expected of Cæsar's wife. Commercially, Mr. Fenton held the unquestioning respect of London's magnates, and the envying admiration of his confidential accountant. The perfectly regulated round of his life, public and private, pursued the even tenor of its honourable way, flawless and without hitch. But on this evening in his study Mr. Morley Fenton was obviously very wearied.

The owner of Weir Lodge laid down his pen, sighed, and leaned far back in his chair to read the letter he had written. It was addressed to George Barnard, and, after a few lines devoted to generalities, this is what the letter contained:

"In a way, I believe I appreciate the wisdom of your advice to allow this phase of Harold's life to work itself out before attempting to further influence him. Indeed it would appear that we can do nothing else. And yet—and yet, old friend, look at the matter eye to eye with me, allowing your memory to run back over the years between to a certain phase in my life; a phase with a bitter end of death and birth, and shame and pain, useless regrets and exhausted energies. No one interfered with that phase in me, save you, George, with your unchanging clean strength, which was foiled by my recklessness, as a fencer's skill is sometimes rendered useless by the passionate onslaught of one who has never before handled sword or rapier. Of the moral consequences I say nothing. Of the mental effect of that dead passage in my life it is hard to judge fairly. Its physical result, I sometimes fancy, was merely indicated by that long and helpless prostration through which you nursed me. Is experience absolutely lacking in utility? Can the past, the dead past, that we pay for in blood and in tears, be of no service to the present, beyond the mere forestalling of calamity by anticipation?

"By the uninforming note which told me of his return to town, I know that Harold has been six days now in London. I have written twice, and been to his lodgings four times. You have done still more. Yet we have not even seen him. He has not been to the hospital. Leo Tarne says he has lost touch with him, after trying all he could to steady the boy. Dr. Wainwright tells me that he overheard a remark made by one of the students at Bartholomew's, who had seen Harold in a West End supper-hall after midnight on Wednesday, a remark which in its suggestiveness is as painful as it is coarse. The student said that 'Morley Fenton's foundling seems to have gone a regular mucker.'

"As you know, the annuity I purchased and settled on Harold when he left the University was three hundred a year. He must be spending a great deal more than that, which may mean that he is in the hands of some money-lender. I cannot help feeling that a personal remonstrance would appeal to Harold's better feelings. Financial aid, of course, I should never let him be without, even though I could not meet him. But beyond that, old friend, I cannot yet lay down my arms. I cannot admit to myself that I

—that we—have definitely failed in our attempt to guide and shape the course of Harold's life. I must see him, if only once, and try the weight of personal influence before I can admit failure, even to you. If that really failed, which, mind you, I cannot believe likely, then I think I should be forced to agree with you that, for the present at all events, Harold's life is something for him to thrash out alone with the devil —that you and I, George, have failed utterly to straighten out a life inherently awry. So, help me once more, old friend. Bohemia, even your hard-working, clean-lived Bohemia, has for many years been a foreign land to me, as you know; how foreign, and yet how near, perhaps you yourself can hardly guess. Find out for me, George, some place in which Harold has been seen. Then I will go alone, and meet him there. Who knows? Some hidden instinct in us both may incline Harold sufficiently toward me. At least, I can try. So much, believe me, I must do. Therefore, help me once more, and add to the debt owing you from   MORLEY FENTON."

Some warmth which had crept into his tired face in the writing of this long letter, faded out from it now, as, having folded the sheets in an addressed envelope, Mr. Morley Fenton rose from his chair, and walked slowly out from the study into the shadowy hall beyond.

"H'm, a quarter to twelve," he murmured, glancing thoughtfully at the hall clock. "I may as well go and post this. I should like Barnard to have it in the morning. Yes."

So Mr. Fenton slipped an ulster over his shoulders and put a soft hat on his head, in the vestibule, where the white light of an incandescent gas lamp shone brightly. Then he opened the outer door and stepped into the complete darkness of a cloudy April night.

Before the door had closed behind him a little ejaculation of nervous surprise escaped Mr. Fenton's lips. He appeared to have stumbled curiously, for he was bending over the doorstep, one knee on the ground, the other hugged under his left arm. He rose, however, his left hand resting on the handle of the door, and felt no sensation of pain, or of any shock.

"Very odd," he murmured, whilst walking down the silent road to the pillar-box. "I must have been thinking of something else, and missed the step, I suppose."

Ten minutes later, Mr. Fenton had completed his usual round of locking up and putting lights out, and was standing before the dead fire in the hall with a bedroom candle in his hand. He lighted the taper, and leaning forward then, turned out the last remaining jet of gas. In raising his hand to the gas bracket, Mr. Fenton accidentally brushed the candle's wick with his coat-cuff. Having been only that moment lighted, the candle was the more easily extinguished by this contact.

Mr. Fenton turned sharply on his heel to relight the taper, and in that same instant he fell at full length, and heavily, on the soft rug at his feet.

Mr. Morley Fenton's head had only grazed the floor, and beyond a slight shock, and possibly a bruise or two, he was in no way hurt by his fall. Rising, with a muttered exclamation of astonishment, to his knees, Mr. Fenton drew a match from his pocket, struck it, and, standing up then, relighted his candle.

"This is really very odd," he said with half a smile. "It is a good thing no one is about. The servants might fairly suspect something." Then the hesitating half-smile died out of Mr. Fenton's face as, moving slowly toward the stairs, candle in hand, he added, under his breath: " Does this mean growing old? Absurd! elderly men don't necessarily fall about. I wonder if it can have anything to do with that mistiness in my eyes. But it was dark when I fell, anyhow. Yes, of course, quite dark. Very odd. I think I must call on Wainwright to-morrow, and get him to prescribe something. Ah, if Harold—Tcha!"

And with something of his customary alertness and precision in walking, Mr. Fenton made his way to his room, and to bed.

"My dear, I am quite sure," said Mrs. Fenton to her husband next morning—" I am quite sure you are getting run down, and in want of a rest. I wish you would call on Dr. Wainwright and ask his opinion. You look dreadfully tired again this morning, and you were awake when I woke for a moment hours ago."

"Well, you may set your mind at rest, dear, for, oddly enough, I had made up my mind to call on Wainwright this morning; though, as Wainwright is really a nerve specialist, I suppose it would be more fitting for me to visit our own good little Brownlow."

"Ah, but Dr. Wainwright is, I am sure, the cleverer. No, go to Dr. Wainwright, dear."

"Yes, I think—yes, I will go to Wainwright."

"Well, Sad-eyes," said Mr. Fenton to Norah, as she accompanied him from the breakfast-room to the vestibule on that same morning. "I wish you could be a little brighter and happier."

"Father," said the girl, looking up into his face half reproachfully, "how can I be bright when you—when you are so ill?"

"Nonsense, sweetheart, I'm not ill. But, anyhow, I am going to call on Dr. Wainwright to-day, so that I may be assured of the fact."

"Oh, I am so glad, father dear. But you will tell me truly what he says, won't you? You'll tell me?"

"Yes, yes, inquisitive one, I'll tell you. He may tell me to take a holiday, and go away, with you to look after me. Eh? How should you like that?"

Norah's big eyes glistened and glowed lovingly. And Mr. Morley Fenton left her happier that morning than she had been for some time. So hope seemed to spring up in her heart, that she had almost asked why Harold Foster made no sign. She had almost asked, but her mind's eyes catching a flash glimpse of the barrier, and her woman's heart making a shrewd guess at the nature of one of Mr. Fenton's worries, she had refrained.

In the early afternoon Mr. Morley Fenton was ushered by a solemn man-servant into the consulting-room of Dr. Wainwright, the eminent nerve specialist and physician. He had spent some little time in the doctor's waiting-room, where a patient, one side of whose face was paralyzed, had exercised a curious influence upon him. This patient had fixed his gaze on Mr. Fenton, and had stared with weak persistence at the owner of Weir Lodge, until the time of his summons to attend in the consulting-room.

The doctor's greeting was friendly, and Mr. Morley Fenton, as he took his seat in the beautifully appointed room of judgment, spoke half apologetically of the trifling causes which had induced him to pay a professional visit.

"I think I am merely a little run down, you know, Doctor," he said. "But I promised my wife I would come and see you. By the way, a rather odd thing happened to me last night—two rather odd things, I may say."

"Oh yes! Let me hear them, Mr. Fenton. You know the value of confidence and detail to a doctor.

But, excuse me, would you mind taking this easy-chair here? Thanks, the light is so much better. It doesn't try your eyes, does it?"

"No; oh no, thanks. But just lately I have noticed a queer mistiness sometimes in my sight. A little indigestion, I fancy, or something like that."

"Quite likely—quite likely," assented the physician suavely. "And now, about last night's adventures."

Speaking in the tone of one who dismissed lightly and by the way, some trivial circumstances, Mr. Morley Fenton described his stumble outside Weir Lodge on the previous night, and, again, his fall on the hearth-rug in the hall. Immediately then, he began to speak of his eyes and general state. The doctor checked Mr. Fenton with a deft interpolation. His eyes had been fixed on his patient's face. Every vestige of the friendly host had gradually faded from out his own smooth features. He was now in every glance, in each changing expression, the shrewd, grave, watchful man of science, held in check, made suavely self-contained, by his professional aplomb, toned down and softened slightly by his life's habit as a healer.

"Permit me for one moment, Mr. Fenton," he said, leaning forward slightly in his chair. His right hand was raised, its white forefinger lifted perpendicularly. "Would you mind letting your eyes follow my finger as I move it—laterally, so. H'm! thank you. Once more, please. Ah'm! thanks. Yes—thank you."

These last exclamations were obviously the physician's vent for unspoken thoughts, the relief channels from which his perfectly trained mind drew its professional equanimity.

"If you will excuse me for one moment, I will ask you to step into another room." The doctor disappeared for perhaps two or three minutes by way of a curtained-off entrance to an apartment opening out of the consulting-room. Then he returned, and again addressed his patient. "I want to have a look at your eyes under the ophthalmoscope, Mr. Fenton, if you will come with me into my dark room here. No, permit me. Let me take your arm. I know the way, you see."

After a few minutes of careful examination, doctor and patient returned to the consulting-room.

"Well, Doctor?" inquired Mr. Morley Fenton, resuming his seat in the easy-chair by the window. He had caught some of the gravity of the physician's expression, and his face was more pale than before his visit to the dark room.

"Well, you mustn't let things frighten you, you know, but—yes, you ought to have come to me some little time back."

"You don't mean that I'm going blind, Doctor?"

Mr. Morley Fenton's voice sounded a little dry and harsh.

"Oh dear no! No, you are certainly not going blind, Mr. Fenton. Just cross your legs for a moment—at the knee—so. Thank you. H'm! exactly. Only, as I say, I should have been the better pleased to have seen you a little earlier. But you need not be alarmed about your eyes. Don't strain them in any way, you know, but—— Yes!"

The doctor was seated at his great writing-table, pen in hand.

"I want you to be very careful in taking the medicine I shall give you. By the way, let S—— make it up, will you? The dose is only one drop, you see, so that—— Yes, that's the prescription, Mr. Fenton. And I want you to come and see me—— Let me see." The doctor ran his eyes over three pages of his engagement book. "To-day is Tuesday, and—— Would this time on Friday suit? Yes; very good. Friday, then. You—er—do you go about much in the City, Mr. Fenton?"

"No, no, not very much, Doctor."

"Ah well, I would patronize the harmless necessary hansom, you know, pretty often, if I were you—always, I think, in London."

"Why, Doctor, you don't——"

"No, I don't, my dear Mr. Fenton. I don't say anything, except 'be careful.' To be sure, you are strong enough, but—well, you know, a sudden faintness or dizziness is a serious matter in a crowded London street. Business? Well, you ought to go away for a change and complete rest. But if you cannot manage that at the moment, you must just take things as easily as possible. Don't walk about, don't spend much time alone, and don't worry about anything. Mind, there must be no worrying, or I shall drive you away from town. Ha! yes—a serious matter for a city magnate. Good-morning, Mr. Fenton. Friday afternoon, two-thirty."

"Very well, Doctor."

So they parted, and it was not until Mr. Morley Fenton reached his inner sanctum in Lombard Street that he called to mind the fact that he had spent half an hour with Dr. Wainwright without once mentioning the name of Harold Foster. He had not up to that moment even thought of Harold. His interview with Dr. Wainwright had been one of some moment. Now, however, Mr. Fenton's thoughts returned sharply to the affairs of his protégé.

A telegram from George Barnard was lying on the desk of the Lombard Street sanctum. It had been opened by Mr. Fenton's secretary. The words it contained were:

"The Castanets—the old place—Arthur Street, before midnight. Shall I meet you?—GEORGE."

Ten minutes later Mr. Morley Fenton's bell rang. A clerk appeared at the door of the sanctum.

"Send that telegram off at once, Harris," said the head of the firm. And as the door of the room closed behind the silently retiring clerk, Mr. Morley Fenton placed his elbows wearily on the desk before him, and covered his face with both his hands.

The wording of the telegram written by Mr. Fenton had been as follows:

"Thank you. But I will try quite alone. Thank you.—MORLEY."

"Quite alone," muttered Mr. Morley Fenton, lowering his hands from a face set now in stern lines of determination. "Quite alone! This thing is—it is too big to divide."

CHAPTER XXVII.

BETWEEN TWO WORLDS.

> "*Festus.* What is your purpose, Aureole?
> *Paracelsus.* Oh, for purpose,
> There is no lack of precedents in a case
> Like mine ; at least, if not precisely mine,
> The case of men cast off by those they sought
> To benefit."
> *Paracelsus.*

MR. MORLEY FENTON left his office in Lombard Street shortly after four o'clock on the afternoon of his visit to Dr. Wainwright. He did this from habit, passing through the outer office only a few minutes after his usual time for so doing. Then he bethought him of the long evening to be lived through before he could hope to accomplish his that night's task. He also thought of Dr. Wainwright's curious caution about not spending much time alone. The caution was not a very necessary one as a matter of fact, for, since his interview with the physician, Mr. Fenton had felt a nervous desire for the company of some presence other than his own.

So he walked back from Lombard Street into the office, and, having reached the enquiry desk, was astonished to see its occupant leisurely lighting a cigarette. The cigarette vanished in a floorward direction. The young man from Brixton blushed, just as ordinary mortals sometimes blush, and addressed three words of incoherent apology to his blotting-pad, as Mr. Morley Fenton, with an inscrutable little smile, asked for a couple of telegram forms.

Having written a message to Weir Lodge to explain that he would be unavoidably detained in town that night, and another to Furnival's Inn, requesting George Barnard to join him at whatever time was most convenient, for dinner at his club, Mr. Morley Fenton handed the forms to the clerk, and said:

"You might take these round to the telegraph office yourself, Mr. Smithson, if you will. It will be an opportunity for a cigarette or a pipe—away from the counting-house."

A subdued and perfectly business-like titter ran, with a sound like the rustling of new bank-notes, round the desks whose occupants had not found time to begin their evening smoke. Mr. Morley Fenton bowed his grave "Good-night, gentlemen," to the staff, and passed out through the swing-doors to the street. Then, having called a hansom, he drove to his club, feeling a little more at ease than he had felt since seeing Dr. Wainwright. Arrived there, he sat down in the smoking-room to think, and to await the arrival of George Barnard.

One of the very few matters in which Mr. Morley Fenton paid no outward tribute to the canons of orthodoxy, a matter, in fact, regarding which he passively ignored the laws of custom, was attendance at any church. As was natural and to be expected in such a man, he showed every possible respect and consideration for the habits of others in this matter. Further, he was a liberal subscriber to the funds and to all interests of the church his family attended. He also contributed freely to other religious causes, and was scrupulous in the matter of providing books, sittings at church and the like, for the use of Weir Lodge domestics. Beyond this, and a quiet, courteous interest which he displayed in any church affairs spoken of by his wife and children, Mr. Morley Fenton's bearing towards matters of religion, faith, or devotion, was impassive, and absolutely inscrutable. With one exception, no member of the Weir Lodge household had ever heard the family's head refer in any way whatever to his own feeling in matters spiritual or sacred. The one exception was his wife. On an occasion, during her early married life, Mrs. Fenton had asked her husband why he did not attend a place of worship regularly?

The reply of this grave man, whose youth was buried, had been:

"That, my dear, is a matter in which I think a man cannot be held answerable even to his wife." Mr. Fenton had paused to stroke the said wife's soft hand. "If I believed that the Creator desired my presence each week at St. Ann's, believe me, I should not hesitate to give it. But I don't. Personally, I think that when the Creator chose the last day of the week as a day of rest, He did so knowing well that rest was the first essential to the state of worship. Now, I—I admit my taste is at fault—cannot rest anything like so thoroughly at St. Ann's as I can in my own study. Consequently, I think that at St. Ann's I should be farther from the state of worship than in my study. Consequently, again, I go to St. Ann's only two or three times a year, and to my study—very much more often. Believe me, dear, there is no cause for you to worry. Go you to the form of worship toward which your greater refinement inclines you, and leave me to—to come and meet you."

So Mrs. Fenton had gone to church, and Mr. Fenton had subsequently walked home with her. And the smooth daily round of both their lives had gone evenly on from that day to this evening of Mr. Fenton's meditation in the smoking-room of the Constitutional Club; if without any great joyousness, then, as certainly, without the smallest shadow of trouble or hitch, and without one reference from the head and guiding spirit of it all, to any subject akin to religion.

Now, it would have been quite foreign to Mr. Morley Fenton's nature, even on such an occasion as this evening, when he sat thinking over what he believed to be a crucial situation in his life, and in that of Harold Foster, to have looked for help from other than purely human agencies. He desired nothing of the sort.

"Harold is flesh and blood," he would have said; "and it is Harold's flesh and blood life, in a very real world of flesh and blood, with which I have to deal. The moral aspect of it is no concern of mine, and a matter about which every man must answer to himself."

But yet, as he sat there waiting for George Barnard, strong, impassive Mr. Morley Fenton grew more and more solemn, and a little over-awed, at the prospects and possibilities of the night before him. His immobility had been severely strained by the events of the past few weeks, and shaken more than he suspected by his interview in Dr. Wainwright's consulting-room. A large share of the latter half of this man's life had been devoted to the work of shaping and shielding another, younger, life, for which he held himself responsible to a stern judge—himself. To this end—the working out in Harold Foster, its living offspring, of what he, Morley Fenton, tacitly regarded as his atonement for the buried portion of his own life—had been devoted rigidly repressed habit and inclination, and a life of absolutely unremitting restraint, of discipline adhered to with unvarying fidelity.

And of late had come a consciousness of the utter

futility of all this. Of late had been forced, like steel, slowly and irresistibly, into Mr. Morley Fenton's mind, a sense of failure in his life's work, his buried half's atonement. And on this night, by his own seeking, he was to face the crisis of it all; he was to make his last throw with Fate; to grasp and hold again in safety the soul of his atonement, or to bow his head before the remorselessness of the penalty of that for which he had striven to atone—to confess himself to himself a failure, in his chosen work.

"Mr. Morley Fenton! Mr. Morley Fenton!"

Three times the page-boy's monotonous cry rang on the ears of the gentleman for whose benefit it was intended. And then Mr. Fenton rose abruptly from his chair, at the same moment that the boy, having recognised the owner of the name he cried, stepped towards him.

"Mr. George Barnard wishes to see you, sir."

"Yes. Quite right. I'll come down. Is Mr. Barnard in the waiting-room?"

"Yes, sir."

Mr. Morley Fenton gained in spirits and in confidence as he sat talking over dinner with the barrister. The two men agreed tacitly in appearing to ignore the subject uppermost in the minds of both, until late in the evening, when they occupied a secluded corner of the great smoking-room.

"This place is too big, Morley. It's like belonging to a Crystal Palace."

"It is a big place, but a good club, Barnard, a very good club," replied Mr. Fenton with disproportionate seriousness. "I dare say you think it peculiar," he continued, without any pause, "that I do not ask you to come with me to-night?"

"Not at all; not a bit, old man, I assure you."

Anything approaching to absence of reserve in Mr.

Morley Fenton was calculated to force respectful consideration from a far less understanding man than big, clean-minded George Barnard.

"Thank you," resumed Mr. Fenton. "After all, I might have known that you would know. You can guess, perhaps, as no one else could, how all these twenty-five years I have lived—fixedly, George—in one world; but yet near enough to its edge to see always, as I walked along, the many-coloured beach of another world, here in London. Once or twice visitors from that world, wanderers, have passed me here in this. But I have made no sign. I have been just a sort of passing shade to them—just a shade. And now that I am going to step back over the edge I must do it alone, George. I—it's a very naked thing, you see."

"Yes, yes; I know. Of course you will go alone. And I will wait here for you, if you like."

"No, I have taken rooms at the hotel—across the square, you know. You see, I can't take Harold down to Sunbury to-night. I shall be very glad if you will stay and sleep there, or go back to Furnival's Inn, as you think best."

"Yes. All right. Anyhow, I'll wait and meet you when you come back. It—it's rather weird that it should be the Castanets, of all places, isn't it? But, to be sure, there's not much likelihood of any of its present frequenters—er——"

"Being old enough habitues to remember my day? No, I don't think so, George; I don't think so. But, perhaps, the chance may be one reason why I don't want you to——"

"Exactly. And, I say, it's after eleven o'clock. Did you say you had engaged these rooms?"

"Yes. I sent word from here. I will walk there with you now."

Mr. Fenton rose from his chair, a little unsteadily, and rested one hand on the barrister's arm.

"It is strange how this thing affects me," he said. "I'm afraid I am not so strong as I was, nothing like so strong as I was, George."

Mr. Morley Fenton had not told the barrister of his visit to Dr. Wainwright. George Barnard smiled cheerily as he took his friend's arm, and walked with him down the great staircase to the entrance hall of the club house. The man from Furnival's Inn was very anxious about his friend's intended meeting with Harold Foster, and had far less faith in it as a means of regaining the lost hold upon the younger man, than had Mr. Fenton. He looked at the situation with the added clearness of vision of a comparatively outside point of view. Therefore, hoping little, he smiled cheerily, and, fearing much, he spoke hopefully.

The two parted in the lobby of the hotel in which Mr. Fenton had engaged rooms, the barrister promising to wait there for his friend's return.

"And then we'll all three have some supper together," said Barnard.

"Yes, yes," replied Mr. Fenton thoughtfully. "And to-morrow I may possibly go away somewhere with Harold. I am a little run down, as you told me the other day. My life has not been a very easy one—of late, anyhow. But—to-night is not going to prove it lived in vain. That could hardly be, George."

"Why, no!" The barrister spoke reassuringly, but a glance at his friend's face showed him that no reassurance was needed. The strong mouth was settling itself in firm lines now, the eyes seemed clearer, brighter than before, and growing, strengthening determination was asserting itself, quietly supreme, over all Mr. Morley Fenton's face.

"No, that shall not be. Good-bye for a little while, George."

Mr. Morley Fenton stepped briskly across the pavement and into a cab which the hotel porter had called for him.

"Drive to the Cas—to the corner of Arthur Street and Regent Street, Cabby."

"Yessir."

The trap in the roof of the cab was closed, and Mr. Morley Fenton started on his way to a place the very name of which had not passed his lips for twenty years.

CHAPTER XXVIII.

"MORLEY FENTON'S FOUNDLING."

"Now what is it?—returns
The question—heartens so this losel that he spurns
All we so prize? I want put down in black and white,
What compensating joy, unknown and infinite,
Turns lawlessness to law, makes destitution—wealth,
Vice—virtue, and disease of soul and body—health?

Ah, the slow shake of head, the melancholy smile,
The sigh almost a sob!"
Fifine at the Fair.

GEORGE BARNARD filled his pipe, and sat down to wait as patiently as might be for his friend's return to the hotel. The barrister had not much hope of seeing Harold Foster that night.

Mr. Morley Fenton drove westward towards the Castanets.

Arrived at the corner of Arthur Street, Mr. Fenton paid his cabman, but told the man that if he were inclined to wait for half an hour, he might probably earn a return fare. The man said he would wait, and looked curiously after Mr. Fenton's retreating figure as it disappeared into the darkness of the quiet side street. Presently this tall, erect figure reappeared to the watchful gaze of the cabman, a couple of hundred yards away and in the blaze of light which fell across the pavement from the entrance to the Castanets.

"Well, I'm blowed!" muttered the cabman, feeling in his pocket for pipe and matches. "Well, I'm damned!" he added, with matter-of-fact profanity, as he struck a match on the rail behind him. And, having lighted his pipe, the cabman dismissed the subject of his ejaculatory comment by saying, with Cockney readiness of deduction, "And a' Sundays 'e 'ands round the plate."

The first obstacle which presented itself to Mr. Morley Fenton was one for which he had quite forgotten to provide.

"Can't let you in, sir, without someone introduces you. You're not a member, sir, are you?"

"A—no; I am not a member at present, I think, but—is M. Dupuy, the manager, here?"

"M. Dewpwee's son is here, sir."

"Ah—Alphonse, eh?"

"Yes, sir."

"Just give him this card, will you? Ask him to —to hark back a good bit, and tell him Mr. Fenton is waiting, will you? Or—wait. Is Mr. Foster in the house. You know Mr. Foster, don't you?"

"Yes, sir. Mr. Foster is upstairs, sir." The porter felt that he was not dealing with a stranger. "You had better step in, sir. I'll call Moosyer Dewpwee."

"Thank you. Yes, I'll come in."

Mr. Morley Fenton stood waiting before a bright fire which burned in the little entrance hall. Presently a fussy little Frenchman, with an embroidered shirtfront and braided evening clothes, tripped forward from a door at the far end of the hall, and with a quick comprehensive glance—the man had been educated in the study of appearances—advanced to Mr. Morley Fenton. The Frenchman's scrutiny brought recognition with it, and some recollection. It was a satisfactory scrutiny to him, and would have been sufficient to justify recognition, even had no vestige of recollection supported it.

"Ah, it ees, it ees," said the man of embroidery,

with no little dramatic force. " I am vare glad to zee you, Meestah Fenton. You will again, ze amus——"

"Yes, yes, quite so, Alphonse—quite so. In the meantime, just for this evening, I am not looking for amusement. To-morrow, perhaps," said Mr. Morley Fenton with suave mendacity. " But to-night I want your assistance."

" Ah, yes, yes, yes—my *assistance*; quite the same as long ago—ees it not so? "

" Not quite, Alphonse," said Mr. Fenton—" not quite the same. However, Mr. Foster is supping here to-night, is he not? "

" Oui."

" In the supper hall? "

" Ah no. En particulier. Mr. Foster has only one friend to-night—ze leetle sister of her, it ees."

" Eh? Oh, someone's little sister, is it? Well, look here, Alphonse, I want you to show me in to Mr. Foster. I—I fancy he half expects me, you know. Which room is he supping in? "

" Ze Fleur-de-lys. He—how you say?—he expect you, eh? "

" Yes—yes, I think he expects me—a little, you know. Anyhow, that will be all right, Alphonse. He will not mind my coming."

So, Alphonse tripping before, with the air of a master of ceremonies, Mr. Morley Fenton walked up the staircase, and down a corridor, every panel in the wainscoted sides of which touched with recollection's cold finger upon some tightly-strung nerve in the grave man who had viewed them so differently, his blood at such an opposite temperature, more than twenty years before.

Alphonse tapped airily at the door of the *chambre fleur-de-lys*. The man who felt like a spirit from another world, haunting now this place of dead memories of hot young blood, dazzling lights, and dancing movement, heard a voice which he barely recognised, and the words: "Come in!"

Then he stepped forward, rigid, erect, colder than any waif in London that night, and felt the door of the room closed behind him by Alphonse.

The room was small, dainty, brilliantly lighted, and upholstered in pale blue and silver, with a fresco of fleur-de-lys, and the atmosphere of a flower-filled hothouse. In its centre, and immediately under a handsome candelabra, stood the supper-table, a sparkling study of flowers, cut glass, plate, and red wine—sparkling Pommard it was—on snowy damask.

A fair-haired woman, with dancing eyes and a curious Dresden-china-like daintiness about her skin and about the flowered folds of her dress, sat at the supper-table, facing the door of the room. The tiniest of yellow cigarettes was between her rather doll-like lips, and her glass was raised and held towards that of her companion. This woman might have been one or two and twenty years in age. But, on the other hand, there were pretty, puckered little lines about her mouth and eyes which might have been the developments of ten or twelve years more than that. On the whole she was a charming picture—very like a piquant figure in a French pastoral print.

Harold Foster sat facing her. He turned abruptly in his chair and glanced sharply over one shoulder, as the door of the apartment closed behind Mr. Morley Fenton's spare figure. Then he started forward, and to his feet, overturning a glass of wine as he did so. The generous wine ran down the snowy cloth's out-curving side, like blood on a woman's arm.

"Good God!" he exclaimed. "Mr. Fenton!"

Then he nervously jerked his chair aside, and

stepped clear of the supper-table. The fingers of his right hand were twisted tightly in the folds of a napkin. Harold was facing the man to whom he owed many things.

"Forgive my coming uninvited, Harold. I have tried to find you at your lodgings, but without success. I heard that you were sometimes here in the evening, so came in, because—I am particularly anxious to have a chat with you."

The lightsome eyes of the girl who suggested Dresden china shepherdesses, widened and widened in their gaze at the new-comer. Her red lips parted, the tiny Russian cigarette still clinging to the under-lip, like the yellow pistil one may see in the bells of some cactus flowers. Mr. Morley Fenton's words cut incisively through the perfumed air of the brilliant little room. Both men remained standing. Harold Foster's face was flushed now, with wine and the heat of the room. Something which looked like anger and resentment blazed out through the filmy moisture of his blue eyes, accentuating the fact that they were bloodshot, and a little sunken, between purple-streaked rims. There was a certain carelessness in his dress—a creased white tie, two wine spots on his shirt-front, grey lines round the button-holes and collar of his dress-coat—which, in so young and so handsome a man, was suggestive of reckless living. His lips twitched in anger or nervousness when they parted, and the words which came from them sounded as though they were uttered merely to give the speaker cover behind which to collect himself—to check and restrain other words which struggled to free themselves.

"I have left my old lodgings," he said. "And I don't think you would be interested in my present residence or way of living."

"You might have given me an opportunity of

trying, Harold. I have some knowledge of more kinds of life than one."

"Evidently, sir!"

The end of Harold Foster's restraint was very near at hand, exactly how near Mr. Morley Fenton recognised more clearly than did Harold himself. Mr. Fenton was always a quick thinker. Essentially man of the world and worldly, he was thinking luminously now, and with rapidity born of nervous tension. He modified the staccato incisiveness of his utterance, lowering and broadening his voice slightly.

"I have apologized for my intrusion, Harold. Af'er all, some liberty I may claim as an old friend. I fear I must not ask now for the—the *tête-à-tête* I had looked forward to. But, perhaps—— May I talk in the presence of this lady?"

Mr. Morley Fenton bowed with old-world grace in the direction of Harold's companion. Here a touch of something more human than all that had as yet transpired, relieved the tension of the atmosphere. A woman's intuition told the Dresden shepherdess that the new-comer was no friend to her or to her interests. A woman's curiosity made her wishful to hear and see more of the relations between her cavalier and his friend. A woman's vanity—and, possibly, some truer, better quality—forced her to return some consideration for the dignified courtliness shown her by the handsome, grey-haired stranger. She responded in her own kind:

"Oh, I say, you know—nonsense, you two! Hal, why don't you ask your friend to sit down and have a glass of wine, if he wants to talk to you? And if you don't care to talk in front of me, I'll go somewhere else till you've finished. And if you won't talk at all, I'll go away altogether. What nonsense! Why don't you both sit down? Ah, footsak!"

With this curious exclamation—presumably a sort of toast—the Dresden shepherdess raised her glass to her lips and lowered it more than half emptied, thereby doing a good deal towards relaxing the strain of the men's attitude each to each.

"I beg you'll stay where you are," said Harold, turning abruptly towards the fair woman.

Bowing again, with the slightest inflection of a smile—his friend had not introduced him—towards Harold's companion, Mr. Morley Fenton placed his hand hesitatingly on the back of a chair which stood beside the door.

"You will permit me?" he said, turning to Harold.

"Oh, please do as you wish. I have an engagement elsewhere very shortly," said Harold; ungraciously enough, but still speaking under strong restraint.

Following up the line of thought which had caused him to modulate his voice after his first few remarks, Mr. Morley Fenton, having seated himself, began now to speak with some easiness, and as though attaching no great weight to his own words.

"You see, Harold, this is your final year at the hospital, and I cannot help following that with interest and some trepidation. I was made a little anxious by your lengthened stay on the Continent with Leo Tarne. And then, when you returned to London, only to immediately set off for somewhere else, and I had a quite plaintive letter about your missed opportunities and spoiled prospects from Dr. Wainwright, I—well, I began to think something must be done, you know."

"Surely this is hardly a suitable time or opportunity for a discussion about my hospital work," said Harold Foster, with ominous calm in his voice, and colour in his somewhat sunken cheeks.

"No; perhaps not. But you see, I had no choice

of opportunities. Now, Harold, for the sake of all the years of all your life—believe me, I have watched them all carefully enough—listen to me to-night, and let me tell you what is in my mind. As a man of the world you might fairly grant some consideration to advice which comes from an experience of double the length of your own. There are some affairs of a man's life, Harold, which he may allow to be guided by caprice, developed according to his whim or desire of each passing moment. There are other matters, again, in which sanity, the world's good-will, and the eternal fitness of things, all demand that a man shall express himself clearly, take a definite stand, and abide by it. These are the portions of a man's life which affect the community. These are the things he is judged on. The adoption of a profession is one of these latter things, one of the matters of definite success or failure. The initiatory steps necessitate a certain prominence, exposure of a clear front to judgment. The thing achieved and decided, much of a man's life may be allowed to subside into the behind-the-curtain freedom with which the world has nothing to do."

"All men may not care for the verdicts of this world you speak of," said Harold, nervously twisting and untwisting his finger-napkin. "Some men may be indifferent utterly, to this question of judgment."

"No; pardon me! I thought I had explained that. In the matters which whims may rule—yes. In this matter—no. A man must live the life he is born to, whether he will or no. The question is how to make it the best possible which its scope permits. The answer is, by careful decision in the important issues, absolute adherence to those decisions when formed, and the sacrifice of smaller matters—whims and the like—in the carrying to achievement of the greater issues."

Harold jerked his watch from his pocket.

"I cannot miss my engagement," he said brusquely.

Mr. Morley Fenton permitted himself to smile slightly. And that was an error of judgment surprising in so astute a man.

"That is precisely the attitude which policy demands of a man in relation to the important steps of which I have spoken. You feel its necessity in the matter of your engagement, and—— But you follow me, I am sure."

Harold muttered something which might have been assent to Mr. Fenton's last remark, but which sounded to the Dresden shepherdess very like, "Damn policy!" Mr. Morley Fenton believed it to be muttered assent. So he continued speaking. The Dresden shepherdess smiled.

"Harold, you know that I can have no other motive than a desire to help you, when I say that the point in your life, which you are now making subsidiary to the behind-curtain trifles, is one of the junction points at which the world you live in demands definite action—that application which holds in its hands success or failure."

Harold moved uneasily. He was sitting on the extreme edge of his chair.

"If I have any knowledge of men and women," continued Mr. Morley Fenton, his didactic tone being unconscious, and induced by depth of feeling and strength of meaning, "this lady will not in any way misconstrue my intention, or take umbrage at my words, when I say that common-sense demands your turning your back just now on—on"—Mr. Fenton embraced the Castanets and its atmosphere with a meaning wave of one hand, a gesture which obviously included the Dresden shepherdess—"you understand me—on this life of the past month or two. Wisdom, policy, your place in the only world you have at present, your whole life's future, demands it, Harold. And I want you to see it, and—and accede. I beg you to."

Harold raised his head with a gesture of overwhelming impatience.

"Some of the secondary matters, the trifles you dismiss so lightly," he said explosively, " may be of infinitely more importance to me than the matters of policy which you esteem so highly. And it is my life —mine—which you are—of which you speak."

Mr. Morley Fenton drew a long, sighing breath. Nervousness, anxiety, impatience and regret were all represented in Mr. Fenton's sigh.

"It is, Harold; it is your life, and not mine, of which I am speaking. But you see, when a man has passed a certain point, his own life is not always a matter so near and dear to him as some other life may be."

Then Mr. Fenton's hand moved forward and upward, as though he would have touched Harold Foster, and his voice rose and broadened in scope and volume, as he said:

" Look at this thing eye to eye with me, Harold, as a man of the real, workaday world. Good God! Don't let us sit here—in this place, stabbing each other with childish cross questions and crooked answers. Put the little sparkling toy—a pretty thing for idle moments, this life, I know—put it aside, Harold, in the face of a flesh-and-blood crisis. Do I ask so very much? Am I inhuman—bloodless—unreasonable? No! Believe me, I know it all. Yes, all of it. See! Be a man of parts, restraint, and policy. Look at your life; not at a London season. I don't ask renunciation, and a life of denial. Nothing of the sort. I ask the momentary exercise of a little of the oil that makes the wheels of the world go round; a little simple policy, for a solid, tangible, permanent end; a knuckling down to finish an almost completed task. And the world—the world of success and honour and repute—which, mind you, is the world which supplies the toys that glitter—the real, great world asks no more than this that I ask. Make this little effort. Take your stand. And then—oh! such slight tribute then, gives you perfect freedom! And without the light gold shackles, is no freedom worth the name. The whims and trifling of a season—— Tsh! Come away with me, now, Harold. You know me. Remember Bishop Blougram. Pay the little price. Put the moment behind you, for the sake of the years. Don't you see it? It is all so clear. For God's sake, Harold, come away with me—now!"

Mr. Morley Fenton had risen to his feet, one hand extended as though to take Harold's, his eyes glowing as perhaps they had not glowed since he was last in the Castanets. The Dresden shepherdess was bending forward, her dainty chin pillowed on one little biscuit-coloured palm, her lips parted, her eyes dancing, and her breast rising and falling with her every quick-drawn breath. She had not heard talk like this before, and her experience, of its kind, was varied, and one covering no inconsiderable period; even as time is reckoned in the world of which Weir Lodge, for instance, was a part.

Harold Foster had for some minutes been moving irritably on his chair, his lips twitching, and his fingers twining in and out the creased and crumpled serviette which he still held. Half a dozen times he had been on the verge of an angry interruption. His sense of proportion was distorted out of all reason by anger; his old feeling of respect for Mr. Morley Fenton was swallowed up completely by his nervous exasperation. Now, as Mr. Fenton ceased speaking, Harold jumped to his feet, and, with hands springing to gesticulation, faced the man of whom he had thought as of a guardian.

"Yes," he said, "I see it all, and hate it for its sordidness." There was too much hysteria to admit of perfect truth in the chord his voice struck; but it rang out clear and loud, and penetrated every corner of the brilliant little fleur-de-lys room. "I do remember Bishop Blougram, and hate him for the damned smugness of his oily adherence to the faith which brought old wines, and many-coursed dinners, and hand-kissing. Faugh! for his policy, do you understand? and the lying, white-handed diplomacy which you would have me emulate. You join with more courtesy in his sneer at the literary man—his guest. And wherein lay his superiority, and all that gave him the power to sneer, and the snobbishness? Why, in the Bishop's princely revenues, the reward of your vaunted diplomacy, and his shameless hypocrisy. Ah, Mr. Morley Fenton, the world's body-grinding old wheels might stop for want of oil, if the world were peopled with men like me; but I would rather live one hour of my purposeless, trifling life, as you see it—yes, here in this place you despise so—than earn a century of the smug respectability you prize. You threaten me with your august world's disapproval. Well, I care not one curse for your world or its disapproval. You ask me to throw aside the moment which I love for its colour, for ·the sake of those years in the world which I loathe for its drabness. You tell me that a little grubbing in the drabness now, will make it safe and possible for me to indulge my whim to live according to the lights of my nature—behind certain fences of diplomatic humbug, of course—later on. Well you see, I have the moment, which is natural and bright to me; I don't want the grubbing even temporarily, and I won't hide behind those white-washed fences, not for an eternity of indulgence, or for any other reward which Blougram and his world could devise under the inspiration of beeswinged port. That's my childish ignorance, my vulgar want of diplomacy. Granted. But it's mine—mine! And if God made me, then He made me so—just so, not otherwise. And if I choose to live my life as He made it and I feel it, in the world He put me in as I see it—why then that's my affair, not yours or Blougram's. He with his pulpit and his port—his ' soul titillations'; you with your beautiful house, your honour, and high-standing, those things you value highest—can't you both go on living the life you love and hold best, leaving me in peace to run through my little, insignificant, unpolitic life with the—the trifles I love best? You can, but you won't, you say? You know best, and for my sake—— Fiddle-de-dee, and *sauve qui peut!* It is I who have to lead my life, not you. Oh God! if You can really hear and see little things like me, and great, hill-faced things like—like Bishop Blougram, who made wine and oil for his table out of folks' duty to Your Church; if You really know of me at all, and if my life and Your beautiful world as I see them, are not my life and Your beautiful world as You made them, then why am I not given the power to see things as they are? Anyhow, this is as I see them—so I live. It is not wise maybe, or politic, or diplomatic; but at least it is not a lie. It is really me. And lie and truckle for the approval of your other world, which I hate, I will not! And that is my last word, Mr. Morley Fenton. If I am ungrateful I am sorry for it. Perhaps I, too, have my little conscience. If I am rude, I ask pardon for that. And—and I leave you to say, sir, whether you or I shall be the first to leave this room."

Harold stepped forward, and opened the door of

the fleur-de-lys room. Mr. Morley Fenton's head was bent low, and as he raised it for a moment his face showed grey and sunken, and his eyes seemed to hold no light. His voice, too, when he spoke sounded empty, fleshless.

"And that is your last word—to me, Harold?"

"Now, and on such a subject always—yes!"

The young man was pale, and seemed to have grown calm and firm. He spoke with all the blind finality of the man who has had his say, and has resisted all persuasion to relinquish his conviction.

"Then I must go. Good-night, Harold!"

"Good-bye, sir!"

Mr. Morley Fenton, his shoulders sunken, and his head bowed, walked slowly from the room, and down the brilliantly lighted corridor, once so familiar to him, to the entrance-hall and the street beyond.

And talkative, volatile Alphonse, he of the embroidered linen and the mincing gait, meeting his old patron in the entrance-hall, bowed, and drew aside with wide, staring eyes, but spoke never a word.

"What did you say his name was?" asked the fair woman in the fleur-de-lys room. There were tears hanging between the lashes of her blue eyes. But her voice was firm enough.

"What earthly interest can his name have for you, child?" said Harold Foster wearily.

"I know him, I'm certain I know him; and I shall remember by-and-by."

"Nonsense, little one; that's impossible. He is—or was—my guardian, my adopted father, and his name is Morley Fenton."

"Morley Fenton, Morley Fenton? Ah!" The Dresden shepherdess tapped her forehead with two taper fingers. "Well, presently, you will see, I shall remember all about him. I remember him, and his name too, now."

When Mr. Morley Fenton drove up to the entrance of the hotel in which he had left George Barnard, the barrister was waiting beside the hall-fire, and Big Ben was chiming half-past one.

The barrister walked slowly upstairs, his old friend's arm linked in his. His was that beautiful sympathy of silence which, perhaps, can only exist between men who have been for many years friends. Supper was laid for three in one of the rooms engaged by Mr. Fenton. The barrister poured out a glass of wine for his friend. Mr. Fenton shook his head.

"No, thanks, George. It is finished. He bade me good-bye. I have failed utterly. We have quite failed, George. And this is the end of it."

"We did our best, old man. We—we are only men, you know. There's Someone else watching over him."

"Ah yes! Yes, George, you always found comfort in that idea, didn't you? A beautiful idea, very beautiful, for a man who can feel it."

"Look here, Morley, old man, have a little supper, and a smoke afterwards with me."

"Not to-night, George; not to-night. To-morrow. I would rather be left alone now. Forgive me, old friend, I would really. There's plenty of time for us to talk to-morrow—plenty of time. I have several things to tell you. And now I am going to my room. Good-night, George."

"Good-night, old chap! I say—damn it, you know! God bless you, Morley—good-night!"

So they parted.

CHAPTER XXIX.

HAROLD FOSTER LOSES HIS WAY.

"For they verily for a few days chastened us after their own pleasure ; but He for our profit, that we might be partakers of His holiness."—*The Epistle of Paul to the Hebrews.*

FOR many minutes after Mr. Morley Fenton's departure from the *chambre fleur-de-lys*, the chill which had crept over Harold Foster remained a potent factor in the atmosphere of the little silver-and-blue apartment.

Then Harold left the place, with his companion, to keep that "engagement" of which he had spoken. This was the beginning of a very riotous night, or morning—a reckless round of visits to a number of gaily-coloured temples of recklessness in that small, lurid patch which represents London's forcing-bed of London's rankest growths. This is a field in which are sown the seeds of disease, moral, physical, and mental —a bed in which upthrusting wild oats jostle and choke down timid conscience buds; a swamp thinly covered by verdure of the greenest, and ablaze with exotic growths and colouring—a patch of the very air above which is cloudy with the flying pollen of sorrows born of Satiety by Pleasure.

The other, big, workaday world—the moorland— was thronged and busy when Harold Foster turned from the day-paled purple lights to take such rest as comes with loss of consciousness in tossing, dream-clouded slumber.

Another day had passed and had given way to

reality-cloaking evening, before Harold moved out again into the world before the curtain. Then, by merest chance, and as he passed out of the entrance to a Turkish bath house, he happened across a fellow-student at St. Bartholomew's, the student who had spoken of "that Morley Fenton's foundling."

"Hullo, Foster!" said the student. "Buck up, old man; you're looking like a corpse! Is this true—this business about Mr. Morley Fenton?"

"Is what true?"

"Why, what the papers say about his illness, you know. I only this minute saw it in the *St. James's* here."

"Let me see."

Harold had been pale enough before. He was a little whiter now, and his hands shook as he took the medical student's evening paper and unfolded it in the light from the entrance to the baths he had just left.

"No, last page but one, near the bottom," said the student. "I expect all the papers will give some version of it, you know."

But Harold Foster was no longer conscious that his fellow-student was speaking. He was reading the paragraph about Mr. Fenton; and this is what it said:

"Financial circles in the City, and his own long list of friends and acquaintances, will very much regret to hear of the serious illness of Mr. Morley Fenton, of the well-known Lombard Street firm of Messrs. Morley Fenton, Son and Co. Being detained in town until a late hour last evening, it appears that the gentleman in question decided to sleep at ——'s Hotel, in Trafalgar Square. Mr. Fenton was late in retiring, and was accompanied by an old friend, a barrister, who also slept in the hotel. This gentleman it was who, having entered Mr. Fenton's room for the purpose of waking him this morning, discovered that he was very seriously ill, and, we believe, in a helpless condition. Dr. Wainwright, the eminent Cavendish Square physician, was shortly afterwards in attendance, and news of the patient's condition was sent at once to Sunbury, where Mr. Morley Fenton has for many years lived with his wife and family. Dr. Wainwright naturally showed some reticence in speaking of Mr. Fenton's condition, but we gather that the illness is something in the nature of a paralytic seizure—lateral sclerosis, it is thought—and that it will for a few days prevent Mr. Morley Fenton's removal to his own home. Mrs. Fenton, with one of her daughters, has taken rooms at ——'s Hotel, and a professional nurse is in attendance. Mr. Fenton is the head and principal of the Lombard Street house, and is regarded as one of the ablest and most successful financiers in the City."

" I wonder you hadn't seen all the papers by now," said the student from Bartholomew's, as Harold Foster raised his eyes, allowing one half the paper to fall from his hands to the pavement. " I suppose it's exaggerated a bit, eh? I bet old Wainwright never mentioned ' sclerosis.' He's not fond enough of reporters. But I suppose Mr. Fenton must be pretty bad, isn't he? "

" Eh? Yes—I don't know. Excuse me, Yorke. I—I've got an engagement. Good-night! "

" Oh, good-night, Foster."

Harold strode off down the busy street.

" 'Pon my soul, I don't believe he knew anything about it," muttered the young man from Bartholomew's. " He certainly is going the pace. Never shows his face at Bart's; and every night—— I wonder where he gets the cash? Heigho! it's good to be an ' able financier's ' foundling! Shouldn't be surprised if he was—really."

HAROLD FOSTER LOSES HIS WAY. 273

The student went into the Turkish baths, and Harold Foster wandered rather aimlessly into Regent Street.

His impulse in leaving the man from Bartholomew's had been to proceed at once to the Trafalgar Square hotel, and ask to see the man whom he had regarded in the light of a father. Then quickly he had recalled the stormy interview of the previous night, his own passionate resentment of Mr. Morley Fenton's attitude, and the bitter, hopelessly final note which had been struck between them in their parting at the door of the *chambre fleur-de-lys*.

"No," he muttered, pausing on the curb-stone at a crowded corner—"no, I'm about the last man he will want to see—or any of the others. God! how they will hate me! George surely knows about last night; and, of course, they will all want to know where Mr. Fenton had been before going to bed. Paralysis, paralysis—Mr. Morley Fenton paralyzed! The thing's not possible; that's the paper's mistake. Nervous exhaustion; he's overworked—run down—and last night upset him. And yet—sclerosis! Good Lord!"

The wheel of a passing cab brushed one of Harold's coat-sleeves.

"Where yer goin', clumsy?" jeered the driver of the cab.

"Eh—what? I beg your pardon," muttered Harold to the street. And he wandered on vaguely, indefinitely, past Piccadilly Circus and Leicester Square, down Long Acre, and so to Bloomsbury and the old Court end of the town.

He paused at last outside a house in which Amelia may have entertained Becky Sharpe, and became conscious that rain was driving against his shirt-front—he was in evening dress—and that the time of an appointment he had made with his companion of the previous evening must be long since past. With a murmured protest against the futility of things, he raised his hands to button the neck of his light evening cape. Then he walked on to the Russell Square cab-rank, and stepped into a hansom.

"Thirteen, Dalmain Crescent, Cabby," he said shortly. "Quickly as you can."

"Yes, sir," said the man.

"Window!" cried Harold impatiently, when the driver had whipped up his horse, and half the length of Southampton Row had been traversed.

The window was lowered, and Harold, leaning far back in one corner, remained without moving a muscle until the cab drew up outside the house in which the Dresden shepherdess occupied a flat. The fair woman said nothing as to Harold's unpunctuality, but led him to the fire in her florid little sitting-room.

"You look as though you'd seen a ghost," she said, "a wet one. But sit down. I've got news for you. I've remembered all about your friend, as I said I should. Look here! Whose writing is that?"

The Dresden shepherdess slipped into Harold's outstretched hand an envelope, yellow with age and dust, but clearly addressed in firm, distinctive handwriting to "Miss Blair, Ivy Cottage, Barford, Surrey." The name of Harold's companion was May Blair.

"Great Scott! That's Mr. Fenton's writing," said Harold excitedly. "You don't mean to say he ever wrote to you, child?"

"No, I was only ten years old when that was written. That was written to my sister, who died. You know, I've spoken to you about my sister Lottie. That was written to her over five-and-twenty years ago— only a week before she died—before her child was born. And it was written by Mr. Morley Fenton, just after he brought Lottie back from abroad. I can remember him as well as possible. How we hated him!"

"Well, but——"

"Yes, I know. I am older than you think. Now, look here, Hal, have you any relations?"

"No—not one, that I know of."

"And who were your father and mother?"

"My mother died when I was born, and my father died soon after. I don't know who they were, except that Mr. Fenton was my father's best friend."

"When is your birthday, Hal?"

"The second of May. That's next Thursday. Why?"

"Yes—yes. And your old nurse was a Scotch woman, called Mary Crichton. And the young nurse who weaned you was a Lizzie Johnson. I know the whole thing. And in this letter Mr. Morley Fenton said that if her child was a boy, it should be called Harold—Harold Foster, because Foster was the name they had taken abroad, Hal."

"Good God, child, don't say things like that! You don't know—— You—— My God! I went to see old Mary Crichton, in Barford, two years ago. But not at Ivy Cottage. She's dead now. I——"

"You were brought up at Barford, Hal. You were—you were her child; and Mr. Morley Fenton is your father, as well as your guardian. I remember him well enough, now. I've a bundle of these letters, Hal. I had them when my mother died. But she would never mention Mr. Morley Fenton's name. He wanted to give her a house, but she wouldn't take it. You know that pearl cross I sometimes wear?"

Harold stared mechanically.

"Well, your father gave that to Lottie—to your mother. See—you can have this letter. Do you understand all I'm telling you?"

The Dresden shepherdess, who looked far more of a girl than a woman, placed one of her little hands with a familiar, *bon camarade* gesture, on Harold's neck. He was sitting on a low chair before the fire. She was standing beside him. As her soft hand touched his neck, Harold threw back his head, and started abruptly to his feet. He had been staring vacantly into the bright fire. The touch of her woman's skin seemed to tear vacancy's veil from his eyes, to bring with it a whole world of reality, consciousness of the things that are. Harold knew. The idea of further inquiry seemed absurd. He felt, in every fibre of him, that what this dainty, doll-like woman at his side had said was truth—absolute truth. This pretty, laughing comrade, with her laces and perfumes, her love of gaiety, her reckless abandon to his whims, his recklessness; she had really known his dead mother; the dead woman—wife, in God's eyes, of Mr. Morley Fenton. And Mr. Morley Fenton, the grave, respected man of high repute and unquestioned position, was his father, and had known it all these years. George Barnard, too. Yes, he must have known it. And on the previous night he had parted, finally, with this grave, worldly man. They had said "Good-bye!" with great bitterness, and in the presence of this fair woman who now touched his neck—this companion of his reckless life, who was really——

"My God! Don't touch me, don't——" He moved back from the Dresden shepherdess with hands upraised. "He is ill—Mr. Morley Fenton. Paralyzed, or something. I—I—it is all true, all of it. I know it is. Only for God's sake, don't touch me, now— child! Forgive me! What can I say? But I want to get out—get out. You must forgive me! Good-bye! God, I must go out!"

"Yes—yes; I knew. Good-bye, Hal."

Harold Foster had snatched his cloak and hat from where they lay, on a chair-back; and carrying them in his hands, he strode out of the pretty, littered little room. The Dresden shepherdess stood watching the door for a minute. Then she sank down on her knees before the fire, holding the faded, creased envelope in her hand, gazing fixedly before her. Then two big, bright tears fell on to the yellowed envelope.

"Yes, yes, I knew," repeated the Dresden shepherdess slowly. "Of course, it's part of my—my business."

Harold strode along in the rain outside, his cloak flying loose over his right arm.

CHAPTER XXX.

HAROLD FOSTER FINDS HIS WAY.

"That man will read you rightly head to foot,
Mark the brown face of you, the bushy beard.
The breadth 'twixt shoulder-blades, and through each black
Castilian orbit see into your soul.
. . . .
He will have understood you, I engage.
Endeavour, for your part, to understand
He knows more, and loves better, than the world
That never heard his name, and never may."
Red Cotton Nightcap Country.

HAROLD FOSTER strode on unseeingly, through the gusty rain of the spring night; on and on, unthinkingly, through the squares and crescents and gardens of Kensington.

There was no doubt that for the time Harold had lost his way. There are doubtless many who would say that he had lost it when he went to Berlin with Leo Tarne, or to the Castanets with the Dresden shepherdess. That would be a mistake. He was following then a very distinct way—of a sort. But on this rainy April night he had made certain discoveries, and he had very completely lost his way.

If a ship be off her course, one of the first steps towards taking her back to it is the ascertaining of her exact bearings. When Harold Foster left the St. Bartholomew's student who had given him the evening paper containing news of Mr. Morley Fenton's illness, he, Harold had not even known that he had lost his way. When he left the house in which the Dresden shepherdess lived, he had realized the fact in every nerve and fibre of himself. Consequently, though he, of course, was not aware of the fact, his position was considerably more hopeful than it had been earlier in the evening.

Harold's decline, from the points of view, say, of Dr. Wainwright, the specialist in nervous diseases, of Mr. Morley Fenton, the man of standing and of unquestioned social and commercial repute, and of any upholder of morality, Christian or otherwise, had, since his return from Berlin, been very marked and rapid. It had not been marked by Harold, but it had by everyone else with whom he came in contact.

Perhaps the most striking proof of this lay in the fact of his being severed from Leo Tarne. Leo Tarne was not a man who had any great care of his reputation. Respect for the conventions had no place in Leo Tarne's creed. Beauty and morality, comfort and virtue, meant to Leo Tarne one and the same thing. Ugliness, immorality, discomfort, and vice—these were synonyms to Leo Tarne.

Yet, almost immediately after their return from Brighton together, to London, these two had parted, with an understanding that their paths for the present diverged. And Leo Tarne had taken the initiative in this parting. He had said:

"Frankly, my dear Harold, no consideration of friendship or obligation would induce me to associate closely with a man whose ways jarred on me. I couldn't afford it. It would destroy the beauty of my life, spoil my work, and make the Carissima unhappy. It would make me unhappy. Nothing in the world, to me, is worth purchase at the price of unhappiness. Far be it from me to interfere with my friend's actions or desires. I have made suggestions. To me it is surprising—your present way of living—because, to me, it seems so grossly inartistic. You seem to divide your time now between doing grotesque things and making hideous resolutions. Your resolutions smack of religious revival meetings, and your actions—forgive me—suggest Saturday night in Piccadilly Circus. It is painful to me—it is really. See! Here is a little finger-post to what I mean. You never drink Rhein wine now. You drink brandy-and-soda in the daytime—brandy-and-soda, Harold!—and sweet, sparkling, red things, at night. I am awfully sorry; but—you are upsetting my life—you are, really, by making me a kind of accomplice in all this."

There had been no banter in this speech, to the man who had made it, or to the man who had heard it. And in that way these two had parted. And their parting had slightly accelerated Harold's descent, which had been fast enough before, as was inevitable to his peculiar temperament. That at which he had shuddered early on one evening, he had merely turned away from at midnight, shrugged his shoulders at in the small hours, smiled at the next evening, and taken part in twenty-four hours later.

Already, as he strode along through the outlying streets of Kensington, it seemed to Harold that a long stretch of life, a wide gulf of time, lay between that evening with its revelations, and the other, past, evening of his parting with Mr. Morley Fenton at the door of the blue-and-silver room in the Castanets. Already, it seemed that, walking along there, through the thin, driving rain, he was living a different phase of his life to that in which the Dresden shepherdess had had a part. He would probably never see her again. They had met for the last time. He had known her, it was true, for a few weeks. Then they had parted. That belonged to the past. Even the fact that Mr. Morley Fenton was his father! Well, of course he was!

Harold came to a standstill suddenly, in a quiet, deserted street. The point reached in his reflections was what had stopped him. But the moment he stood still he realized that he was carrying his cape-coat instead of wearing it, and that he was already very wet. He drew on the coat slowly, and buttoned it over his wet shirt and limp collar.

To seek to disclose the mind-workings of just such a young man in just such a condition as was Harold Foster's at this moment, would surely be unfair—if the disclosure were an offering up for judgment. The most self-satisfied among Pharisees would hesitate to judge a man on the utterances of his delirium. But a wise physician, a kindly doctor, will sometimes listen most attentively and thoughtfully to a patient's raving.

"He was very anxious about my worldly success," muttered Harold, whilst he stood still in the rain; "very much afraid of my offending the proprieties; but he didn't care to own me as his son—even as a foundling—all those years. Oh no! that wouldn't have been diplomatic; and—— Psh! But I will never trouble him. If I disgrace myself, he needn't fear my disgracing him. Oh, God! What am I talking about? And he is——"

Harold resumed his walk, but more slowly and less blindly than before.

Once again he stopped abruptly in his walk, and, raising his eyes in the darkness, said, with the tone of a man who makes a discovery:

"Then I am absolutely alone—much more alone than before. Leo Tarne, and the Carissima, and George Barnard, and—and the child, and Mr. Morley Fenton—they're all gone. And Weir Lodge—— Psh! And—Norah! Why I am just—— My God! and even my name isn't my own."

As before, a mental break brought cognizance of physical surroundings. Looking round him, Harold saw that he was approaching a bridge over the river. He was in the suburbs.

"I don't want that place," he muttered; and, turning sharp round then, he began to walk back over the ground he had covered up to that point. Then his mind resumed its troubled working, and he ceased to take note of his surroundings.

Eleven o'clock was passed when Harold had left the sitting-room in which he had seen that yellow, creased envelope. He had felt no weariness whilst trampling along the suburban roads, groping in his mind for that course which he had lost. But at last, whilst he retraced his steps without noticing where they were leading him, his pace slackened, his shoulders began steadily to droop, his arms hung listlessly beside him, and, looking up wearily once, as the hour of one boomed out from St. Stephen's, he murmured:

"That sounds like Big Ben. Half-past something —no, one o'clock. I am very tired."

He wandered on, dejectedly now and with no protest, no suggestion of battling, in the weary lines his figure took. Rather was there in his crouching gait an implied desire to escape unnoticed—to escape even from himself, perhaps. And, later, as he still crept on through one street after another, even this suggestion faded out from his movements and appearance, leaving apparent only weariness—great weariness.

Harold had not dined that night, and he had taken no food, save a very little fruit, during the day. For days and weeks he had been growing more nervously feverish, more physically listless, and on this night there was no very great store of vitality left in Harold to respond to the strain he put upon himself.

"Just give us a lift up with this, mate, will yer?" said a voice at Harold's elbow. "Ah, thank ye— thankee, sir! I thought ye wor ——, seein' ye 'ere, like. Thankee, sir."

Harold passed on with a murmured "Don't mention it." He had just strained every muscle in his weary body to aid a market-gardener in dragging a sack of turnips on to a little raised platform. Looking round now, Harold saw that he was at one of the entrances to Covent Garden market. His only desire just then was to sit down somewhere and rest. For a few minutes he walked on over rough cobble-stones, which were strewn with leaves of broken vegetables and flower stems. Then he reached the piazza, and sat wearily down in the shadow of one of its stone supports.

"I must go somewhere and sleep," he muttered, stretching out his legs on the damp stone.

But in the meantime he sat there, in the shadow of the pillar.

The rain of the night had ceased during the first hour of morning, and spring was in the air, whispering, like a glad child on the eve of a child's holiday, of coming dawn. In the streets beyond, tired night would hold her sway for two or three hours yet. But there, in the great market, night seemed already to be drawing her sable skirts about her, half abashed by the joyous, soft whisperings of new life, and the floating breaths from country pastures, which strove to assert themselves in the London air.

Now and again came the slow rumbling of a cart or waggon, earlier than its fellows—tarpaulins spangled over with mingled rain and dew from outside the Charing Cross radius; horses, the matted hair of whose fetlocks carried fragments of wet clean earth, foreign quite to the refuse of wood pavements; earthy vegetable smells, suggestive of wide, wet bovine nostrils; fruity smells calling up visions of sun-kissed orchard slopes, flecked over with snowy dimples of fallen blossom, and of warm old lofts where apples mellow and develop the skin-creases of kindly old age; flowery, budding smells, which embodied faintly all the moist loveliness of spring, and roused fancies about lads and lasses, sun-bonnets, rosy plumpness, cream, dimity, and tiny windows.

Harold Foster decided to go somewhere and sleep. Meanwhile, he sat on the damp stone of the piazza, leaning against a dark pillar, his legs outstretched over wet cobble-stones, his nostrils inhaling languidly that air, its fancies, whisperings, and perfumes, which made tired night to gather about her her sable drapery.

"Thanks all the same, my young friend. I thoroughly appreciate your kindness, but—a Bond Street hotel is a little out of my line. With the coming of the springtime, no doubt, your thoughts turn lightly to—to Bond Street, and love. Mine frequently meander heavily towards Covent Garden—this very spot— where I have a weakness for playing death's head at the feast of dawn. Damn poor taste, you think? Why, yes; it's some time since I've read my Shelley, certainly. But, que voulez vous? You and your good friends toasted me as the King of Bohemia. Voila! C'est le roi! vive le roi! In these days, my young friend—to be honest, it was always so—the path to such a throne is—well, not Bond Street. Shall I tell you something that one of your clever set said the other day? Ha! He said: 'Old man Carroll is mellowing like some fine old pear. If he only lives long enough, be gad! he'll found a school of philosophy.' Not bad, was it? A fine future for 'old man Carroll,' eh? Ha, ha! No, don't sit down, my friend—my very kind-hearted young friend. To begin with, I—I really don't want you, you know, and, further, this stone is damp—very damp. I? Oh, I am immune, thanks! Yes——"

"But, I say, Mr. Carroll, you know, of course I haven't known you long, you know, and—er—that sort of thing; but—er—are you sure you won't—er—eh? Because I should be only too——"

"Yes, yes, I know, my young friend. I'm not joking; I count it an honour that you've made your offer—and—and, yes, I'm quite sure, thanks. Good-night."

Harold Foster, curiosity and interest overcoming his languor, peered round the side of his pillar, and saw, occupying exactly his own position at the next pillar, the figure of a man whose long beard glistened with moisture and greyness; and facing the recumbent figure stood a young man in evening dress, his overcoat unbuttoned and hanging loosely.

"Well, of course, if you're sure—er—you won't let me——"

"No, thank you," interrupted the man who was sitting on the piazza.

"Well, then, I'll say good-night!"

"Good-night, my friend."

And Harold saw the young man walk slowly away over the cobble-stones, towards one of the market entrances.

For some minutes Harold sat thinking of the words he had listened to. He remembered quite well having heard George Barnard and a young doctor at St. Bartholomew's each speak of Carroll, the old Bohemian. Then he thought he ought to have made his presence known in some way. But yet, he was not in a private place. He felt strongly interested in the old man, whom he could distinctly hear now in the act of lighting a pipe. Harold Foster coughed loudly, as one who announces himself.

"Hullo, there! Who's that?"

The question came in the thick, deep voice of the man called Carroll. And it carried authority. Harold rose to his feet, half shamefacedly. Weariness had some part in this. .

"It's me," he said, with almost childish lack of confidence, and grammar.

"Well, who are you, my friend?"

"My name's Harold Foster."

"Harold Foster! Is it now? What an odd little world! Sit down, Harold Foster, if you don't mind the damp. Let me have a look at you.—Well, really! It is damned odd!—you must excuse me. Yes! And so you are Morley Fenton's foundling, eh?—Well, well! You appear to be beginning where I leave off, my friend—on the piazza."

Harold Foster stared in amazement at the old man, whose authoritative gesture of invitation he mechanically obeyed. Perhaps his weariness had something to do with this, too.

"But—but how is it you know me?" he asked as he sat down beside the man Carroll.

"Eh? Oh, bless you! I know most people, including George Barnard, who came to have a talk with me the other day about the Castanets and—things. My name's Carroll. Now, look here, tell me about yourself, Harold Foster. You're rather alone just now, aren't you? There's no one holding cotton-wool round you any longer. You've stampeded round a little without the Morley Fenton curb or the George Barnard snaffle, and now you don't quite know where you are. Steady! So then, steady, sonny! No one wants to hurt you. Tell me all about it—come! You and I will sit and see the spring come—the light creep over the gloom of things. You're in luck's way. We've nothing to do with any of 'em. We'll just look over the ball of the earth together."

Then they began to talk, these two, "old man Carroll" saying very little at first, but listening mightily, the while a largely comprehending smile played under his grey moustache, and his eyes glowed and beamed dull fire below their eaves of moist straggling hair. Harold warmed towards the old outcast with every word which he, Harold, spoke. He felt no shadow of restraint in unbosoming himself to Carroll. To be sure he was ripe for unbosoming. And he had never before met a man who understood quite as Carroll understood, with such sweeping breadth of tolerance, such minute grip of trifles, such instant seizure of loosely indicated large facts; and, above all, such power of showing, with passive ease and obviousness, just how all-embracing was this understanding of his.

Soon Harold ceased to explain his thoughts; such supererogation seemed in bad taste. He simply gave them utterance. And the thoughts of such a mind as was Harold Foster's, unexplained, are tight-packed images. They dismiss massed facts, indicate serried events, advance premises, sequences, deductions, by little pungent gusts of atmospheric suggestion, by carelessly out-flung splashes of vivid word-colouring.

And all this was absorbed by the big man recumbent beside Harold—understood with that evidence of understanding which cannot be denied or simulated, since itself is the current across which one man makes such hot communications to another. The great grey beard rose and fell gently. "Ah!" "H'm!" "Ye-es!" "And—" "So?" "Ha!" "I know!" "Oh Lord! I know!" These and similar murmured ejaculations were the rest-houses, the restoring stations, at which Harold paused momentarily, with sails half-hoisted, wings aflutter, on his voyage of explanation.

Now and again Harold would beat his wings impetuously against the glass of some barrier the far side of which he saw clearly enough, but knew not how to reach. Then the big man would seem to bend down over Harold, and with his catholic knowledge press aside some sash which held the barrier of glass, drawing Harold through then to the clearer, freer air of his own understanding.

Everything in his mind Harold Foster poured out for the inspection of the big man on the piazza, with the exception of his discovery as to Mr. Morley Fenton's real relation to him; and of that the big man's memory, freshened by much that he heard now and had thought of late, told him a good deal, and suggested more, of which he made no mention to Harold.

And then Harold ceased speaking, and the two rose to their feet on the piazza's edge, just as the first nacreous hints of coming dawn began to ripple, opalescent-wave-like, over the sky citywards.

"A foretaste of spring, Harold Foster," said Carroll, raising his lean right hand, and pointing to the east.

Harold looked, and saw insistent purpling colour stealing out and up over the grey, sighing bosom of night—night as she lay a-dying, on a blue-fringed bed of pearl. The morning star was paling, stepping backward before day's joyous advance.

"See the troubled mist of things not understood, fade silently out, and truth rise with the dawn and springtime," said the big man, with a queer little smile. "Look at it all, sonny, and soak it in; for—for of such is the real kingdom of heaven. The wide sweep that takes it all in—not a street or a house, or a class or profession, but the 'good gigantic smile o' the brown old earth,' Harold Foster.

"'And a bird overhead sang *Follow*,
And a bird to the right sang *Here*;
And the arch of the leaves was hollow,
And the meaning of May was clear.

"'I saw where the sun's hand pointed,
I knew what the bird's note said——'

That's some of what your mind's got to take in and thrive on, to make a whole man of you, outside cotton-wool and Morley Fenton—good man—and George Barnard—better man. And it's going to take it in, too, sonny. You start a clean page with the day-dawn that's coming, and you start it alone—*alone*, by the eternal catholicism of things! You start it alone, and you're going to make a real book of your life: a big book men may read, not a little diary of Lombard Street and Suburbia; not a ten to four journal of any spit-turning little round, nor even a record of Harley Street and Bartholomew's, but a great big leather-backed book of a white man's life, sonny. That's what you're going to begin, when the sun gets up. And a man can't do that in a cotton-wool waistcoat, so don't be cast down at the loneliness of things. You were stark, staring naked when you sat down here— and a damned good thing for you, my son. For to get anywhere near the brown old earth—that's your white man's catholicism—a man's got to begin naked; and that's just what you're going to do. Why, look here, Harold Foster, when I——"

And then, while the market was beginning to fill, while the spring day's rose-dimpled feet tripped with life's joyousness over the night's mauve-coloured grave-clothes, this big old man called Carroll rolled out a few yellowed-over scrolls of his seamed and cross-seamed past, for the aid and benefit of Harold Foster—Harold Foster, who was beginning his life that morning, quite alone, and the object of no man's protection. It was light thrown with absolute impartiality over portions of—not a good life— a life full of stains and blemishes, but a life which, in the living as in the telling, had been one long lesson, one unceasing gleaning of knowledge, one unending round of varying experiences—a broadly catholic storing up of understanding and wisdom.

And all this Harold listened to and drew into himself whilst standing in the dawnlight on the edge of the piazza; his limp, stained coat buttoned closely under his pallid chin, his eyes gleaming brightly between flushed cheek-bones, which seemed to thrust redly through the rain-washed whiteness of his face.

"And you look at me," said the big man; "and you wonder where it has all led me. And you—— But no, you don't sneer. You have learned too much already, this morning, for that. And then I know you're white and clean underneath. The cotton-wool naturally set up a little irritation, and left a few patchy marks. But I know you're clean. Besides, God forbid that I should tell you to do as I've done. I didn't have anyone who'd done it to tell me; and I didn't see the dawn early in my life as you are seeing it now. No; I crippled myself just so much in one of the patches—you know it: you've passed through it already—just so much as to prevent my finally coming out on the other side; but—but—not enough to prevent my seeing, watching, and learning to understand the big horizon outside. Oh no! I had my dawn. I saw the rim peer over the ball of the earth. But I saw it late—very late. You see it early. You have sloughed your cotton-wool. You have skimmed through the lurid, weedy patch, learning it—for there's a heap to be learned there, where so many stick, as you've found out in the last month or two. And one should learn all. And you have reached the brown earth outside, naked, in the dawning. It's magnificent. Those are the two great preliminary quicksands. And you've crossed 'em, and learned 'em. And now you stand in the dawnlight, watching. You look down at the little lurid patch which some folk call Bohemia

—that's a mistake, of course, because Christ was the first Bohemian—and you see that, with all its splashes of colour and perfume, it is still only a very small patch of your brown old earth, the great horizon where your book's to be made. It is, as a matter of fact, a small patch. But it's not quite so small as another patch you look at now. Some call that Nonconformity. That, too, is a mistake in labelling, because Christ was the first Nonconformist. It contains the cotton-wool process, and ten to four respectability, Mr. Morley Fenton's life, and the religion of appearances; and it's even worse to get stuck in—because smaller—than the lurid patch. But what you've to remember, sonny, is that this, and all the other patches—conventionality and unconventionality, five o'clock tea and small hours Burgundy, ten to four appearances and the Castanets abandon, Sunday-school teaching and decadent art exoticism—all these are only little patches. But, understand, they *are* patches of your great brown earth—the big windy-skied, sweet-heather-smelling world, in which you are going to make your book. You spoke of Blougram and his dinner-table philosophy. That's a patch, Harold Foster, the patch Morley Fenton wanted you to live in. I suppose he chose it in mistake for the world. But don't despise it, sonny, because it's a piece of your earth, remember. And, for God's sake, don't get stuck in it, else you'll grow too fat to ever get out of it."

The big man paused and smiled in the baby day's face.

"And even looking at me," he continued, "I told you how I was crippled—you needn't be frightened of the new life you're beginning. All the world knows I'm a failure. My dawn came too late. But, sonny, do you fancy for a moment that, as I am, I'd change places with any millionaire in Christendom—stuck fast in one of the patches?"

Carroll was a fine figure of a man. Broken, gnarled and seared by the life he had led, he yet reared up his grey head like a lightning-blasted elm, and with a large nobility that was fine to see. Harold did not answer the question, unless with his eyes.

"So now you will start, and alone," resumed Carroll. "You will fear nothing, shun nothing, despise nothing, and—you will be governed by nothing. Do you understand? No lying down and closing your eyes to classic Greece, while you worship dainty Byzantium, or blind yourself with Moorish high lights. You must move about over the brown earth, learning all—all—loving all, helping all, and being helped by all. You have seen the dawn this morning, the life you must learn alone. And, sonny, you will do it; you will do it. Go right away from all the influences, and start clear. You can go up for your final examination in a month or two. Well, go to Hargreave at Bartholomew's, and ask him to arrange for you to put in the rest of your time at another hospital, one farther east, say. He'll do it. I'll write him. You have enough money for food and living. Go and work in a new place. You must pass the examination. You will, of course. And then you will go on, and on, and on—ah, sonny, it is a beautiful life, this that I have told you of, on the big earth's rought breast. And the book of it—the big, russet-leather-covered book of your life—it shall· be a classic, my friend, a classic. See! There's the sun, clear of all the mist now. Your life's begun. You've seen truth dawn. Go on! They called you 'Morley Fenton's Foundling.' That's all dead now. And in the life you're going to, Harold Foster—

ah! they shall call you 'God's Foundling.' Goodbye."

So the big man called Carroll disappeared among the throng of waggons. And Harold Foster turned and walked slowly away, his head held high, his eyes looking upward and onward.

CONSEQUENCES.

PART I.

THE PASSAGE OF TIME.

"'Tis the weakness in strength, that I cry for ! my flesh that I seek
In the Godhead ! I seek and I find it. O Saul, it shall be
A Face like my face that receives thee ; a Man like to me
Thou shalt love and be loved by, for ever : a Hand like this hand
Shall throw open the gates of new life to thee ! See the Christ stand !"
Saul.

THOSE newspaper reports which had spoken of Mrs. Fenton's hastening, with one of her daughters, to the Trafalgar Square hotel in which Mr. Morley Fenton lay stricken and helpless, had to all intents and purposes been perfectly accurate. Norah Fenton was practically one of Mrs. Fenton's daughters—something more, perhaps, to Mr. Morley Fenton. And Norah it was who accompanied Mrs. Fenton, on that morning of consternation and alarm, from the smooth-running calm of Weir Lodge, through London—a London hurrying with fixed, unseeing eyes to its daily toil and moil—to the hushed, heart-chilling, half-darkness of the room where Mr. Morley Fenton lay.

They came, as David came to his king's tent when Saul's trouble was heavy upon him, these women; one a wife and a mother, the other in reality neither, but yet with native understanding and intuitive woman's wit enough for both. And as David paused in fear and wonder when he saw Saul,

" Hung there as, caught in his pangs
And waiting his change, the king serpent all heavily hangs "—

so these two women paused, blanched and fear-struck, at the entrance to the chamber of Mr. Morley Fenton's helplessness, and listened to the trained nurse's grave and kindly words of warning sympathy.

Mrs. Morley Fenton shivered, and sat down for a moment in the sitting-room from which the bedroom was approached. The nurse moved to her side. Norah, white and fearful to her finger-tips, but firm and showing no slightest tremor, stepped on into the sick room—

"Then once more I prayed,
And opened the fold skirts and entered, and was not afraid,
But spoke, ' Here is David, thy servant !' And no voice replied."

In this way and alone, Norah first faced the tragic fact that he who to her had been, if in one way less, then in another way more, than had her real father; this strong, impassive man the finest chords in whose nature she had touched upon understandingly, the mere policy in whom had in the course of circumstance never been made to touch her; this adopted parent, so close to whose heart she had lived, was unable now to speak to her—perhaps, so far as she could tell, to recognise her. For, though the sunken, half-opened eyes gazed up at Norah's face when she bent over him, their expression did not change. No muscle governed by intelligence moved in the dark, finely-chiselled face. But veins and muscles on one side of it were twitching vaguely, and with a suggestion of helpless irresponsibility. The grey lips made no sign.

Later on, days afterwards, at Weir Lodge, Miss Matthews—the deft-handed, large-bodied professional nurse engaged by Dr. Wainwright to attend on Mr. Morley Fenton—this skilled craftswoman added much to her store of knowledge. She learned to recognise the beauty of art's union with craft. She learned that there is in nursing, to the student who studies it lovingly, something much greater, much more all-soothing and all-embracing, than is even the important corner-stone of technical knowledge. And this she learned of Norah. In this study her teacher, primer, and modestly silent demonstrator was Norah—a mere girl.

Mrs. Fenton with her two daughters, full of sympathy and a genuine desire to help, hovered constantly about the room where the owner of Weir Lodge lay. They were ready and anxious to do anything, endure anything, for the patient. They were ready and anxious, to do and to endure. Norah did and endured, saying little and showing no weariness. Everyone appreciated this in Norah. But no one else understood the beauty of it to the same extent as did the nurse and the doctor. And so strongly impressed by it all was Nurse Matthews that when, on a certain day of great sorrowing, her services being no longer required, the nurse left Weir Lodge, she could not refrain from saying to Norah:

"Oh, Miss Fenton, if you only realized the wonderful power your heart puts into your eyes and your fingers, you would give up all the ties of your own life, and make sick creatures happy by going round to their bedsides. You have no need of hospital training. You have something bigger and better to give than that. And—don't think me rude—I think you would be happier, too!"

Norah always remembered what this usually calm and apparently emotionless woman said to her, on that day of weeping in Weir Lodge.

Before this occasion, however, came a day during the morning of which, when George Barnard was sitting with bowed head at his bedside, Mr. Morley Fenton asked very definitely for Harold Foster. The barrister, who had been severely cautioned by Dr.

Wainwright against saying anything to distress or excite the patient, was painfully perplexed. His efforts to ascertain Harold Foster's whereabouts had, since the first morning of Mr. Morley Fenton's illness, been almost unceasing, and quite unavailing. He had even approached the big old man called Carroll, on the subject. But Carroll had merely smiled, in his satirical, half-sympathetic, half-derisive way, and had said:

"I fancy it's better to let sleeping dogs—not to mention dead dogs—lie, you know. I rather fancy that young man's life, as Harold Foster and Morley Fenton's foundling, must have ended. And isn't it just as well, don't you think? Morley Fenton's foundling was a bit of a mistake—a bit of a failure, eh? Anyhow, I haven't the remotest idea where Harold Foster may have buried himself—unless, perhaps, in Covent Garden."

And then Carroll had asked George Barnard to drink some whisky, and himself had declined to pursue farther the subject of Harold Foster's probable whereabouts.

So, sitting by his stricken friend's bedside, the barrister stammered in his perplexity, and finally said that he would take immediate and decisive steps towards bringing Harold Foster to Weir Lodge.

He took all manner of steps, but he found no trace of Harold Foster, save that the young man had obtained authority to pursue his studies at some other hospital, and had left St. Bartholomew's. And two days later, a good deal to Dr. Wainwright's surprise, the disease which held the owner of Weir Lodge enchained, took an unexpected stride in the remorseless and resistless path of its advance.

On that morning, seated on one side of her husband's bed, and facing George Barnard on the other,

Mrs. Morley Fenton received certain intelligence regarding which no breath of suspicion had ever crossed her mind. She learned of the buried phase in her strong husband's career; that phase which had come before policy or diplomacy had entered into Mr. Morley Fenton's life. She learned of the real relationship between her husband and Harold Foster; and, all the good woman and devoted wife rising in her and brushing aside the resentment-pricks of a life's habit of littleness and custom-worship, she assured the masterful man who lay dying, that when Harold Foster crossed her path again he should cease to regard himself motherless.

It was goodness to be expected of some women. In this gracious mistress of Weir Lodge, with her bird-like voice and her smiling, unvarying devotion to the small matters of a small life, it was magnificent. It earned for her the undying respect of George Barnard, and the dying gratitude and love of her husband, a yielding up to her in impressive silence, of portions of this man's heart, which, in all the years of their married life, had never even been shown to Mrs. Fenton. It is true they had never been looked for, asked for, or felt for. Perhaps Mrs. Grundy does not teach even the most select among her disciples any of the many methods of plumming human hearts, of tracking emotional streams to their sources, of setting free and seizing the wealth of hidden springs, rock-bound, but readily responsive to the divining-rod of understanding, wielded clear of conventionality's restraint, and in catholic good faith.

Two weeks afterwards, when the period of strain was ended, and Weir Lodge, as it were, sank back to draw the long breath of submission to weariness, before weeping at finding itself without a master, Dr. Wainwright, seeking with professional courtesy to show his sympathy with the bereaved wife of his patient, said to her:

"My dear Mrs. Fenton, everyone who ever came into contact with—with him, must needs miss him—miss him sorely. But there are many consolations. As a doctor, I cannot but find many consolations. I had looked for months of great and quite hopeless pain, Mrs. Fenton, months of ever-increasing helplessness, and—and, I do assure you, the end was a very merciful one—though so sad for you and all of us, yet a very merciful one."

And as time wore on, far more speedily than she could have believed possible, Mrs. Fenton adapted herself to the great change in her life. Her widowhood sought consolation in many small ways and channels—and found it. So, too, with Maud and Lucy Fenton, who, returning to London with Norah and their mother after ten months spent in South-Coast watering-places, found many new interests in life at the pretty little Mayfair house, which, at Mrs. Fenton's request, George Barnard had obtained for them. Many associations were cut off with the giving up of Weir Lodge. Many new ties and associations were formed with the beginning of a London season in the Mayfair house. These were keenly appreciated, at all events, by Maud and Lucy. Mrs. Fenton was rich. She was not without ambitions, as far as her daughters were concerned. And these ambitions were, in the nature of things, to her full of small interests.

Norah at this time, was less understood, more isolated, and probably less happy, than at any other period of her life.

Though the events of Mr. Morley Fenton's illness had added to the affectionate admiration with which Mrs. Fenton and her two daughters regarded Norah, and, perhaps, to their closeness of touch, yet by his death it seemed that a slowly widening gulf, an ever-strengthening wall of reserve, had been brought into being between Norah and the dead man's family.

Almost unconsciously, and entirely without recognition of the feeling, Mrs. Fenton had shared with Maud and Lucy, her daughters, certain vague resentments. Mr. Morley Fenton's inclinations and actions during all the strong, evenly-lived period of his life which these three women had known, had been subject to, and cloaked by, the man's never-failing tact and sense of fitness. On the bed of his sickness, every fibre of him the child of his disease, all this had been changed. Many of Mr. Morley Fenton's inmost thoughts had then carelessly announced themselves; his every passing desire had been readily apparent and instantly acted upon.

He had seldom asked for his wife, he had only once looked for his children, and rarely, during this sad time of his helplessness, had Mr. Morley Fenton opened his eyes, or turned wearily on his bed, without looking and asking for Norah, the daughter of his dead brother—the girl whose unvarying deftness and inspired ability to soothe, had been a study and a marvel to Nurse Matthews.

Then had come the end—of sickness, of nursing, and of Mr. Morley Fenton. And with it the causes of the small resentments had been removed. In their place had opened out the gulf afore-mentioned; rose then, between Norah and her kinsfolk, a misty veil born of a great devotion, out of different points of view. And this was a far more real thing to Norah than it was to Maud and Lucy or to their widowed mother. The giving up of Weir Lodge, the settling down to a new life full of new interests and new pleasures, in the Mayfair house, the social ambitions which brought absorption to Mrs. Fenton and forgetfulness to her daughters—all this, to the girl who had loved so well and been so well beloved of the man now dead, served to widen the gulf and give substance to the veil, which hung between herself and her only relatives.

Norah was very much alone, a state felt keenly by all deep-rooted natures whose intimacies are few and close. She could not escape from her daily, hourly consciousness of the final loss of that life which had been so close, so intimate, to her own. Mr. Morley Fenton had entered and filled the grief-hung place left in her heart by his weak elder brother's death. His strength had enlarged this place, filling and dominating it amply. Now he had gone. And to fill the space his loss left empty, Norah was offered—the little ties and pleasures of a London season, in a woman-ruled house in Mayfair.

So Norah sat in the no-man's-land to which calamity sometimes introduces deep-feeling natures, wondering at the greyness of her life, groping with outstretched hands, which shrank from much they came in contact with, groping through a mist of sadness in a waste of littleness.

George Barnard, his dead friend's executor, could only sympathize. This he did with all the kindness of his big heart. And Norah, in her misty, between-whiles place, was very grateful. The barrister was nearer and more real to her then than was anybody else. But breezy, blue-eyed George Barnard had not the faculty of imparting, dominating, absorbing, which had enabled the strong man whom these two had both loved, to give to Norah a new hold of her life.

And Harold Foster, toward whom so much of Norah's understanding heart had instinctively gone out in sympathy, Harold Foster made no sign. He had disappeared utterly from out the horizon of Norah's life. His loss seemed as real and complete a thing as was that of the older, stronger man, who, having led him into Norah's presence, had then set a bar between them, which had matured into what appeared to be final separation.

Then came a morning when Norah woke calm and rested, filled and dominated by a loving determination to step out from her place in the mists of passive sadness, and to act. Norah's mind was very clear in the matter. She would set out to bring into other lives some of that happiness which Fate had been pleased to take from hers. This was her inmost nature's assertion of its superiority over the dictates of circumstance—a quiet, great triumph.

Norah wrote to George Barnard. Then she tore up the letter she had written, and went to see Nurse Matthews.

Nurse Matthews listened and smiled.

"I knew you would come," she said. "I don't think one can be given all that you have, without feeling bound to use it. It wouldn't be right—or kind."

Mrs. Fenton, in her pretty little Mayfair drawing-room, raised her eyebrows deprecatingly when she heard Norah's announcement of her intention to enter a training school for nurses.

"Of course it is very good of you, Norah dear, very good and sweet of you; but——" And Mrs. Fenton's expression of opinion ended vaguely in the gentle deprecation afore-mentioned.

"Well, do you know, I always had an idea that Norah would do something—something peculiar, you know, like that," said Lucy Fenton in the course of subsequent conversation.

"I don't know about 'peculiar,'" said Maud, quickly; "but the fact is, she's a great deal too good for any of us. I'm quite sure of that. We never half-understood her, you know, Lucy, and it's because she's so much better than we are that you think Norah peculiar."

So Norah ceased to be an inmate of the house in Mayfair. She took up her abode instead at a certain nursing institute, where she quickly became the close friend of Nurse Matthews and the affectionately admired associate of many good women, who were impressed deeply by that in Norah which had led Nurse Matthews to say, " I knew you would come."

In her new life, too, Norah saw more of George Barnard, himself a man rich in the instinct which makes healers and nurses of men and women. Nurse Matthews grew to regard the barrister in the light of a comrade, and these three passed many pleasant hours together, in an atmosphere more genial and more hopeful than anything Norah had found in Mayfair. The woman in her—the catholic, all-loving woman—grew and broadened out in ever-brightening, ever-widening eddies of human faith and human understanding.

Norah did not enter a hospital, but chose rather to enrol herself on the books of a little, unsectarian organization of which Nurse Matthews had become a devoted member. This little colony of workers had its modest head-quarters in a rather sordid quarter of that curious world in which all roads lead to the Docks. The members of this obscure association knew no professional etiquette. They lived, and helped others to live, on their own small means, and nursed all and sundry, with and without medical assistance, with and without thanks. Norah lived on a small portion of the small annuity which had been left her by Mr. Morley Fenton. Her visits to the house in Mayfair were brief ones now, and paid at infrequent intervals. She was losing touch with the few intimates of her old life, always excepting the man from Furnival's Inn, and was gaining, in the place of this lost touch, the admiring comradeship of some dozen of workers, and the grateful devotion of a few men, women and children, in one small corner of the wilderness called London's East End.

Her life at this time was genial and deep-breathing, if somewhat lacking in directness of aim and method. She was not quite content, and certainly not entirely happy. She felt the absence of much—the want of many things. But she was growing in heart and mind, and was influencing lives round her from day to day. In moments of depression—wholesome, hopeful depression—she tried sometimes to explain to George Barnard and to Nurse Matthews the sense of limitation which, whilst denying her positive content, and lending a certain vagueness to all her work, yet had not robbed her efforts and projects of their spirit.

"We seem so hemmed in," she would say at times, wearily, to this sympathetic couple. "What we do is so tiny, after all. And—and sometimes, you know, it makes me wish I were a man. I believe I could have saved that red-haired woman's husband last week, if I had been a man and a doctor. They think a woman cannot really know. And even if we ease their bodies, they—they smile at me afterwards, as though I were a child—a good child, you know. And I have no influence that lasts. When they are well, they—I think they rather resent me. It makes me feel very small and weak."

Then George Barnard would glance over Norah's head to Nurse Matthews, and that large-minded woman would smile back at him, with a little reassuring pursing up of her lips which said:

"Yes, yes; exactly. We know, do we not? But wait. All is well, as you will see. It will come; it will come."

And Norah would ask to be forgiven for complaining; or perhaps she would resume, as on one occasion when she said:

"If only one could be like that man they are always talking of in Stepney, that young doctor. Ah, that would be beautiful—beautiful!" And the white light of inspiration fell across, and seemed to illumine, Norah's beautiful face and dark, wave-clouded head. "Do you know what Mrs. Gunning's husband said to me yesterday?—the man who broke his leg on the P. and O. wharf, you know. It sounded rather dreadful, of course, but he didn't mean to be irreverent. He said: 'I reckon if that there Dr. Stephens had been alive 'way back in the old days, God wouldn't have bothered sending Christ down here. There wouldn't have been any need.' That's what he said," continued Norah, with eyes aglow and rising breast. "And he did not mean any irreverence, but only love and gratitude. Why, the man was just a brute, till he broke his leg, and that Dr. Stephens took him in hand and cured him. And look at him now. He is quite the best man in Geranium Court—quite the best man. And I have heard lots of them talking in the same way. They are close to him for a few weeks, this doctor, and then their whole lives seem altered. He heals their bodies, and asks nothing of them—not even a promise. And they come away wanting to help others. Oh, no wonder they think him like Christ. Like Christ—to be thought like Christ! Ah!"

And Norah turned away, her eyes brimming with tears. But she won through all her little phases of sadness, and went on striving, and loving, and learning, hopefully and helpfully, in the small circle through which her influence was felt.

So Norah lived and grew, while time wore on, till the fifth anniversary of Mr. Morley Fenton's death had passed. A few days' break came in the routine of her life, when Lucy Fenton was married to Sir Arthur Barstairs; and no one congratulated Maud on her engagement to Captain Lefevre, of the Seventh Hussars, more sincerely than did Norah.

"You dear, sweet Norah," Maud had said impetuously. "You make me feel absolutely ashamed of my useless little silly self, when I think of your giving up your life to—to those funny people at the docks, and—things. But you're not ashamed of me, are you, dear?"

Mrs. Fenton's only sister was living with her in Mayfair, now. There had been a vague rumour of Mrs. Fenton's intention to marry again. The name of the vicar of a certain fashionable church had been mentioned in this connection. And during the whole of these five years, Harold Foster's disappearance had remained a thing unexplained. George Barnard, as Mr. Morley Fenton's executor, held in trust for the young man who had been called "Morley Fenton's foundling," the sum of twenty thousand pounds. But George Barnard had been absolutely unable to trace the whereabouts of the heir to this legacy. And, partly because of certain carelessly suggestive words which the man called Carroll had spoken, the barrister had practically given up his search.

"The boy was badly bitten by the cotton-wool complaint," Carroll had said in answer to renewed inquiries from George Barnard. "You didn't mean any harm, I know, but you nearly swamped Morley Fenton's foundling with influence. The influence was a dead failure, and left him pretty raw and naked. When he's healed, and sure of himself, I expect he'll come and look us up. As for the money, he's better without it. If half what Hargreave at Bartholomew's said about him is true, he's far too clever a doctor to ever want money."

So George Barnard had gone on with his work at Furnival's Inn, his heated discussion of trifles with Nurse Matthews, his stormy interviews with Mrs. Greet, his confidential unbosomings to his mongrel dog, and his admiring study of Norah Fenton; and had determined to await patiently the return of the man whom Carroll thought might have been buried "in Covent Garden."

Late one night, just five years and one month after the morning on which Harold Foster had stood on the Covent Garden piazza, watching a spring sunrise, the big man called Carroll meandered heavily up the ill-lighted stairway which led to George Barnard's chambers in Furnival's Inn.

The old man declined the barrister's invitation to sit down and smoke. He staggered slightly as he stood there in the open doorway of George Barnard's den. His eyes were glassy, and his voice hoarse and thick. The last five years of his life had told very markedly on the strength of this storm-stained old man.

"Look here, George Barnard," he said. "You wanted to find that young man they called 'Morley Fenton's foundling,' didn't you? You were very keen on it."

The barrister nodded.

"Well, you know, he might have changed his name—without losing very much, mightn't he? Just as he might have changed his life, when he stopped being 'Morley Fenton's foundling.'"

"Yes. Well?"

"Well, did it ever strike you to inquire at the bank that paid his annuity in the old days, whether——"

"Well, I—well, I'm damned!"

"Not yet, surely," chuckled the old man. "You forgot that? Yes. Well, look here, George Barnard, he's had five years now to get healed and set. I reckon he must be well on with whatever he meant to do. You go and see the people at that bank, George Barnard—that's my advice. Good-night!"

And the old man wandered out again, and down the narrow staircase into the street, and the warm spring night.

PART II.

THE TRIUMPH OF TIME.

"So, take and use Thy work,
Amend what flaws may lurk,
What strain o' the stuff, what warpings past the aim !
My times be in thy hand !
Perfect the cup as planned !
Let age approve of youth, and death complete the same !"
Rabbi Ben Ezra.

WHEN Mrs. Greet made her appearance at George Barnard's chambers, somewhat later than usual, on the morning following the visit of the old man Carroll, the good woman was astonished to find that her employer was absent.

" H'm! " she muttered, with a certain virtuous glee, " p'r'aps he never slept here."

A hurried inspection of the barrister's bed caused a look of unmistakable disappointment to flit across the lumpy lines of the worthy housekeeper's face. Such disappointment is not unknown to pious members of certain societies formed for the discovery and trumpeting abroad of hidden vices—vices so deeply hidden as to be mistaken by ordinary mortals for innocent amusements and the like. The barrister had without doubt slept in his own bed, and, further, Mrs. Greet observed, had burned a hole in the cover of his pillow with his " filthy terbacker." Apparently, too, he had breakfasted, in some haste, on the mantelshelf, on his dressing-table, and on the back of an easy-chair. With a scornful curl of her hirsute upper lip,

Mrs. Greet began gathering together fragments of digestive biscuits and potted game.

At that moment the barrister, attended by his disreputable dog, was patiently awaiting admission at the outer door of the bank from which Harold Foster had, in the old days, drawn his annuity.

" Why, no," said the manager, when in due course he had arrived at the bank and the barrister had been ushered into his room. " No; Mr. Foster has not drawn upon his annuity since—let me see—since one year after Mr. Morley Fenton's death. At that time his account was considerably overdrawn, you know. I say this in confidence, of course, regarding you as Mr. Morley Fenton's executor."

" Exactly. Oh yes, I am not asking from mere curiosity. As a matter of fact, I—— But, however, perhaps you can give me Mr. Foster's address? "

The manager called a clerk and asked for Mr. Harold Foster's address.

" The last we have, sir, was given us four and a half years ago. ' Harold Foster, Esq., care of H. Stephens, Esq., Royal Free Hospital, Stepney.' That is the entry I have."

" Ah! Thanks, very much—thanks, very much! " And two minutes afterwards George Barnard was hurrying eastward, bound for the Royal Free Hospital, Stepney.

Arrived at that huge and dingy building, in which some of the foremost medical men of the age may be seen at times patiently tending the needs of the most sordid among London's sick and ailing, George Barnard breezily inquired of a hall-porter for Mr. Harold Foster.

" Don't know th' gen'elman, sir. Is he one of the students? "

" Well—er—now you mention it, no; I think not. Is Mr. H. Stephens here? "

"What, Dr. Stephens, sir? 'E won't be 'ere till three o'clock to-day, sir. I did 'ear that Sir Charles Mathieson 'ad called 'im in fur a consultation on Lord Burgher's case to-day. But I'm not sure, sir. 'Tain't horfen he goes out West now, sir—only for some real tip-top case."

"Ah! Perhaps you can tell me where his private house is?"

"I can that. 'Tisn't more'n half a mile from 'ere, sir. Th' Maner-rouse, top o' Brook Road. Anyone 'll tell yer, if yer jest follow this road till yer come to th' Wesleen Church."

"Ah, thanks—thanks! What number did you say?"

"I didn't say no number, sir. I never 'eard it 'ad one."

So George Barnard, after giving a little monetary proof of his gratitude for information afforded him, hurried on down the wide, gritty, shabby Stepney highway till he came to a blue and chilly-looking building, which he assumed was the "Wesleen Church" referred to by his friend at the hospital.

"Do you know where Dr. Stephens lives, sonny?" he asked of a small but responsible-looking urchin, whom he found some few minutes later, sitting on a high curbing and poring over a ragged copy of "Robinson Crusoe."

"Do I what?" replied the urchin, looking up with fine scorn from Defoe's pages to the face of his questioner. "Ain't this 'is book? You're a-gettin' at me, that's what you're doin'!"

"No, really," said the barrister, humbly, whilst feeling in his pocket for a copper. "I do want to know."

"Well, I'm blowed!" exclaimed the urchin, rising from his place on the curb and tucking his classic under one small arm. "Well, bli'me! But—oh yus, you're a stranger, you are. You 'aven't been in London long, 'ave yer, sir?" asked the boy with a quaint mixture of impudence and respect. "Well, 'ar docter, 'e lives in th' Maner-rouse, an' if it wasn't fur 'im I sh'd be at school wif me 'ed splittin' ag'in t'dye. I'll take yer t' 'ar docter's, sir, if y'll let me; an'—an' I won't tike nuffin fer it, neither. I thort everybody knew 'ar docter. Come on, sir."

So the barrister stepped out beside the small student of fiction, having wonderingly replaced the penny he had drawn from his coat-pocket.

As they walked together over the paper-strewn pavement, the man and the boy, a sudden idea came to George Barnard.

"Why, bless me," he muttered, "this Dr. Stephens of Stepney, whom everybody knows, he must be Norah's Christ-like young doctor, the man they swear by in Geranium Court—the healer of souls and bodies! I hope Harold's living with this man. It must be the same. What's he like, sonny, your Dr. Stephens?"

"*My* Dr. Stephens! Bli'me, 'e's everybody's docter! Well, 'e ain't like anyone, as I know, 'less it's Gawd."

"Unless it's who?"

"Gawd! Well, 'e's jest like the pictures uv Christ wot's 'angin' in th' misshun 'all; jes' th' sime, beard an' all."

"Good heavens! But, sonny, Christ is in heaven, you know."

"Yus; that's all right. P'raps that's the nobs' Christ. 'Ar Christ, in Stepney, 'e lives at Maner-rouse. Eny'ow, that's what 'ar docter's like; an' 'ere y'are, sir! 'Ere's Maner-rouse."

"Thank you, sonny. Here—— Well, get some

sweets for your friends with it, if you don't want it yourself. Good-bye!"

"Good-bye, sir! Bli'me! I s'y, mister! Tell 'ar docter as Dick Tate showed yer th' wye, will yer?"

Then the small boy sauntered off, still clutching Defoe's masterpiece under one arm; and George Barnard pushed open the crazy wooden gate which bore upon it, in faded black lettering, the words, "Manor House."

Manor House, Brook Road, Stepney, was one of the many curious dwelling-houses which display their decaying fortunes to the prying eyes of encroaching jerry-buildings in most of the northern and eastern suburbs of London. When a tenant can be found for these once substantial residences—decaying aristocrats among self-assertive plebeians—they are permitted to very gradually fall to pieces, and often are not finally swept away on the outrushing tide of consumptive lath and plaster, of draught-wheezing villa-ets, until their very sides gape and cry out for burial. In most cases their lives—these landmarks of a forgotten generation—were begun in roomy surroundings, including kitchen-garden, orchard, and sometimes a paddock. First the paddock was sacrificed to the maw of the relentless, conscienceless jerry-builder. Then orchard and poultry-yard gave place to a huddled mass of rickety, two-storey cupboards. Then the kitchen-garden was yielded up; and finally, in some places, one may see the hoary wreck of a last-century dwelling-house, hemmed in to its very porch, jeered at in its own stable-yard, by little rudimentary abortions in stucco and plaster, which have risen up with the rapidity said to characterize the creation of fairy palaces, and the crumbling instability of the most vulgar variety of fungus.

Such a bankrupt gentleman among vulgar peddlers was Manor House, down whose grass-grown gravel drive George Barnard walked toward the door upon which appeared Dr. Stephens' name.

But Manor House, though tottering toward lingering dissolution, was yet propped up, and, as it were, smartened to face the world, by all sorts of quaint evidences of young life in its surroundings. The kitchen-garden was still intact, and straggled out to meet a roughly-mown lawn. The coach-house and stable held up its grey old head bravely, if its nether limbs were a little uncertain. The narrow conservatory on one side of Manor House still clung to its parent wall, though in places its parent wall did shrink weakly from it, as though half inclined to disown its yellow panes, by way of expressing contempt for its humble uses as a lumber place and storehouse.

In the side garden, beyond the dingy greenhouse, stood two substantial children's swings. Over the coach-house door were painted, in white letters on a dark board, the words, " Play-room." On the great red lamp over the front entrance, appeared two painted hands, pointing in opposite directions. Under one was written, " To the medicine room." Under the other appeared, " To the doctor's room."

" Aha! " murmured George, as he raised his hand to an old iron bell-pull. " So he's a family man, this Dr. Stephens. Apparently it would be difficult to hit upon anything that he is not. Hullo! why, this bell doesn't act."

It was an indisputable fact that the rusty old bell-chain moved nothing, save a loose staple in the wall over the barrister's head.

" Queer, too, since there's no knocker."

George Barnard put out his hand, and found that the door facing him stood ajar. He pushed it open and stepped into the entrance-hall of the old house.

At that moment he heard a thin, querulous voice

issuing from some hinder portion of the house, and the words:

"Well, aren't our doctor at 'ome, Mary?"

Then, in a slightly stronger voice:

"No, daddy, he ain't; but 'e will be in half an hour. What's wrong, daddy? Is th' rheumatiz bad again?"

"No, no; the rheumatiz is all right. Our doctor don't let me 'ave nothin' wrong wi' me these days. Oh, ay!" The speaker seemed half regretful.

"Are ye short of food, then, daddy?"

"No, no, bless ye, Mary; our doctor don't let us old uns go short fur food. He—he'd go short first, I'm thinkin'. It's about my son Joe, Mary; he's that bad wi' th' drink, that I—I——"

"Yes, yes; I know—I know; an' so our doctor must go to him, instead o' him comin' here; an'—— Hark! There's someone in front. Sit down, daddy; sit down, while I go an' see who it is. Our doctor 'll be back soon."

Then a bent, virile little old woman, with a dusky bloom on her shrivelled cheeks, and curious indurations on her hands, like those of lizard-skin, came slowly out from a dark doorway, and down the wide hall to where George Barnard stood waiting.

"Why, to be sure," said the old lady cheerily, in answer to the barrister's questions. "To be sure ye can come in an' rest till our doctor's back. It must be near one now, an' he said he'd be in by one."

So the barrister was shown into a big, shabby room, the very chairs and walls of which announced to workman George Barnard that this was the den of a hard-working, work-loving man. Medical books, instrument-cases, graduating glasses, diagrams, half-filled medicine-bottles, stethoscopes, a faint but penetrating odour of antiseptics, and a huge anatomical figure on a pedestal, were sufficient to tell of the nature of the work and study to which this apartment was devoted.

Whilst George Barnard stood in the centre of the great littered room, gossiping with the cheery old dame who spoke of "our doctor" as a personal and much-loved friend, there came to them the sound of a firm tread and of a deep, ringing voice in the hall beyond.

"Mary! Mary! Where are you? Come and say you're glad to see me! Come and——"

"Bless me—bless me!" muttered the old gossip at George Barnard's side. "Coming, sir; coming, Doctor dear! That's our doctor back, and I——"

But, gently forcing Mary aside, George Barnard strode past her and into the hall from which the ringing voice came. He saw a tall man, with a fair, pointed beard; eyes bluer than his own eyes, shoulders almost as broad as his shoulders, and a face full of clean strength, softened by a light of tenderness such as that with which painters love to glorify their canvas ideals of masculine sainthood. The man was bending over one raised foot and loosening the laces of his boot.

"Harold!"

"What—George! Dear old George! How—— Why, dear old George, come in here."

So the two men walked into the big working-den, by the door of which old Mary stood.

"Oh, Mary! This is Mr. George Barnard, my— my very dear friend. George, this is Mary—that is— yes, Mary. 'Kind Mary' the children call her. My good, wise housekeeper, George. We'll have lunch in here, Mary; and if anyone comes send them in, and—— Well, well, George, it is good to see you. Come and sit down and talk."

Then these two men sat down among the working

débris of the doctor's den, and talked freely and fluently for two hours. At the end of that time Harold had to hurry round to the hospital, accompanied by the barrister, and talking still, as they walked along a road in which almost every passer-by had some respectful word of salutation for the young doctor.

Then, after an hour spent in the hospital and half an hour at the house of the old man whom Harold's housekeeper called "Daddy," the two returned to the working-room in Manor House, to talk again and far on into the spring evening.

"You see," said the golden-bearded man whom George Barnard had known as Harold Foster, and whom everyone in the neighbourhood of the Royal Free Hospital and of Manor House, appeared to know as "our doctor"—"you see, I felt bound to go to that consultation this morning, or I should have had more leisure this afternoon. A thirty-guinea fee, you know, George; and my people down here want it—want it all. If it weren't for that I think I should never go West at all any more, for doctors are plentiful enough there—clever doctors, too. I often wonder that they have faith enough in an outsider to offer me the fees they do. But I'm glad of it, because my own people need it all, and badly. I do my best to earn it, you know, George, of course."

"Well, but bless me, Harold, there's twenty thousand pounds of yours lying idle because I couldn't find you."

"Twenty thousand pounds, eh! Well, well! What a place I could make of the old Manor House! And my people are ripe for it now, George—they are ripe for it. And they are very good and grateful—very good people."

"Well, then there's your annuity, Harold."

"Ah! Yes, there's the annuity. Well, you know,

George, I meant to have come to you soon, and asked you if you thought—if you thought I deserved the use of that. I didn't care to use it after I had qualified, because it—— Well, it seemed to be all part of the——"

"Yes, yes! I understand, Harold—I think I un- derstand. Well, you will have so much the more to use now. And—God bless you, old chap!—I'm so glad you've done it all alone. All this beautiful work of yours—all this love and respect from men, women, and children! Why, Harold, do you know I have heard talk of your influence upon men and women— only I didn't know it was you—miles and miles away, where Norah is at work. I've heard Norah speak of it. People about there told her that Dr. Stephens was like Christ in his life and work. And her eyes—faith, her eyes glowed like a saint's eyes, Harold!"

The young doctor's face was crimson. His eyes were very moist.

"Ah, George," he said, "don't ever talk like that. You make me ashamed. What is my one little life of these five years, among so many, where so much is to be done? George, there are men and women among my own people who in all their lives have never known as much happiness as comes to me in every day of mine. And they are far more patient with it all than I am, George—far more uncomplaining. My greatest trouble so far, has been want of capital to start any help for my people on a systematic basis. But now——"

"Now you will use what—what he left for you? And—and you can't help doing honour to his memory in using it."

So they talked on and on through the evening, while George Barnard learned gradually a good deal of the breadth of influence, the broad, ever-increasing scope, the kindly, loving catholicism, of the big life which "our doctor" was living. At last he rose to return to Furnival's Inn, promising himself a renewal on the following day of this, his insight into Harold's life.

"You'd rather I came to you than that you should come to me, wouldn't you, Harold?" he asked, as they were walking together to the railway-station.

"Well, yes," replied Harold, "I would. You see, I've generally half a dozen sick children, and other folk about Manor House. It's awkward for me to be long away from Stepney. I—I suppose it's selfishness, really, you know, because I'm never anything like so happy anywhere else. You see I began with these people, and—oh! I love them, George, all of them. That's why they like me, and why I am able to—to help them a little."

"Yes, yes; you—oh yes, it's pure selfishness, Harold, I've no doubt, that makes you refuse West End practice. Well, then, I'll come down to-morrow afternoon, and in the morning I will go and see the lawyers. You can lay your plans for the restitution of that— that great old house of worship you live in, at once, Harold. There's over twenty thousand pounds at your disposal, you know. And, Harold, I may tell Norah who Dr. Stephens is, mayn't I?"

Added colour crept up from under the doctor's beard to his temples.

"Well, if you don't mind, George, I should very much like to leave that until you have seen a little of the change I will make at Manor House with some of that money. I should so like Norah to—— Do you mind?"

"Why, no, of course not. It's as you choose. Here's my train. Till to-morrow, then, good-bye, Harold!"

"Good-bye, dear old George; good-night!"

. . . .

Just a week after this meeting between the new Harold and his old friend, George Barnard left his chambers in Furnival's Inn, to pay a visit to the decaying house in Stepney, on which builders were already at work. The time was just two o'clock, on a warm, bright afternoon in early June, and London, despite its whirr and rush of business, seemed softened and sweetened by the joy of young summer.

The barrister had a call to pay in Fleet Street. This done, he walked slowly down the great highway of the newspaper world, smiling over the heads of its many wayfarers at the beauty of the world he lived in. Suddenly he paused, on the threshold of a famous tavern. He had caught a glimpse of the figure of the old man called Carroll, approaching him from the far side of the road. Pushing young men made way for old Carroll, for in that part of London his gaunt figure was better known than in any other, and it commanded a certain deference. The warm wine of June seemed to have entered the old man's veins on this sunny afternoon. His head was held erect, his eyes were unusually bright, and his voice rang clear and mellow when he saluted the barrister.

"Hullo, George Barnard! Well, did you find the 'foundling?'"

"I did. I found him living a great workman's life in the East End."

"Aha! Well, I hope you didn't interfere with him."

"No," said George Barnard, humbly enough. "No; I only admired. I'm just off to his place now. Come down with me, will you? He'd be very glad to meet you, I know."

"Eh? You think so? Let me see! Five years— H'm! Yes. All right! Come along, George Barnard. I'll go with you, and see the 'foundling.' H'm!

Gad—five years! I'm growing old, George Barnard; but it's a grand world, a brave old world, with its pain and pleasure, and success and failure, and wide brown earth! Eh? Come along, George Barnard."

So these two journeyed down to Stepney together, in the June sunshine.

As they walked through the over-grown old garden to the side entrance of Manor House, the ringing laughter of children's voices reached them from the clump of trees by the green-house, where the swings stood. There were sharp sounds, too, of tapping hammers, and busy sounds, as of wood-sawing. The scent of old-fashioned flowers filled the air. A belated bee was droning about the side of the shabby coach-house. Queen June, who embodies the joy of living, was abroad and about the old Manor House, and Mary, the housekeeper, whose cheeks were like late, winter-ripened fruit, stood in the side-doorway, shading her bright eyes under one wrinkled hand, and gazing out into the sunlight. Mary and the barrister were close friends.

"Oh, yes, sir, he's at home. Our doctor's inside. He's in his room. Come along, sir!"

Mary had dropped a quaint curtsey to Carroll, and now, as she preceded the two on their way to the doctor's den, she seemed to be labouring under some unusual strain of happy excitement. She chuckled and muttered to herself as she walked through the shadowy hall.

"Ye'll find our doctor inside, Mr. Barnard," she said, nodding her silvered-over head, as, having first tapped upon it, she pushed wide open the door of her master's working den. George Barnard smiled at the old dame's enthusiasm. Then, followed by Carroll, he stepped past her into the big, littered room.

Beside the open French window at the far end of

the room, the two men from Fleet Street saw standing Norah Fenton and the tall, yellow-bearded man who had once been called "Morley Fenton's foundling." The picture was a fascinating one. Neither of the two men from Fleet Street spoke. Harold was holding Norah's two hands, outstretched, in his own. Norah had found the man who was thought "like Christ," and that without George Barnard's assistance.

Harold released one of Norah's hands, and, still holding in his the other, turned to greet his visitors. Then George Barnard and Carroll stepped forward; and there were no apologies between these four.

"Mr. Gunning was away at the docks," murmured Norah, to the barrister. "And his wife did beg me to take her little boy to—to Dr. Stephens, because he was so ill. So I brought him, and——"

"And Norah doesn't mind my name being changed. And she knows everything about—everything, in fact," said Harold, with feeling, if without much coherence. "And Norah forgives me for everything."

"There is nothing to forgive," murmured Norah, her dark eyes full of tears.

"And you are very happy?" added the barrister, half questioningly.

"And I—Norah—we are very happy. And, you see, George, and Mr. Carroll, you—you Christian! we both love our people, and our work, and we think—well, you see, I shall be able to do ten times as much with Norah's help. Perhaps I can help Norah a little, too. Anyhow, she is going to let me try. I must try to deserve it. George, Norah has promised to be my wife."

"I am so glad, Norah! Harold, I am very glad! You will both be very happy, and you will make hundreds of others happy."

THE TRIUMPH OF TIME.

"I congratulate you, Doctor," said Carroll; and his rich deep voice seemed to fill every corner of the big room. "You've seen the dawn, and the morning is yours. The first part of that russet-leather-backed book has been written—written as a classic should be written. You will go on living in 'the gigantic smile o' the brown old earth.' It's a beautiful life, you big young doctor, a beautiful life. Miss Fenton"—the old man turned his sunken, bright eyes towards Norah—"you will be very happy. You will have a beautiful life, as is fitting. You will not marry a man who lives in a little patch of the earth, but a man who is a citizen of all the world. Your husband will not be 'Morley Fenton's foundling.' He has won clear, and he's 'God's foundling.' George Barnard, you old bachelor fool! come out with me, and talk to the children in the garden!"

George Barnard smiled when Carroll called him a "bachelor fool." The barrister was thinking of Nurse Matthews, and of a certain conditional promise she had given him. The condition had borne upon Norah's prospects, and that afternoon's events made Nurse Matthews' promise free and absolute.

So Norah and Harold were left together, in the broad wave of sunlight which fell through the open French window on to the floor of "our doctor's" workroom.

THE END.

APPLETONS' TOWN AND COUNTRY LIBRARY.
PUBLISHED SEMIMONTHLY.

1. *The Steel Hammer.* By LOUIS ULBACH.
2. *Eve.* A Novel. By S. BARING-GOULD.
3. *For Fifteen Years.* A Sequel to The Steel Hammer. By LOUIS ULBACH.
4. *A Counsel of Perfection.* A Novel. By LUCAS MALET.
5. *The Deemster.* A Romance. By HALL CAINE.
5½. *The Bondman.* (New edition.) By HALL CAINE.
6. *A Virginia Inheritance.* By EDMUND PENDLETON.
7. *Ninette:* An Idyll of Provence. By the author of Véra.
8. "*The Right Honourable.*" By JUSTIN MCCARTHY and Mrs. CAMPBELL-PRAED.
9. *The Silence of Dean Maitland.* By MAXWELL GRAY.
10. *Mrs. Lorimer:* A Study in Black and White. By LUCAS MALET.
11. *The Elect Lady.* By GEORGE MACDONALD.
12. *The Mystery of the "Ocean Star."* By W. CLARK RUSSELL.
13. *Aristocracy.* A Novel.
14. *A Recoiling Vengeance.* By FRANK BARRETT. With Illustrations.
15. *The Secret of Fontaine-la-Croix.* By MARGARET FIELD.
16. *The Master of Rathkelly.* By HAWLEY SMART.
17. *Donovan:* A Modern Englishman. By EDNA LYALL.
18. *This Mortal Coil.* By GRANT ALLEN.
19. *A Fair Emigrant.* By ROSA MULHOLLAND.
20. *The Apostate.* By ERNEST DAUDET.
21. *Raleigh Westgate;* or, Epimenides in Maine. By HELEN KENDRICK JOHNSON.
22. *Arius the Libyan.* A Romance of the Primitive Church.
23. *Constance,* and *Calbot's Rival.* By JULIAN HAWTHORNE.
24. *We Two.* By EDNA LYALL.
25. *A Dreamer of Dreams.* By the author of Thoth.
26. *The Ladies' Gallery.* By JUSTIN MCCARTHY and Mrs. CAMPBELL-PRAED.
27. *The Reproach of Annesley.* By MAXWELL GRAY.
28. *Near to Happiness.*
29. *In the Wire Grass.* By LOUIS PENDLETON.
30. *Lace.* A Berlin Romance. By PAUL LINDAU.
30½. *The Black Poodle.* By F. ANSTEY.
31. *American Coin.* A Novel. By the author of Aristocracy.
32. *Won by Waiting.* By EDNA LYALL.
33. *The Story of Helen Davenant.* By VIOLET FANE.
34. *The Light of Her Countenance.* By H. H. BOYESEN.
35. *Mistress Beatrice Cope.* My M. E. LE CLERC.
36. *The Knight-Errant.* By EDNA LYALL.
37. *In the Golden Days.* By EDNA LYALL.
38. *Giraldi;* or, The Curse of Love. By ROSS GEORGE DERING.
39. *A Hardy Norseman.* By EDNA LYALL.
40. *The Romance of Jenny Harlowe,* and *Sketches of Maritime Life.* By W. CLARK RUSSELL.
41. *Passion's Slave.* By RICHARD ASHE-KING.
42. *The Awakening of Mary Fenwick.* By BEATRICE WHITBY.
43. *Countess Loreley.* Translated from the German of RUDOLF MENGER.
44. *Blind Love.* By WILKIE COLLINS.
45. *The Dean's Daughter.* By SOPHIE F. F. VEITCH.
46. *Countess Irene.* A Romance of Austrian Life. By J. FOGERTY.
47. *Robert Browning's Principal Shorter Poems.*
48. *Frozen Hearts.* By G. WEBB APPLETON.
49. *Djambek the Georgian.* By A. G. VON SUTTNER.
50. *The Craze of Christian Engelhart.* By HENRY FAULKNER DARNELL.
51. *Lal.* By WILLIAM A. HAMMOND, M. D.
52. *Aline.* A Novel. By HENRY GRÉVILLE.
53. *Joost Avelingh.* A Dutch Story. By MAARTEN MAARTENS.
54. *Katy of Catoctin.* By GEORGE ALFRED TOWNSEND.
55. *Throckmorton.* A Novel. By MOLLY ELLIOT SEAWELL.
56. *Expatriation.* By the author of Aristocracy.
57. *Geoffrey Hampstead.* By T. S. JARVIS.

APPLETONS' TOWN AND COUNTRY LIBRARY.—(Continued.)

58. *Dmitri.* A Romance of Old Russia. By F. W. Bain, M.A.
59. *Part of the Property.* By BEATRICE WHITBY.
60. *Bismarck in Private Life.* By a Fellow-Student.
61. *In Low Relief.* By MORLEY ROBERTS.
62. *The Canadians of Old.* A Historical Romance. By PHILIPPE GASPÉ.
63. *A Squire of Low Degree.* By LILY A. LONG.
64. *A Fluttered Dovecote.* By GEORGE MANVILLE FENN.
65. *The Nugents of Curriconna.* An Irish Story. By TIGHE HOPKINS.
66. *A Sensitive Plant.* By E. and D. GERARD.
67. *Doña Luz.* By JUAN VALERA. Translated by Mrs MARY J. SERRANO.
68. *Pepita Ximenez.* By JUAN VALERA. Translated by Mrs. MARY J. SERRANO.
69. *The Primes and their Neighbors.* By RICHARD MALCOLM JOHNSTON.
70. *The Iron Game.* By HENRY F. KEENAN.
71. *Stories of Old New Spain.* By THOMAS A. JANVIER.
72. *The Maid of Honor.* By Hon. LEWIS WINGFIELD.
73. *In the Heart of the Storm.* By MAXWELL GRAY.
74. *Consequences.* By EGERTON CASTLE.
75. *The Three Miss Kings.* By ADA CAMBRIDGE.
76. *A Matter of Skill.* By BEATRICE WHITBY.
77. *Maid Marian, and Other Stories.* By MOLLY ELLIOT SEAWELL.
78. *One Woman's Way.* By EDMUND PENDLETON.
79. *A Merciful Divorce.* By F. W. MAUDE.
80. *Stephen Ellicott's Daughter.* By Mrs. J. H. NEEDELL.
81. *One Reason Why.* By BEATRICE WHITBY.
82. *The Tragedy of Ida Noble.* By W. CLARK RUSSELL.
83. *The Johnstown Stage, and other Stories.* By ROBERT H. FLETCHER.
84. *A Widower Indeed.* By RHODA BROUGHTON and ELIZABETH BISLAND.
85. *The Flight of a Shadow.* By GEORGE MACDONALD.
86. *Love or Money.* By KATHARINE LEE.
87. *Not All in Vain.* By ADA CAMBRIDGE.
88. *It Happened Yesterday.* By FREDERICK MARSHALL.
89. *My Guardian.* By ADA CAMBRIDGE.
90. *The Story of Philip Methuen.* By Mrs. J. H. NEEDELL.
91. *Amethyst: The Story of a Beauty.* By CHRISTABEL R. COLERIDGE.
92. *Don Braulio.* By JUAN VALERA. Translated by CLARA BELL.
93. *The Chronicles of Mr. Bill Williams.* By RICHARD MALCOLM JOHNSTON.
94. *A Queen of Curds and Cream.* By DOROTHEA GERARD.
95. *"La Bella" and Others.* By EGERTON CASTLE.
96. *"December Roses."* By Mrs. CAMPBELL PRAED.
97. *Jean de Kerdren.* By JEANNE SCHULTZ.
98. *Etelka's Vow.* By DOROTHEA GERARD.
99. *Cross Currents.* By MARY A DICKENS.
100. *His Life's Magnet.* By THEODORA ELMSLIE.
101. *Passing the Love of Women.* By Mrs J. H. NEEDELL.
102. *In Old St. Stephen's.* By JEANIE DRAKE.
103. *The Berkeleys and their Neighbors.* By MOLLY ELLIOT SEAWELL.
104. *Mona Maclean, Medical Student.* By GRAHAM TRAVERS.
105. *Mrs. Bligh.* By RHODA BROUGHTON.
106. *A Stumble on the Threshold.* By JAMES PAYN.
107. *Hanging Moss.* By PAUL LINDAU.
108. *A Comedy of Elopement.* By CHRISTIAN REID.
109. *In the Suntime of her Youth.* By BEATRICE WHITBY.
110. *Stories in Black and White.* By THOMAS HARDY and Others.
110½. *An Englishman in Paris.* Notes and Recollections.
111. *Commander Mendoza.* By JUAN VALERA.
112. *Dr. Paull's Theory.* By Mrs. A. M. DIEHL.
113. *Children of Destiny.* By MOLLY ELLIOT SEAWELL.
114. *A Little Minx.* By ADA CAMBRIDGE.
115. *Capt'n Davy's Honeymoon.* By HALL CAINE.
116. *The Voice of a Flower.* By E. GERARD.
117. *Singularly Deluded.* By SARAH GRAND.
118. *Suspected.* By LOUISA STRATENUS.
119. *Lucia, Hugh, and Another.* By Mrs. J. H. NEEDELL.
120. *The Tutor's Secret.* By VICTOR CHERBULIEZ.

APPLETONS' TOWN AND COUNTRY LIBRARY.—(Continued.)

121. *From the Five Rivers.* By Mrs. F. A. STEEL.
122. *An Innocent Impostor, and Other Stories.* By MAXWELL GRAY.
123. *Ideala.* By SARAH GRAND.
124. *A Comedy of Masks.* By ERNEST DOWSON and ARTHUR MOORE.
125. *Relics.* By FRANCES MACNAB.
126. *Dodo: A Detail of the Day.* By E. F. BENSON.
127. *A Woman of Forty.* By ESMÉ STUART.
128. *Diana Tempest.* By MARY CHOLMONDELEY.
129. *The Recipe for Diamonds.* By C. J. CUTCLIFFE HYNE.
130. *Christina Chard.* By Mrs. CAMPBELL-PRAED.
131. *A Gray Eye or So.* By FRANK FRANKFORT MOORE.
132. *Earlscourt.* By ALEXANDER ALLARDYCE.
133. *A Marriage Ceremony.* By ADA CAMBRIDGE.
134. *A Ward in Chancery.* By Mrs. ALEXANDER.
135. *Lot 13.* By DOROTHEA GERARD.
136. *Our Manifold Nature.* By SARAH GRAND.
137. *A Costly Freak.* By MAXWELL GRAY.
138. *A Beginner.* By RHODA BROUGHTON.
139. *A Yellow Aster.* By Mrs. MANNINGTON CAFFYN ("IOTA").
140. *The Rubicon.* By E. F. BENSON.
141. *The Trespasser.* By GILBERT PARKER.
142. *The Rich Miss Riddell.* By DOROTHEA GERARD.
143. *Mary Fenwick's Daughter.* By BEATRICE WHITBY.
144. *Red Diamonds.* By JUSTIN MCCARTHY.
145. *A Daughter of Music.* By G. COLMORE.
146. *Outlaw and Lawmaker.* By Mrs. CAMPBELL-PRAED.
147. *Dr. Janet of Harley Street.* By ARABELLA KENEALY.
148. *George Mandeville's Husband.* By C. E. RAIMOND.
149. *Vashti and Esther.*
150. *Timar's Two Worlds.* By M. JOKAI.
151. *A Victim of Good Luck.* By W. E. NORRIS.
152. *The Trail of the Sword.* By GILBERT PARKER.
153. *A Mild Barbarian.* By EDGAR FAWCETT.
154. *The God in the Car.* By ANTHONY HOPE.
155. *Children of Circumstance.* By Mrs. M. CAFFYN.
156. *At the Gate of Samaria.* By WILLIAM J. LOCKE.
157. *The Justification of Andrew Lebrun.* By FRANK BARRETT.
158. *Dust and Laurels.* By MARY L. PENDERED.
159. *The Good Ship Mohock.* By W. CLARK RUSSELL.
160. *Noëmi.* By S. BARING-GOULD.
161. *The Honour of Savelli.* By S. LEVETT YEATS.
162. *Kitty's Engagement.* By FLORENCE WARDEN.
163. *The Mermaid.* By L. DOUGALL.
164. *An Arranged Marriage.* By DOROTHEA GERARD.
165. *Eve's Ransom.* By GEORGE GISSING.
166. *The Marriage of Esther.* By GUY BOOTHBY.
167. *Fidelis.* By ADA CAMBRIDGE.
168. *Into the Highways and Hedges.* By F. F. MONTRÉSOR.
169. *The Vengeance of James Vansittart.* By Mrs. J. H. NEEDELL.
170. *A Study in Prejudices.* By GEORGE PASTON.
171. *The Mistress of Quest.* By ADELINE SERGEANT.
172. *In the Year of Jubilee.* By GEORGE GISSING.
173. *In Old New England.* By HEZEKIAH BUTTERWORTH.
174. *Mrs. Musgrave—and Her Husband.* By R. MARSH.
175. *Not Counting the Cost.* By TASMA.
176. *Out of Due Season.* By ADELINE SERGEANT.
177. *Scylla or Charybdis?* By RHODA BROUGHTON.
178. *In Defiance of the King.* By C. C. HOTCHKISS.
179. *A Bid for Fortune.* By GUY BOOTHBY.
180. *The King of Andaman.* By J. MACLAREN COBBAN.
181. *Mrs. Tregaskiss.* By Mrs. CAMPBELL-PRAED.
182. *The Desire of the Moth.* By CAPEL VANE.
183. *A Self-Denying Ordinance.* By M. HAMILTON.
184. *Successors to the Title.* By Mrs. L. B. WALFORD.

APPLETONS' TOWN AND COUNTRY LIBRARY.—(*Continued.*)

185. *The Lost Stradivarius.* By J. MEADE FALKNER.
186. *The Wrong Man.* By DOROTHEA GERARD.
187. *In the Day of Adversity.* By J. BLOUNDELLE-BURTON.
188. *Mistress Dorothy Marvin.* By J. C. SNAITH.
189. *A Flash of Summer.* By Mrs. W. K. CLIFFORD.
190. *The Dancer in Yellow.* By W. E. NORRIS.
191. *The Chronicles of Martin Hewitt.* By ARTHUR MORRISON.
192. *A Winning Hazard.* By Mrs. ALEXANDER.
193. *The Picture of Las Cruces.* By CHRISTIAN REID.
194. *The Madonna of a Day.* By L. DOUGALL.
195. *The Riddle Ring.* By JUSTIN MCCARTHY.
196. *A Humble Enterprise.* By ADA CAMBRIDGE.
197. *Dr. Nikola.* By GUY BOOTHBY.
198. *An Outcast of the Islands.* By JOSEPH CONRAD.
199. *The King's Revenge.* By CLAUDE BRAY.
200. *Denounced.* By J. BLOUNDELLE-BURTON.
201. *A Court Intrigue.* By BASIL THOMPSON.
202. *The Idol-Maker.* By ADELINE SERGEANT.
203. *The Intriguers.* By JOHN D. BARRY.
204. *Master Ardick, Buccaneer.* By F. H. COSTELLO.
205. *With Fortune Made.* By VICTOR CHERBULIEZ.
206. *Fellow Travellers.* By GRAHAM TRAVERS.
207. *McLeod of the Cumerons.* By M. HAMILTON.
208. *The Career of Candida.* By GEORGE PASTON.
209. *Arrested.* By ESMÈ STUART.
210. *Tatterley.* By T. GALLON.
211. *A Pinchbeck Goddess.* By Mrs. J. M. FLEMING (Alice M. Kipling).
212. *Perfection City.* By Mrs. ORPEN.
213. *A Spotless Reputation.* By DOROTHEA GERARD.
214. *A Galahad of the Creeks.* By S. LEVETT YEATS.
215. *The Beautiful White Devil.* By GUY BOOTHBY.
216. *The Sun of Saratoga.* By JOSEPH A. ALTSHELER.
217. *Fierceheart, the Soldier.* By J. C. SNAITH.
218. *Marietta's Marriage.* By W. E. NORRIS.
219. *Dear Faustina.* By RHODA BROUGHTON.
220. *Nūlma.* By Mrs. CAMPBELL-PRAED.
221. *The Folly of Pen Harrington.* By JULIAN STURGIS.
222. *A Colonial Free-Lance.* By C. C. HOTCHKISS.
223. *His Majesty's Greatest Subject.* By S. S. THORBURN.
224. *Mifanwy: A Welsh Singer.* By ALLEN RAINE.
225. *A Soldier of Manhattan.* By JOSEPH A. ALTSHELER.
226. *Fortune's Footballs.* By G. B. BURGIN.
227. *The Clash of Arms.* By J. BLOUNDELLE-BURTON.
228. *God's Foundling.* By J. A. DAWSON.

Each, 12mo, paper cover, 50 cents; cloth, $1.00.

For sale by all booksellers; or sent by mail on receipt of price by the publishers,

D. APPLETON AND COMPANY, NEW YORK.

D. APPLETON AND COMPANY'S PUBLICATIONS.

"The Story of the Year."
HALL CAINE'S NEW NOVEL.

THE CHRISTIAN. By HALL CAINE, author of "The Manxman," "The Deemster," "The Bondman," etc. 12mo. Cloth, $1.50.

"One of the grandest books of the century-end."—*New York Home Journal.*

"The public is hardly prepared for so remarkable a performance as 'The Christian.'... A permanent addition to English literature.... Above and beyond any popularity that is merely temporary."—*Boston Herald.*

"Must be regarded as the greatest work that has yet come from the pen of this strong writer.... A book of wonderful power and force."—*Brooklyn Eagle.*

"The best story Hall Caine has written. It is one of the best stories that have been written for many years. It is emphatically the strongest and best story that has been written during the past twelve months.... A masterpiece in fiction."—*Buffalo Commercial.*

"This extraordinary piece of fiction. None who read it will gainsay its power and effectiveness.... The remarkable book of the summer."—*New York Times.*

"Of powerful and absorbing interest. The reader is irresistibly fascinated from the very beginning.... A remarkable book."—*Philadelphia Press.*

"A noble story ; one of the best half-dozen novels of the decade ; a splendid piece of writing ; a profound study in character, and a series of thrilling portrayals."—*Chicago Evening Post.*

"A book that has assuredly placed its maker upon a pedestal which will last well-nigh forever.... Powerful, thrilling, dramatic, and, best of all, intensely honest in its every line.... A truly wonderful achievement."—*Cincinnati Commercial-Tribune.*

"By long odds the most powerful production of his very productive pen, and it will live and be read and re-read when ninety per cent of the books of to-day are forgotten."—*Boston Daily Globe.*

"Though the theme is old, Mr. Caine has worked it up with a passion and power that make it new again.... Can not fail to thrill even the most careless reader."—*New York Herald.*

"'The Christian' is one of the strongest novels of the year, and is in some respects the greatest work this author has yet produced."—*Philadelphia Evening Telegraph.*

"Indisputably Mr. Caine's strongest and most important work."—*Philadelphia Bulletin.*

"A powerful story.... The portrait of the pure womanliness of Glory Quayle is beyond any praise we can bestow."—*N. Y. Mail and Express.*

"By far the strongest novel that has been brought out this year.... If you once dip into it you must stay with it until the end. It lays hold upon your heart and compels attention."—*San Francisco Chronicle.*

D. APPLETON AND COMPANY, NEW YORK.

D. APPLETON AND COMPANY'S PUBLICATIONS.

THE STORY OF THE WEST SERIES.
Edited by RIPLEY HITCHCOCK. Each, 12mo, cloth, illustrated, $1.50.

"Histories, many of them, have been written about the Western country, but most, if not practically all, by outsiders who knew not personally that life of kaleidoscopic allurement. But ere it shall have vanished forever we are likely to have truthful, complete, and charming portrayals of it produced by men who actually knew the life and have the power to describe it."—HENRY EDWARD ROOD, *in the Mail and Express*.

THE STORY OF THE INDIAN. By GEORGE BIRD GRINNELL, author of "Pawnee Hero Stories," "Blackfoot Lodge Tales," etc.

"In every way worthy of an author who as an authority upon the Western Indians is second to none. A book full of color, abounding in observation, and remarkable in sustained interest, it is at the same time characterized by a grace of style which is rarely to be looked for in such a work, and which adds not a little to the charm of it."
—*London Daily Chronicle.*

"Only an author qualified by personal experience could offer us a profitable study of a race so alien from our own as is the Indian in thought, feeling, and culture. Only long association with Indians can enable a white man measurably to comprehend their thoughts and enter into their feelings. Such association has been Mr. Grinnell's "—*New York Sun.*

THE STORY OF THE MINE. As illustrated by the Great Comstock Lode of Nevada. By CHARLES HOWARD SHINN.

"The figures of the prospector and the miner are clearly outlined in the course of the romantic story of that natural treasure-house which more than any other embodies the romance, the vicissitudes, the triumphs, the excitement, and the science of mining life."—*San Francisco Examiner.*

"The autho ' written a book not alone full of information, but replete with the true romance of the .American mine."—*New York Times.*

THE STORY OF THE COWBOY. By E. HOUGH, author of "The Singing Mouse Stories," etc. Illustrated by William L. Wells and C. M. Russell.

The very picturesqueness of the cowboy has subjected him to misinterpretation, and his actual story and a picture of the great industry which he has conducted may be said to be presented adequately for the first time in Mr. Hough's spirited and fascinating pages. The story which he tells is a strange and romantic one, impressive on the practical side by reason of the magnitude of the business described, and very valuable from the historical point of view, because this book preserves in permanent form a typical figure of Western life, and also the development and the passing, or rather transformation, of a vast industry almost within a generation.

IN PREPARATION.
THE STORY OF THE TRAPPER. By GILBERT PARKER.
THE STORY OF THE SOLDIER. By Captain J. McB. STEMBEL, U. S. A.
THE STORY OF THE EXPLORER.
THE STORY OF THE RAILROAD.

D. APPLETON AND COMPANY, NEW YORK.

www.ingramcontent.com/pod-product-compliance
Lightning Source LLC
Chambersburg PA
CBHW021155230426
43667CB00006B/414